午後2時46分
すべてが変わった

quakebook.org 編

2:46

Aftershocks:
Stories from the Japan Earthquake

#quakebook

語研

246: Aftershocks: Stories from the Japan Earthquake #quakebook
Copyright © 2011 Patrick Sherriff All Rights Reserved
Book Design: Yuko Sawamoto
Cover Illustration: Mari Kurisato
Typeset in Fanwood Text & League Gothic for English
  Yu Mincho Medium & Yu Gothic Bold for Japanese

Published by Goken Co., Ltd.

4th FL Orimoto BLDG 7-17 Sarugaku-cho 2-chome, Chiyoda-ku, Tokyo 101-0064, Japan

ISBN 978-4-87615-422-7

2011.03.18 9:13am
Have asked @fatblueman (of Christmas in Japan video fame) to start writing a song for Japan quake survivors, and it got me thinking...

2011.03.18 9:18am
I want to compile a book of quake experiences and publish it like within a week and donate all profits to Red Cross. We have the technology.

2011.03.18 9:22am
If everyone wrote 250 words — one page — or submitted their favourite (original) tweets, pics or artwork, I could edit, publish it in days.

2011年3月18日午前9時13分
日本の地震被災者のために、(Christmas in Japanで知られる) @fatbluemanに
作曲を依頼する。そこから思いついて……

2011年3月18日午前9時18分
今回の地震体験を一冊の本にまとめて、1週間以内にでも出版したい。
利益はすべて赤十字社へ寄付する。我々にはテクノロジーがある。

2011年3月18日午前9時22分
1ページ250語の原稿、あるいはお気に入りの(オリジナルの)ツイート、写真、
イラストなどを送ってくれれば、自分が編集して、何日かで出版する。

Contents

Names / 地名	Yoshiko Ikeda	17
Alive / 生きている	Steve Nagata	18
Another / もう一度	Masumi Nabekawa	20
Awakening	Yoko Ono Lennon	22
Beautiful / 美しい	Christopher Maurer	24
Birthday / 誕生日	Jonas Neergaard-Nielsen	25
Bravery / 任務	Yoshie Sherriff	27
Cakes / ケーキ	Arun Vemuri	28
Care / 心配事	Yuki Watanabe	30
Ceiling-light / 天井の灯り	Brian Wood	32
Ceremonies / セレモニー	Wesley Cheek	35
Changed / 変容	Florian	36
Close / 遠すぎず、近すぎず	Debora K Ohnishi	36
Contrast / 温度差	Aurelio Asiasin	38
Conversation / 小さなつぶやき	Michael Gakuran	39
Cushions / 座布団	Shaun Hickox	42
Dark / 暗闇	Andy Heather	44
Debris / 瓦礫	Greg Harbin	46
Decisions / 決断	Ted Taylor	47
Determination / 決意	Andy Sharp	49
Disappeared / 消えてしまった	Brighid Rader	51
Distance / 遠方より	Brent Stirling	51
Encouragement / 鼓舞	Grandfather Hibiki	53
Engage / 関わり方	Tokyo Twilighter	55
Escape / 逃避	James Hou	55
Evacuated / 避難	Takanori Hayao	57
Exactly / きっかり	Mark Rende	62
Expectations / これからのこと	Miho Nishihiro	64
Experience / 良い機会	Kosuke Ishihara	66
Facebook / フェイスブック	Joel David Neff	68
Faculty / 教員	Rodney Van Meter	70
Forget / 置き忘れたもの	Michiko Segawa	72
Forward / 前へ	Maxamillian John	75
Ganbaro / がんばろう	Lowlypoetic	75
Gesture / しぐさ	N Cobayne	76
Goal / 目標	Naomi	78
God / 神様	John Janzen	78
Graduation / 卒業式	May Arai	80
Harmony / 調和	Tom Hope	82
Heart / こころ	Victoria	83
Help / いま私ができること	Yui and Shizue Nonaka	84
Home / うちへ	Kimberly Tierney	85
Illusion / 幻想	Hiromi Sakai	87
Leaving / 離れてみて	Sandra Barron	89

目次

Lingering / いつまでも	Soso Bureau staff	91
Lost / 僕じゃない	Matthew Holmes	93
Loving / 愛をもって接すること	Shehan Raban	94
Lucky / 幸運	Stephen Lyth	95
Morals / モラル	Yuichiro Ito	96
Mountain / 山	Edan Corkill	97
Muenbotoke / 無縁仏	Jake Adelstein	100
Neighbors / ご近所さん	Yumiko Takemoto	107
Normal / いつも通り	Laurent Fintoni	109
OK / 返信	Naotoshi Nabekawa	109
Options / 選択肢	Jason Morgan	110
Overwhelmed / 圧倒	Corey Wallace	111
Pajamas / パジャマ	Mark Warschauer	113
Photographs / 写真	Mari Aquarian	114
Positive / ポジティブ	Arthur Davis	115
Precious / 愛しきもの	Keiko Fujii	117
Prepared / 準備	Annamarie Sasagawa	119
Radioactive / 「放射能」	Ian Martin	120
Really? / うそでしょ?	Chikae Singleton	121
Rebuilding / 再建	Mr Salaryman	122
Recovery / 復旧	Yoko Kobayashi	123
Relief / 安堵	Don Myles	124
Remoteness / 遠くで	Sybil Murray	125
Same / 同じ存在	Baye McNeil	126
Scenarios / シナリオ	Miles Woodroffe	128
Shaken / 動揺	James Simpson	129
Signs / 前兆	Terrie Matsuura	130
Strength / 前に進む	Ai Hinton	131
Strong / 強靭	Robert Ouwehand	132
Television / テレビジョン	Richard Smart	133
Together / ともに	Jesse Johnson	134
Tremors / 余震	Iain Hair	136
Trousers / ズボン	Joseph Tame	138
Underground / アンダーグラウンド	Bigger in Japan	139
Underneath / 下にあるもの	Yuko Kato	140
Understanding / 理解	Mari Kurisato	144
Values / 大切なもの	Kaoru Raban	145
Vertical / タテ型コミュニティ	Philip Brasor	146
Voices / 声	Jessica Tomoko Perez	149
Waiting / 待ちわびて	Kevin Wood	150
Want / ここにいたい	Dan Castellano	152
Window / 窓	William Gibson	153
Test / 試練	Yushi Tabe	156

This book was written as a record of the disaster that befell Japan, as well as a way to provide relief for the survivors. If you received this copy for free, please consider donating to the Japanese Red Cross at *www.quakebook.org*

本書は日本を襲った震災の記録として書かれ、被災した人々に支援金、支援物資を送るために刊行されます。本書を無料で入手した場合は、*www.quakebook.org* 経由で日本赤十字社に献金なさることをお考えください。

Foreword to the bilingual edition

We are not alone.

11 March, 2011. The day the world changed entirely. We all recall in vivid detail the shock, the sadness, the fear and the uncertainty.

The scale of the disaster was unprecedented. The sadness we feel for the lives lost and all that was swept away will never fade. We have a responsibility to remember. As long as we do, those who are gone will remain alive in our hearts.

I was lost for words when I visited the disaster areas of Ishinomaki, Onagawa, and Sendai. The damage was simply too great. I walked around Iitate, a village that is now being evacuated. In the face of a situation so grave that it threatened to chill me to the core, I realized how vital it is that we share each other's warmth.

We must move forward. We must share our stories. We must help one another. What we need most at the moment is to listen to the voices that well up like sighs from deep within our fellow human beings.

Quakebook brings together the myriad voices of a multitude. The road ahead may be filled with challenges, but how wonderful to know that we do not face them alone.

Kenichiro Mogi
Tokyo, May 2011

2か国語版への序文

一人じゃないって感じること。

2011年3月11日。そして、世界はすっかり変わってしまった。衝撃、哀しみ、怖れ、不安。あの時からの心の刻みを、私たちは鮮明に思い起こす。

未曾有の大震災。失われた命、流されてしまったすべてに対する哀しみは決して消えることはない。いつまでも覚えていなければならないことがある。記憶している限り、私たちの心の中で息づいている。

石巻、女川、そして仙台の被災地を訪れたとき、言葉を失った。余りにも大きな被害。計画避難をする飯舘村も歩いた。向き合っていることの重大に魂が冷えそうになった時、お互いの温もりの大切さに気付いた。

私たちは前に進んで行かなければならぬ。さまざまな声を響き合わせながら。手を取り合って。私たちが今もっとも必要としていることは、他者の魂からかすかに聞こえてくる、そのため息のような声に耳を傾けること。

Quakebook。ここに、ありったけの気持ちが集まった。私たちのこれからの道のりは試練に満ちているかもしれないが、一人じゃないって感じることは、何て素晴らしいことなのだろう。

茂木健一郎
2011年5月　東京にて

Foreword

For me, Tokyo was metropolitan love at first sight. It was 1992, and the government sent me for a language homestay. I got off the Skyliner at Ueno Station from Narita and that was it, I was done for. I could try to tell you why—the energy of the place, its strangeness, the feeling of method to the madness—but really, you might as well try to explain your first crush, your first love, the attraction of a lifelong romance. Whatever you can explain in words won't quite be it. The real connection is always too deep, too elusive, too mysterious ever to be corralled by language. The words will never get it right.

Still, if you're in love and you're a writer, you have to try. You might even create a character, say, a half-Japanese, half-American assassin, to help you:

"At first light, the whole of Shibuya feels like a giant sleeping off a hangover. You can still sense the merriment, the heedless laughter of the night before, you can hear it echoed in the strange silences and deserted spaces of the area's twisting backstreets. The drunken voices of karaoke revelers, the unctuous pitches of the club touts, the secret whispers of lovers walking arm in arm, all are departed, but somehow, for just a few evanescent hours in the quiet of early morning, their shadows linger, like ghosts who refuse to believe the night has ended, that there are no more parties to attend."

If my books have been love letters to Japan, this one is an SOS. I'm both proud and humbled to be part of it, to be in a position to reach others who love Japan and long for Japan so that together we can give back some of what we've received, and to do something to help Japan back to her feet.

Barry Eisler

序文

僕は大都会東京に一目惚れをした。1992年、米国政府が語学ホームステイに僕を日本に行かせてくれた。成田空港からスカイライナーに乗って上野駅に降りたったとき、僕はもうやられた。その場所のエネルギー、違和感、だけど混沌とした裏に何か合理性を感じたところ―と、いろんな理由を並べてみても結局、初めての片思い、初めての恋、生涯をかけての大ロマンスを説明するのと同じぐらい無駄な作業だ。言葉での説明は本質を捉えないのだ。本当のつながりは深すぎて、とりとめのないもので、あまりにも不思議で、言語でそれを突き止めることができない。言葉では正しく伝えられない。

でも、恋をしている小説家だったらがんばって言葉にしてみないと。もしかして米国と日本のハーフの殺し屋というキャラクターを作って彼に手伝ってもらうことだってあるかも。

「夜明けの渋谷は二日酔いの頭を抱えて眠りこんだ巨人のようだった。歓楽の余韻はまだ漂っている。ねじれ、くねる細い裏道の不似合いな静寂と人気のない空間に、先夜の無思慮な笑い声がこだましているのが聞こえるような気がする。カラオケ屋でのお祭り騒ぎを終えた酔客の声、クラブの呼びこみの上滑りした口上、腕を組んで歩く恋人たちの秘密めいたささやき声―すべてが帰途についたあとでも、不思議なことに、早朝の静けさに包まれた束の間、彼らの影は、パーティが終わったことを疑っているかのように、ぐずぐずと居残っている。ちょうど、夜が終わったことを頑として認めない幽霊のように」

僕がいままで書いた本がもし日本に対する恋文だったとして、この本は日本のためのSOSだ。このプロジェクトを通して、日本を愛し、日本を思い求める皆様ともつながり、みんなで微力ながら日本復興のために何かお手伝いができることを恐縮ながら光栄に思っている。

バリー・アイスラー／小説家
(本文中の引用部分は小説『雨の牙』から抜粋)

Introduction

The idea for this book came out of desperation; desperation to do something for a country on its knees.

As I write this, intense aftershocks still force me out onto the street with my daughter in my arms, even though we live far from the hardest-hit areas of the country, and far more comfortably than the thousands in refugee shelters.

After nightfall, my city is dark, as we all try to use the least electricity possible to save energy for more important uses. We wear coats in our homes against the cold. We sleep in our clothes in case our homes collapse and we have to run for our lives. We've forbidden our children from drinking tap water for fear of poisoning them with radiation. And we are the lucky ones.

Those of us who live in Japan are in a state of war. But not a war against a nation, or even nature. We are fighting defeat, worry and hopelessness. The question is: Are we strong enough to overcome?

If Japan is to lift itself from disaster, enormous effort will have to be expended by a great many people. Tens of thousands are already working together under extreme pressure toward this goal, in the hardest hit Tohoku region, around the nuclear reactors in Fukushima, and throughout the nation and world. Millions more have donated generously, and wish they could do more.

For the many people around the world who care deeply about Japan, this book is a snapshot of a nation in crisis, told by the people affected, in their own voices.

Our Man in Abiko, Editor
Chiba

はじめに

本書を考えついたのは必死の思いからだった。惨状を前に膝折れた国のために何かできることはないか。

これを書く今も、強い余震があると娘を抱いて外に出なければならない。もっとも深刻な被害を受けた地域からは遠く離れて暮らし、避難所に暮らす数千の人々に比べればはるかに恵まれているにもかかわらずだ。

日が暮れると、私の街は暗い。みんなはなんとかして電気を節約して、もっと大切なことのために使ってもらおうとしている。家の中ではコートを着て、寒さをしのぐ。家が倒壊して逃げ出さなければならない場合に備えて、服を着たまま床につく。子どもには水道の水を飲ませないようにした。放射性物質を摂取させないためだ。それでも、私たちは幸運だ。

日本はいま戦争状態にある。ただし、敵は国家でもなければ自然でもない。敗北、不安、そして絶望との戦いだ。私たちには勝利するだけの強さがあるか。それが問題だ。

日本がこの震災から自ら立ち上がるには、多くの人々が果てしない努力を続けなければならない。この目的のために、すでに何万もの人々がすさまじいプレッシャーの中で協力して働いている。最大の被災地である東北地方で。福島原発の周辺で。そして、日本中で、世界中で。さらに数百万の人々が惜しみなく義援金を差し出し、もっとできることがあればと願っている。

日本に対して深い心遣いを示す世界中の多くの人々に、本書を通じて危機に直面した国のありのままの姿を伝えたい。被災した人々が語る言葉で、彼ら自身の声を通して。

Our Man in Abiko　編者

千葉県

Names

Here is a photograph, dated 13 March, by Kiyomu Tomita, one of the first independent journalists who entered the area after the quake and tsunami. "A girl huddles herself," he tweeted. "She has lost her family. In Nobiru."

I had barely known these place names. Some "bigger" names such as Sendai, Ishinomaki and Rikuzen-Takata were quite familiar, but I didn't know anything about smaller towns. It was just like how I came to know the name Omagh, Northern Ireland, when the Real IRA bomb killed 29 people in 1998. There would have been far better ways to get to know the name of a town or city. The fact is, whether you know the name or not, there are people living there.

How old is she? 11 or 12? I wept, for the first time after the quake. Then I realized that there's another person in the photo. Somebody wearing black socks is sitting right next to her. So, the girl is not alone, at least. I prayed, and remembered the place name "Nobiru." I googled and found it was a famous beach town in Miyagi Prefecture. The girl wore a green top. I shut off my computer.

Another name is "Futaba, Fukushima." On Saturday, 12 March, I went to my local supermarkets. The bigger one was virtually empty. I could buy some ginger though. The smaller store seemed to have had fewer panicked shoppers. They had almost as many kinds of fresh vegetable as usual. Good, I thought, and then I saw the name "Fukushima" on the package of ordinary shungiku. At the time, partial meltdown had already been reported. I bought it. I cooked, praying for the safety of the farmers. It was delicious.

As I found out later, Futaba was where the first cases of radiation were reported. I'm quite sure this is the last time we see a Futaba vegetable at my local supermarket.

Yoshiko Ikeda
West Tokyo

地名

ここにある写真(左ページ)は、津波と地震に見舞われた地域に最初に足を運んだフリージャーナリストのひとりであるキヨム・トミタ氏により、3月13日に撮られたものです。「女の子がうずくまっている」と彼はツイートしました。「彼女は家族を失った。野蒜で」

私はこれらの地名をほとんど知りませんでした。もっと「大きな」都市、たとえば仙台や石巻、陸前高田ならわかりますが、小さな町については何も知らなかったのです。そう、北アイルランドのオマーという町を初めて知ったのは、29人が死亡した1998年のIRAによるテロ爆破事件でした。町や都市の名を知るには、もっと良い方法がたくさんあるでしょうに。ただ、事実として変わらないのは、なじみのある地名であろうとなかろうと、そこには住んでいる人たちがいるということ。

彼女は何歳だろう？ 11歳か12歳？ このとき、地震が起きてから初めて私は泣きました。ふと、その写真にもうひとり写っているのに気づきました。黒い靴下をはいた人物が彼女の隣に座っています。少なく

とも女の子はひとりではなかったのです。私は祈り、「野蒜」という地名を胸に刻みました。グーグルで調べると、宮城県の有名な海水浴場とありました。少女はグリーンのパーカーを着ていました。私はパソコンの電源を切りました。

もうひとつの地名は「福島県の双葉」。3月12日の土曜日、私は近所のスーパーへ出かけました。大きいほうの店はほとんど何もなく、ショウガだけ買うことができました。小さいほうの店は、どうやらパニック買いをする客はあまり訪れていないようで、たくさんの新鮮野菜がいつもとほとんど変わりなく陳列されています。良かった。いつもの春菊のパックを見ると「福島産」と記されています。そのとき、原子炉で一部メルトダウンが起きているとすでに報道されていましたが、かまわず購入。農家の人たちの安全を祈りながら、それを料理しました。とてもおいしかったです。

後になって知ったことですが、双葉は放射能汚染が最初に報告された地域でした。これからは双葉産の野菜を地元スーパーで見かけることはないのでしょう。

Yoshiko Ikeda
西東京

Alive

It's become a ritual that when earthquakes hit Tokyo, people announce on Twitter as soon as they feel them. So I opened up Twitter and sure enough, pages of "Oh, felt that," "Shaking," "Earthquake!" filled my screen. Then things got weird.

As I joined the online crowd, people were commenting on how long it was going on when things started getting rough. The intensity increased and I held on to my desk. I can remember hearing water sloshing around in a bottle inside my refrigerator and thinking to myself, "This is not good." Things fell off my shelves. Everything in my apartment started to move freely. The TV, my china cabinet, bookshelves, even the chair I was sitting in. Honestly, running or hiding never even entered my mind. I felt frozen, watching as things around me were all falling. I felt like it wasn't real. When it was over, it looked like someone had gone on a rampage in my apartment. I was still sitting in my chair, trembling a little.

After a moment I turned back to Twitter and messages were flying past. It was clear now that something huge had just happened. I flipped on the TV and soon learned some of the basics: The quake was centered in northeast, and we only got a small taste of the full force. People outside of Japan were asking what had happened. News hit of a huge earthquake in Japan, but there were few details. Rummaging through the mess on the floor I found my video camera and a laptop and set up a quick livestream broadcast of the news on TV. For hours I kept the video running as I started to clean up my apartment. I stayed on Twitter throughout the night, as aftershock after aftershock rocked my building, each threatening, then backing down. Soon hundreds of people had logged onto my video as I continued passing information on Twitter to people at work, walking home, or outside of Japan altogether.

I kept at this for the days following, taking few breaks even to sleep as constant aftershocks would soon bring me back to my desk. Together we learned of the tsunami and the terrible damage, the towns washed away into the ocean. Together we learned of the problems with the nuclear reactors in Fukushima. Together we learned that the entire world had heard of the disaster and that planes were on their way to help those in need. Together with thousands of people in my online community, most of whom I have never met, I felt fear, gratitude and sometimes despair, but I never felt alone.

Steve Nagata
Tokyo

生きている

　東京では、地震が起こり、揺れを感じたらすぐにツイッターで報告することがお約束になっている。思った通り、ツイッターを開くと「あっ、感じた」「揺れてる」「地震だ！」といったつぶやきが何ページも画面を埋め尽くしていた。そして、そこから妙な展開になっていった。

　私がオンライン上の仲間に加わったとき、皆は揺れの長さについてコメントしていたが、そこから一気に状況が悪くなっていった。揺れの激しさが増し、机にしがみついた。冷蔵庫にあるボトルの水がバチャバチャとはねる音を聞いて、「これはまずいな」と思ったことを覚えている。棚からものが落ちた。アパートにあるものすべてが勝手に動き始めた。テレビ、食器棚、本棚、そして座っていた椅子までもが動き出す。正直なところ、逃げたり、隠れたりすることが頭に浮かぶことすらなかった。身を凍らせたまま、身の回りのものがすべて落ちていく様子を眺めた。まるで現実とは思えなかった。地震が終わると、だれかが私のアパートを荒らし回ったかのような状態だった。椅子に座ったまま、少し震えていた。

　すぐにツイッターに戻った。そこにはメッセージが飛び交っていた。たった今、大きな何かが起こったことは明らかだった。テレビをつけ、すぐに基本的な事実を知った。地震は東北を震源地としており、私たちが経験したのは威力全体のほんの一部でしかなかった。国外にいる人たちは、一体何が起こったのかを尋ねてくる。巨大な地震が日本を襲ったというニュースが流れたが、詳しいことはわからない。ものが散乱した床を引っかき回して、ビデオカメラとノートパソコンを探し出し、すぐさまテレビのニュースをライブストリーム放送するためにセットアップした。何時間もビデオを放映し続けながら、アパートの片づけを始めた。余震に次ぐ余震が私の住む建物を揺らし、脅し、そして静まっていくなかで、私は一晩中ツイッター上に留まった。そのうち何百人もの人が私のビデオストリームを視聴してくれるようになり、私はツイッターで、仕事中の人、家まで歩いて帰る人、あるいは国外にいる人たちに情報を提供し続けた。

　これを数日間続けた。眠るための休憩すらあまり取らずにいた。絶えることのない余震がすぐに私を机に呼び戻すからだ。津波について、ひどい被害について、海に呑み込まれた町について、私たちは共に知った。福島の原子力発電所の問題について、私たちは共に知った。全世界がこの災害のことを聞き、助けを必要としている人たちのために飛行機が向かっていることを、私たちは共に知った。ほとんど会ったことのない、オンライン上のコミュニティの何千人もの人たちと共に、私は恐怖と感謝の気持ち、そしてときには絶望を感じた。だが、孤独を感じることはなかった。

Steve Nagata
東京都

Another

When the earthquake struck, I was in the waiting room of a small clinic with my 5-year-old twins. The TV switched over to a broadcast about the quake.

Suddenly the building started to shake violently. I took my children and ran out of the clinic and onto the sidewalk, since I was afraid the building would collapse. Everyone, including doctors, office staff and nurses from the clinic also rushed outside.

The floor above the examination room of the clinic held a rehabilitation center. Elderly patients, and one of their doctors who was blind, came quickly out of the emergency exits. The elevators were out of service, so the patients had to rely on the support of young staff members.

As the violent trembling continued, everyone huddled together on the sidewalk. The shaking was so bad that all anyone could do was cling to the ground. My children were so scared that they clutched a nearby tree and held on. Street signals and power lines swayed like crazy. It only lasted for a few minutes but it felt like a very long time.

After everything settled, everyone filed back into the clinic. Just as we arrived, an aftershock came. I grabbed my son's hand and was about to run out again, but I couldn't find my daughter. I told my son to go out without me. As I headed back inside to search for my daughter, one of the doctors appeared carrying her in his arms. Apparently she'd gone back to get my handbag and coat that I'd left behind.

"I can buy another bag or coat, but I can't buy another one of you if you die, so just leave those things behind!" I told her.

Finally, after seeing the doctor and picking up our prescriptions, we walked home. CDs and books were strewn about the living room. Our big, old television set had fallen off the shelf. Everything looked so different that the kids were upset. It was getting late and the air was chilly, but we decided to wait in the garage. I turned on the radio to hear that the trains weren't running. My husband commutes to work by car, so I figured he'd still be able to make it home, but my cell wouldn't connect, I couldn't text and the house phone was dead.

Night fell and it got cold so we went back into the house. My husband called. "I'm fine, but I have to stay and support other workers who can't go home, so I'll be pretty late." Even though it was cold I was too fearful of any aftershocks to use the heater, but hearing from my husband made me feel cozy and warm.

A water main had been damaged in the quake so we couldn't run the tap. Our only choice was to have rice balls for dinner. The kids fell asleep while waiting for daddy to come home. He finally arrived, three hours later than usual. He looked exhausted.

Masumi Nabekawa
Abiko, Chiba

もう一度

　地震が起きたとき、私と5歳の双子は小さな病院で診察の順番を待っていました。
　待合室で見ていたテレビから、突然地震のニュースが流れました。そのとき、激しい揺れが襲い、子どもたちと病院を出て歩道に避難しました。その病院はビルの中にあり、ビルが崩れることも考え、ビルから離れた歩道に避難しました。病院の中から事務の人、看護師、先生、みんなが歩道に避難してきます。
　診察室の上の階にいたリハビリ中のお年寄りたちや、目の不自由なリハビリの先生も非常口から避難してきました。エレベーターが使えないので、男性職員に支えられていました。
　激しい揺れの中、みんなで身を寄せ合い歩道に座り込みました。揺れがひどく、地面にしがみつく形でしか姿勢が保てません。子どもたちは、怖さのあまり歩道の植木を強く握りしめていました。街頭や電線が激しく揺れています。数分の揺れでしたが、ひどく長く感じました。
　揺れが収まり、もう一度病院の待合室へ戻りました。するとまた、激しい地震です。私は息子の手を握り、また病院の外に出ました。逃げようとすると、娘がなぜか見当たりません。歩道に息子を避難させて、病院の中に娘を探しに行こうとしたとき、避難するために外に出てきた先生に娘は抱きかかえられていました。娘は、荷物を置いて避難した私のために、荷物を取りに行ったのです。
　「バッグやコートはまた買えばいいけど、あなたの命はなくなったら買えないから、置いてきていいんだよ」と伝えました。
　診察を終え、薬をもらい、徒歩で帰宅しました。部屋の中はCDや本が散乱し、大きなブラウン管のテレビが棚から落ちています。普段とは違う部屋の様子に、子どもたちは動揺しています。時刻は夕方で肌寒かったのですが、車庫にいることにしました。ラジオをつけると、電車が動いていないという情報が流れています。車通勤の主人は帰宅できるに違いないと思いました。でも、メールも携帯電話も自宅の電話も通じません。
　夜になり、寒くなったので家の中に移りました。そのとき、主人から電話が入りました。無事だけど、帰宅できない人のサポートがあるので帰りは遅くなる。余震が怖くてストーブが使えず寒い部屋が、主人からの電話で少し温かくなった気がしました。
　主人を待つ間に子どもたちは、おにぎりを食べると安心したように寝てしまいました。市から、水道管が破損したので水道の使用を控えるようにとの放送があったので、夕食はおにぎりですませたのです。
　いつもより3時間くらい遅れて、主人が帰宅しました。その顔は、ひどく疲れていました。

鍋川真澄
千葉県　我孫子市

Awakening

I feel numb now, as if I was there myself and hit with this disaster as you have been. Only just recently I visited Tokyo, and was delighted how beautiful, clean and quiet the city was! I didn't expect a disaster like this to happen to the country I love so much.

One year, John, my husband, Sean and I, were in a hotel in Tokyo. It was in the morning, and the earthquake suddenly hit the three of us. I immediately grabbed Sean, who was still a little boy then. I went into an open closet, holding Sean tightly, and sat in there, kept repeating "Namyohorengekyo". After the earthquake subsided, John laughed and said he didn't understand why I sat in an open closet. I explained to him that it was important to be protected by a structure. Well, at least, that was what I was told when I was a child. The earthquake John, Sean and I experienced was not at all like the one you just experienced. But still my body is now shaking tonight from the memory of it.

So I feel deeply for you for having experienced the earthquake that was the severest in the history of Japan. It must have been so, so horrible. I extend my sympathy and love to each one of you. I'm very sorry that you had to go through what you went through. My heart is with you all the way.

Yoko Ono Lennon
New York City, 11 March 2011

愛する日本のみなさん、私は今、私自身がそこにいて、みなさんと一緒にこの大災害に襲われたように、ぼう然としています。私はつい最近、東京を訪れて、この街がいかに美しく、清潔で、平穏であるかを喜んでいました。私がとても愛しているこの国に、このような大災害が起こることは、まったく予期していませんでした。

ある年、私の夫ジョンとショーンと一緒に東京のホテルにいました。朝のことでした。突然、地震が私たちを襲ったのです。私は当時まだ小さかったショーンをすぐに抱いて、扉が開いたクローゼットの中に入り、しっかりとショーンを抱きしめてうずくまり、南無妙法蓮華経を唱えつづけました。地震がおさまった後、ジョンは笑って、なぜ、私が扉が開いたクローゼットの中に座っていたのか理解できないと言いました。私はそれは、骨組みによって守られるので、重要なことなのだと言いました、少なくとも、私が子どものときに教わったことでした。ジョンとショーンと私が経験した地震は、みなさんが経験したようなものでは、まったくありませんでした。でも、そのときの記憶で私の身体は今、震えています。

日本の歴史上もっとも甚大な被害を及ぼした地震を経験したみなさんのことを、私は深く感じています。どんなに怖かったでしょう。みなさんのおひとり、おひとりに、私のお見舞いの気持ちと愛を伝えさせてください。どうしてこんな怖いことを、みなさんが経験なさらなければならなかったのだと苦しく思います。私の心は、いつでもみなさんとともにあるのだということを知ってください。

愛をこめて、ヨーコ。
オノ・ヨーコ 2011年3月11日
(日本語も本人)

Beautiful

In the midst of all the concern and fear, my wife and I received a bit of very happy news: a photo of my mother- and father-in-law. It was taken by my wife's high school friend, who made the long and potentially dangerous drive from Tokyo to their hometown in suburban Sendai. The photo shows our teary Mom and Dad smiling, happy and safe. It's easily the most beautiful photo I've ever seen.

Christopher Maurer
Chicago, Illinois, USA

美しい

不安と恐怖のさなか、私たち夫婦はとてもうれしい知らせを受け取りました。それは義理の両親の写真でした。妻の高校時代の友人が、危険が予想される中、東京から仙台郊外にある妻の地元まで、長い道のりを車で行って撮影してくれたのです。この写真は涙ぐんでいる両親の笑顔、そして彼らが幸せで無事であることを伝えてくれます。間違いなく、これは私が今まで見た中で最も美しい写真です。

Christopher Maurer
米国　イリノイ州　シカゴ

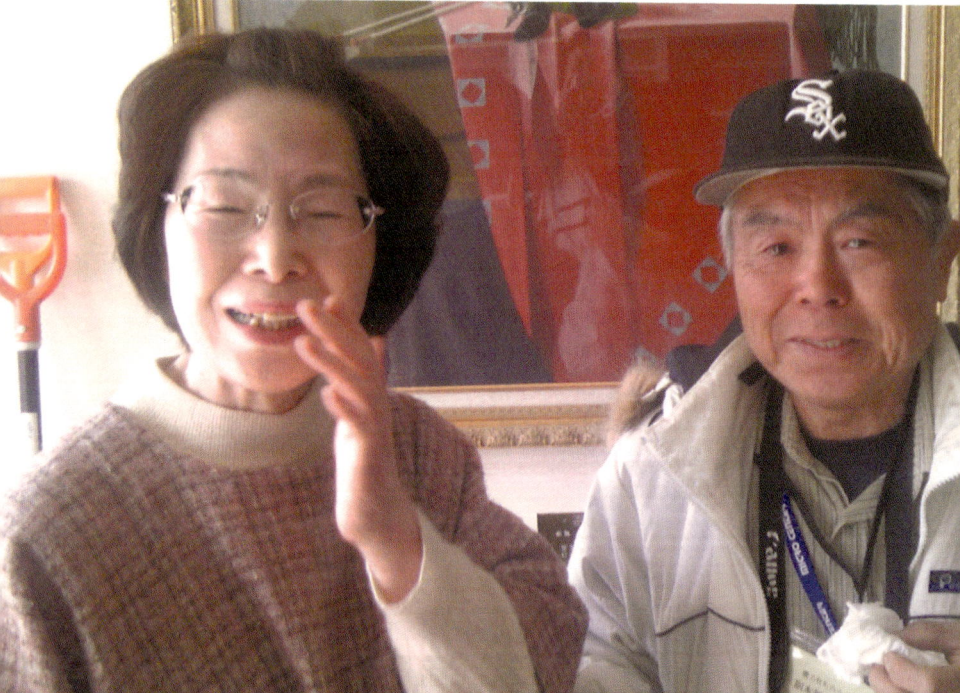

Christopher Maurer

Birthday

I was working alone in my optics laboratory in Koganei, in a single-story building where quakes are rarely felt. When the shaking started it didn't take me long to sense that this was a Big One. Everywhere around me, equipment was rattling more and more violently and a few small things fell to the floor. I quickly convinced myself that there was no immediate danger of being hit from above and whipped out the mobile phone camera. I filmed the optical table heavily wobbling on its pneumatic vibration damping legs, gas canisters beating against their stands, 19" racks swaying and posters in the hallway swinging synchronously from side to side.

After the shaking had died down, I went outside with people from the other labs and heard over the loudspeakers that the quake had been rated a 7 on the Japanese scale in Miyagi. Back in the lab, with NHK on, I could soon watch in terrified disbelief the destruction wreaked by the tsunami on the northeast coast.

A few hours later I did a superficial inspection of the experiment, turned off the laser and measurement gear and went back to my office. When learning about the total shutdown of public transportation, and being 30 km away from home, I prepared to stay overnight, while my wife was walking ten km to get home to a terrible mess in our 13th floor apartment.

I called my horrified parents, and then sat down with some colleagues for dinner and a beer. Around 3:00, exhausted from following Twitter and watching doom on NHK, I fell asleep on the office floor. It was my 31st birthday.

Jonas Neergaard-Nielsen
Tokyo

誕生日

私は小金井市にある光学研究室でひとり作業をしていた。研究室は平屋の中にあり、地震が起きても揺れを感じることはほとんどない。だから、揺れ始めてすぐに、これは大地震だと察した。周囲で実験器具が荒々しく猛烈な音をたて始め、小物がいくつか床に落ちた。頭上からの落下物の危険はないととっさに判断した私は、カメラ付き携帯電話をさっと取り出した。光学実験用テーブルが、空気圧式除振制御機能を持つ脚の上で激しくぐらつく様子や、ガスボンベが収納スタンドに激しく打ち付けられている光景、19インチラックが揺さぶられ、廊下に張ってあったポスターが一斉に左右に大きく揺れている有様を動画撮影した。

揺れが収まってから、他の研究室のスタッフと一緒に屋外へ避難した。スピーカーの放送で、地震は宮城県沖を震源とし、日本の地震尺度で震度7だったと知った。研究室に戻りNHKをつけると、東北地方沿岸が津波によって破壊されていく様子が映し出されいる。私はそれを、恐怖のあまり信じられない思いで見ていた。

数時間後、私は心ここにあらずの状態で実験に立ち会い、レーザーと計測機器の電源を切って、オフィスに戻った。しかし、交通機関がすべて運行停止になっていると聞いて、自宅から30キロ離れたこの場所で夜を明かす準備を始めた。そのころ妻は10キロ歩いて自宅にたどり着いたが、マンションの13階の部屋はすさまじいほどにめちゃくちゃになっていた。

Chris MacKenzie

私は心配する両親に電話をかけ、オフィス内で同僚らと夕食をとり、ビールを1缶飲んだ。ツイッターをフォローしながらNHKで惨状を見ることにも疲れて、3時ごろにオフィスの床で眠り込んだ。31歳の誕生日だった。

Jonas Neergaard-Nielsen
東京都

Bravery

I know little about the Fukushima 50 as the Japanese media haven't focused on them yet. I don't know if they really volunteered to stay there to complete their mission or they were ordered to stay there because they're too old to have children. Either way, I'm so proud of them, that they're ready to sacrifice their own life to try to save all of us.

I've been telling our daughters when we spot any of the Fukushima 50 on TV that they are the bravest men in the world. The place could explode at any time. I just can't imagine how their families can cope with everyday life. They must be terrified every time they turn on TV.

We still experience some earthquakes everyday and they make me so nervous. Even a tiny rattle frightens me. *This might be the biggest one. This might be it. I don't want to lose my family. I don't want to die.* My heart beats so fast. I just cannot believe it is actually happening to us. It feels like it's never-ending.

But all I can do is send encouragement to the Fukushima 50 and pray for them. We have to believe that the Fukushima 50 will complete their mission and save all of us. I have to believe that every single man can come home to hug their wife and children who have been dying to see them.

Yoshie Sherriff
Abiko, Chiba

任務

海外でFukushima 50と呼ばれている人たちに関して、日本ではあまり注目されていないのが現状だ。彼らは、本当にボランティア精神で任務を果たすべく福島原発に残ることにしたのか？ あるいは、ある程度年齢がいっているので、健康上それほど影響なしと勝手に判断され、滞在命令が出たのか？ 現状では情報不足でよくわからない。どちらにしても、私はFukushima 50と呼ばれるメンバーを心から誇りに思う。どんな状況だったにしろ、自分たちの命を犠牲にしてまでも私たちを救おうとする精神、しかもものすごいプレッシャーの下で。頭が上がらない。

Fukushima 50のメンバーがテレビに出ると、「このおじさんたちは、世界で一番勇気ある人たちなんだよ」と娘たちにいつも話している。あの危険な場所はいつ爆発事故が起きたっておかしくない状況だ。彼らの残された家族は、いったいどのように思い、心配し、毎日を過ごしているのか想像を絶する。福島原発でまた何か違うことに挑戦するたびに、ハラハラして居ても立ってもいられない心境だろう。

まだまだ毎日余震が続き、心が壊れそうになる気がする。微震が来ただけでもドキドキし始めて、怯える自分がわかる。

「今度こそデカイ地震かも！」

「これが最後かも！」

「家族と離れ離れになりたくない！」

「死にたくない！」

短時間にあれこれ考え、鼓動は瞬く間に早くなっていく。こんな生活が今現在こうして実際に起きていること自体、信じられない。ましてや終焉なんて果たして来るのだろうか？

しかし、いま私にできることはFukushima 50を心から応援し、そして祈ることのみ。彼らが任務を無事に果たし、私たちを救ってくれることを信じよう。そして、死ぬほど会いたがっている家族のもとに全員が無事で戻ることを信じよう。

シェリフ由恵

千葉県　我孫子市

Cakes

My daughter, during the earthquake, was in her piano class. Her teacher held her tight while she continued playing "Row row row your boat, gently down the stream."

Most soothing and reassuring were our building's owners who called Neeraja and Hema down for tea and cake, saying, "It's OK, relax, stay indoors, the house is well built and protected."

All this while I was having a swinging time 30 floors above in Yebisu Garden Place Tower with my colleagues. I returned their smiles for the first minute (knowing that the building was one of the safest in Tokyo). But then I was one of the first to dive and duck promptly under my desk.

The building swayed and shook wildly. I dialed Neeraja to check the family's whereabouts then switched the phone off to save them from hearing the screams in the background.

After what seemed like an eternity and an apocalypse—computers strewn, desks swept clean, printers toppled and presentations mixed up—the more seasoned people suggested we march down 30 floors. No rushing of feet or stomping of ground, no racing through or overtaking, just a good old smiling saunter as if going down for a quick cup of coffee.

Outside everyone was gathered in groups looking up at the still-swaying building, posing for pictures (flashing the recognizable V-sign). After 30 minutes of exchanging frustrations over not being able to reach loved ones, I headed home while some of my inimitable colleagues prepared for the 30-flight climb back up to tie up loose ends.

Phones didn't work, a small glitch in an otherwise extraordinarily efficient disaster management system. I had to walk for a while with no taxis stopping. Apparently part of the drill was to keep the roads clear for fire engines, ambulances, police cars and buses. I took a bus (free of charge) and finally reached home. I'd been already slightly assured that the family was safe (I had checked Neeraja's message on Facebook), yet feared the worst for the precious possessions (TV, iPod, Tolly/Kolly/Bolly/Hollywood DVDs).

And what a sight, when I reached the building!

The landlord, Akaishi-san, opened the door, smiled benevolently in his fatherly manner. He bowed politely and said, "Come come come, the tea is hot, and we've got cakes from Holland, which you'll like. Hema-chan likes them very much."

Inside, the only sign of all the drama outside (which was still unfolding, as we had not yet heard about Sendai and the second disaster to hit Japan) was the swinging chandelier and the excited and reassuring voices of my wife and daughter chattering first to Mrs. Akaishi-san and then rushing to me and rattling off their adventures of the day, which will forever be fresh in our memories. Two things stand out: The zen-like demeanor of the Japanese amidst such a huge disaster, and the realization that if there is a place on earth that I want to be with my family and friends (current and extended), when (God forbid) such a disaster ever struck again, then it's this country, Japan.

Arun Vemuri
Tokyo, Japan

ケーキ

地震が起きたとき、娘はピアノ教室の最中だった。「Row Row Row Your Boat」を演奏し続ける彼女を、先生がしっかり抱きしめてくれた。

家族の気持ちをだれよりも癒して、落ち着かせてくれたのは、住んでいるビルのオーナー夫妻だった。ニーラジャとヒーマを下に呼び、お茶とケーキを出し、「大丈夫。落ち着いて、中にいなさい。この建物は頑丈だから、安心だよ」と言ってくれた。

そのとき、僕はというと、恵比寿ガーデンプレイスの30階で同僚と一緒に揺れに揺れる体験をしていた。東京でいちばん安全な建物のひとつであるとわかっていたので、最初のうちは同僚と笑い合っていた。でも、次の瞬間、僕はいち早く机の下に飛び込んで身を守ろうとした。

ビルは激しく揺れ動いた。家族がどこにいるか確認しようとニーラジャに電話をかけたが、周りの叫び声が聞こえないようにあわてて切った。

永遠に続くように感じた揺れのあとは悲惨な光景だった。パソコンは散乱し、机の上のものは姿を消し、プリンターは倒れ、プレゼン資料はどれがどれだかわからない。落ち着きを失わなかった同僚が、30階下の地上まで降りようと言った。だれもあわてず、大きな足音もたてなかった。急ぐこともなければ、人より先に出ようとすることもない。笑顔でゆっくりと、ちょっと下にコーヒーでも飲みにいくという感じで降りていった。

ビルの外では数人ずつグループを作って揺れ続けるビルを見上げ、おなじみのピースサインを出して写真を撮ったりしていた。大切な人に連絡がつかないというもどかしさを語り合って30分、僕は家に向かうことにした。強者の同僚は30階上へ戻って、仕事を片付けようと準備していた。

電話が通じなかったのは、非常に効率よく動いていた災害管理システムの唯一の欠点だった。タクシーが止まってくれないので、しばらく歩くしかない。消防車、救急車、警察車両、バスのために道を空けておくのが災害時の決まりだったようだ。無料で乗れるバスを使ってやっと家に着いた。ニーラジャがフェイス

ブックに残したメッセージを確認できていたので、家族が安全だったことはそれなりに確信していたが、家の宝（テレビ、iPod、インドからハリウッドまでさまざまなDVD）が最悪のことになっていないか心配だった。

建物に着いた。なんという光景だろう！

オーナーのアカイシさんがドアを開け、父親のように親切な笑顔で出迎えてくれた。丁寧に頭を下げて、「いらっしゃい、いらっしゃい。温かいお茶も入っているし、オランダのおいしいケーキもある。ヒーマちゃんはとても気に入ったみたいだ」

中に入った。外で起きている一大事（そのときはまだ仙台のこと、地震に続いた次の災害のことは知らなかった）を感じさせるのは、揺れているシャンデリアと、興奮してはいるが私を元気にしてくれる妻と娘の声だけだ。アカイシさんの奥さんとおしゃべりしていた彼女たちは私のところに飛んできて、どんなにたいへんな一日だったかを口早に話してくれた。この日のことを私たちはいつまでも鮮明に覚えているだろう。2つのことがはっきりした。まず、大災害に見舞われても、日本人は「禅の心」で冷静に振る舞う。そして、もしこのような災害が再び訪れたとき（訪れないことを祈りたい）、私が家族や（現在、そしてこれからの）友人とともにいたいのは、ここ日本だ。それがわかった。

Arun Vemuri
東京都

Care

I don't know where to start to write... ten days have passed since the earthquake. My parents' house is within 40 km of the Fukushima nuclear plant. They've been told they must stay indoors. Although the house wasn't greatly damaged by the earthquake or tsunami, as the house is built on solid ground, they have to contend with the problem of radiation.

Although this is far from the worst case of losing a family member or home, they have scarcely any information regarding radiation. All they can do is watch news on TV. They don't know really if they are in danger or if they are safe, and fight against an invisible enemy inside the house. Even if they decide to evacuate, they have no gasoline, so they don't know how far they would get. The trains aren't running, either.

My 70-year-old mother refuses to go to a shelter and insists on staying at home. She says she's not bothered by magnitude 3 earthquakes. Even though the government seems to have forgotten her, she is perfectly calm. What is the government doing? Don't they care about the people in Fukushima? When people living towards the coast were confronted with the threat of radiation, the whole town decided to evacuate without waiting for government instructions. Nobody in my hometown will evacuate. Why? What's more, they took in people evacuating from the town next-door, so now they feel they can't evacuate themselves and leave those people behind.

People of the Tohoku region are stoic, compassionate, calm and humble. They have always just dealt with the situation without complaining. Of course they have questions and fears, but they hesitate to show them as they know other people are experiencing far worse.

They don't expect the government will help them, but they've made up their minds to stay here and fight. Rumors about radiation pollution continue to grow. What have we done to deserve this? We are suffering like others in disaster affected areas. The difference is we have an unnatural and unseen danger to deal with. Please don't abandon Fukushima. Please see the reality. Please give us accurate and timely information. Please get this nightmare power station under control as soon as possible. And please know that Fukushima is doing its best.

Yuki Watanabe
Tokyo (hometown Tamura, Fukushima)

心配事

何から書いたらいいのかまとまらないけれど、地震から10日以上経ちました。うちの実家は、福島原発から40キロ圏内です。いちおう屋内退避地域です。うちの辺りは地震に関して言えば、津波にも遭わず、地盤も硬くて有名なところなので無事だったのですが、その後の原発問題で困っています。

もちろん、津波で家をなくしたとか、家族が亡くなったとか、そういう事態ではないけれど、地震以降ほとんど情報がなく過ごしています。原発に関しても、危険なのか安全なのかまったく情報がありません。ただただニュースを見て、家から出ないようにするしかなくて、ずっと家の中で目に見えない敵と戦ってます。逃げようにもガソリンがないし、列車も走っていないので、どこまで逃げられるかわからない。

70歳になる母は不便な避難所生活はいやだと自宅待機していますが、毎日の余震にも「震度3ぐらい慣れちゃった」と言い、何よりもまったく指示も情報もなくて、すでに見放されてるような生活にも慣れて、逆に落ち着きを取り戻してるような状況です。国は何をやってるのでしょうか。福島県民はどうでもいいのでしょうか。津波被害を受けた沿岸部では、その後の原発被害を受けても何の指示もなくて、町ごと自主避難をしたところもあります。うちの町も全体で避難とならなければ、だれも逃げないと思います。なぜか？

隣り近所、ほとんどの人たちが逃げてないからです。自分だけ逃げるわけにはいかないのです。そのうえ、他の町から避難してくる人たちも体育館などにいて、自分たちだけ逃げることは申し訳ないからです。

東北の人は粘り強いし、思いやりもあって、穏やかで、遠慮深いので、この状況でも黙って我慢、堪え忍んでいるのです。文句は言いたいけれど、言ったところで自分たちの状況よりももっとひどい人がいるって思って、我慢しているのです。

政府が何かしてくれるとはもはや思っていません。でも、だからこそもう少しこの状況でやれるだけやってみようと、逆にがんばろうって思って留まっているのです。放射能汚染の風評被害がまた出てきましたが、福島の人たちは何も悪くないし、他の被害地と同様に被害にあっているのです。これ以上放ったらかしにしないでください。現実を見てください！　とにかく適切な情報をあげるようにしてください！　原発を早く、安全にストップさせてください！　福島はがんばっています！

渡辺由紀
東京都（福島県田村市 出身）

Fernando Ramos

Ceiling-light

I'm sitting here in my high-rise apartment at 5:30 a.m. after being woken up an hour and a half ago by aftershocks of yesterday's big earthquake. The first thing I saw when I woke up was the ceiling-light swaying overhead. Luckily we are safe, thanks to our high-tech apartment building. It sits on some sort of hydraulic system that prevents the building from shaking too violently.

When I got home from the office yesterday, the only sign there had been an earthquake was a puddle of water on the floor from the fish tank. However, the building where I work had a huge crack in the stairwell. We have been in constant sway for the past 15 hours. As I am writing, another aftershock is rocking the building. Many new buildings and skyscrapers are built to withstand such quakes and are probably one of the safest places to be when one occurs.

However, up north they are not so lucky. The quake was stronger up there and many more buildings were damaged. But it was the tsunami that was truly devastating. It was a wall of water marching its way overland destroying everything in its path, incredible to watch on TV. Tokyo was relatively protected by its location at the inner tip of a large bay, but there are no such sheltering bays on the northeast coast of Japan. Most of it is totally exposed to the open Pacific.

This quake was the largest I have experienced in almost ten years in Japan, and from what I hear, the largest pretty much any Tokyoite had ever experienced. We often feel small tremors that gently sway buildings. It is just part of daily life here and people hardly take notice. If you are walking, you probably wouldn't notice one had even hit.

But yesterday's was different. Once my office building started to shake from an aftershock, I knew it was going to be a big one because of the recent quakes in the past week. Yesterday's quake just kept intensifying and intensifying until a couple of us were forced to crouch under our desks. My older office building is not as flexible as my apartment, so the shakes were probably far more violent.

Now, from the relative safety of this apartment, I remember how I quickly left my office and got a taxi to check on things here. The trains and subways were all automatically shut down, so a cab was my only option. I work about 7 km from home even though my office and apartment are both in central Tokyo. The city closed the elevated expressway that snakes through the city, so the city roads were jammed. The first big aftershock happened during my taxi ride near the Imperial Palace. It was surreal. The road was heaving up and down and the cars were hopping on it. I felt bad for my taxi driver, who voiced serious worry about his family. Since the cell networks were over capacity, he could not get in contact with them. Eventually, I had to get out a few kilometers from home and walk. Walking was probably quicker anyway.

I finally arrived home but, the elevators were shut down, so I had to walk up 23 flights of stairs. I can look out my window across the street to a much taller skyscraper called the Park Tower, which houses the Park Hyatt Hotel of Lost in Translation fame. Hundreds of office workers were forced to stay in their offices overnight since many live out in the suburbs and had no way home. The lights remained on in the tower for the employees. Office towers all over the city were brighter than usual because of all the employees stranded there. The elevators in my building were still out last night when I did the trek downstairs to walk my dog. The sidewalks were packed with people walking home. This constant human train lasted throughout the night. Everyone was calm and polite and took everything in their stride.

The aftershocks have been a constant at night. For several hours after the first major quake, my building felt like it was in continuous, swaying motion. You get kind of paranoid and feel like you are swaying even when nothing seems to be moving. Looking at something hanging or dangling from the ceiling or walls is a good way to tell if a quake is real or not.

While I wait for aftershocks, I keep looking at that hanging ceiling-light.

Brian Wood
Tokyo, Japan

天井の灯り

午前5時半、高層マンションの自宅でこれを書いている。昨日の大地震に続く余震が1時間半前にあって、目が覚めた。まず目に入ったのは、頭上で揺れる天井の灯りだった。幸いにもハイテクな建物のおかげで安全だ。ビルの揺れを軽減するため、基礎部分に油圧装置のようなものが取り付けられている。

昨日オフィスから帰宅した際に唯一気づいた地震の痕跡は、水槽から水がこぼれて床にたまっていたことだ。だが、オフィスのあるビルでは、階段の壁に大きな亀裂が入った。この15時間ほど余震がずっと続いている。こうして書いている最中にも、また余震で建物が揺れている。新しいビルや高層建築物の多くは耐震設計で建てられており、地震が起きたときにいる場所としては最も安全だろう。

　しかし、北方の人たちにとってはたいへんな事態になった。震度はここより強く、はるかに多くの建物が被災した。しかし、何より壊滅的な被害をもたらしたのは津波だ。水の壁が陸地に押し寄せ、行く手にあるものをことごとく破壊して突き進んだ。テレビ画面に映る光景はすさまじい。東京は、大きな湾の内側先端に位置するため比較的安全だが、日本の東北沿岸にはシェルターになるような湾は存在しない。ほぼ全域が太平洋の外海にさらされている。

　今回の地震は、私が日本で10年近くの間に体験した最大のものだ。聞いたところでは、東京都民のほとんどがこれまでに経験したことのない規模だという。建物が少し揺れる程度の小さな地震はよく起きる。それは日常茶飯事で、ほとんどだれも気にもとめない。歩行中であれば、おそらく地震が起きたことに気づきもしない。

　しかし昨日のは違っていた。前震に続いてオフィスのビルが揺れ始めると、これは大きくなりそうだとわかった。先週に何度か揺れが来ていたからだ。昨日の地震は激しさを増していき、私ともうひとりは机の下に潜り込まなくてはならなかった。職場の建物は古くて自宅マンションほど柔軟性がないので、揺れはずっと激しかったのだろう。

　いま、この比較的安全なマンションで、急いでオフィスを出てタクシーをつかまえ、自宅の様子を調べに帰ったときのことを思い出している。電車も地下鉄も自動停止したので、タクシーしか方法がなかった。オフィスと自宅はどちらも都心に位置しているが、7キロほど離れている。都内をうねるように走る高架式高速道路が閉鎖されたため、一般道は渋滞していた。タクシーで皇居のあたりを走っているとき、最初の大きな余震が来た。現実とは思えなかった。道路が上下に大きくうねり、車はその上で跳ねる。家族のことを心配そうに話すタクシーの運転手が気の毒になった。携帯電話の回線が許容量を超えて、家族と連絡を取ろうにもつながらないのだという。そうこうするうちに、自宅から数キロのところで車を下りて歩くしかなくなった。いずれにしても歩いたほうが早かっただろう。

　やっとのことで家にたどり着いたが、エレベーターは停まっていたので、23階まで階段を上がった。うちの窓からは、通りの反対側にあるパークタワーと呼ばれる、さらに高い高層ビルが見える。ここには映画『ロスト・イン・トランスレーション』で有名になったパークハイアットホテルもある。オフィスで働く数千人が、職場で一夜を過ごすことを余儀なくされた。多くの人は郊外に住むため、帰る手段がなかったのだ。パークタワーの灯りも、中のオフィスで働く社員たちのためについたままだった。都内の至るところでオフィスビルは普段以上に明るい光を放っていた。帰れない社員がいるからだ。自宅マンションのエレベーターは、昨夜犬の散歩に出ようしたときもまだ停まっていて、下まで歩いて降りた。歩道は家路を歩く人々で混雑していた。切れ目のない人の流れは夜通し続いた。だれもが、落ち着いて礼儀正しく、淡々と行動していた。

　余震は、夜も絶え間なく続いた。最初の大きな揺れから数時間にわたり、職場のビルはずっと揺れているような感じがした。疑心暗鬼のような状態で、何も揺れていないようなときでも、自分が揺れているような気になる。天井から吊り下がってたものや、壁にぶら下がっているものを見れば、本当に揺れているかどうかがよくわかる。

　余震に備えて、私は天井の灯りを見続けている。

Brian Wood
東京都

Ceremonies

Friday afternoon and the kids had all graduated. We sat around the teacher's office in hakama and suits, the principal in formal tails. I felt it first. I always feel it first. I always jump up and look dazed and everyone will laugh at me when it stops. But it didn't stop and everyone said, "You're right. It's an earthquake."

Someone inside turned on the TV and said, "It's Miyagi." That's far away from us in Kansai, but an English teacher who'd traveled to America to come to my wedding pulled out his phone to call his family in Sendai. "My family is OK, but no one can get a hold of my brother."

Everyone wandered off and changed out of their suits and hakama.

On Saturday the first bullet train ever from Kagoshima rolled into Osaka. There had been a ceremony planned, but it was cancelled. My wife's grandfather, a WWII veteran who'd been a lifelong Japan Rail employee, had been waiting for this day for years. He had had his ticket for the first train for months. He told me, "Isn't it terrible about the earthquake. I am old, but I don't feel like dying yet."

Wesley Cheek
Kyoto

セレモニー

金曜日の午後、卒業式は終わっていた。我々は袴やスーツに身を包み、教員室周辺に座っていた。校長はモーニングを着ていた。私が最初に揺れに気づいた。地震になると私はいつも飛び上がって、気を失いそうになるので、揺れが収まったときには皆に笑われてしまう。しかし、揺れは収まらず、「本当だ。地震だ」と皆が言った。

教員室にいるだれかがテレビをつけ、「宮城だ」と言った。我々がいる関西から宮城はかなり遠い。しかし、米国での私の結婚式に出席してくれた英語の教師が携帯電話を取り出し、仙台にいる家族に電話した。「うちの家族は無事でした。だけど、弟とは連絡がつかない」と言った。

皆、卒業式どころではなくなり、スーツや袴を着替えた。

土曜日、鹿児島まで行く新幹線の一番列車が大阪へ到着した。開業セレモニーが計画されていたが、中止になった。第二次世界大戦で軍人だった妻の祖父はJRの職員を定年まで勤め上げ、何年もの間この日を待ち望んでいた。彼は何か月も前から一番列車の切符を手配していたのだ。「地震って本当に恐ろしいなあ。年は取ったが、まだ死にたくはないな」と私に言った。

Wesley Cheek
京都府

Changed

The Tohoku Earthquake didn't affect me physically, but it changed the way I perceive mass media forever.

Florian
Osaka

変容

東北地方太平洋沖地震で物理的被害をこうむったわけではない。しかし、この地震はメディアに対する私の見方を永遠に変えてしまった。

Florian
大阪府

Close

I am an American-Hungarian living in Japan, married to a Japanese man. I'm from Los Angeles, so earthquakes were usually not a big deal to me. But now, I will never be so flippant about them again.

On Friday, March 11, 2:40-something in the afternoon, I was at home in my apartment in Utsunomiya, Tochigi prefecture (north of Tokyo, south of Sendai). I was rushing about gathering my son's things for baseball practice. I felt the slightest of motion at 2:46 p.m., kind of like the feeling you get when you are jet-lagged and the world starts to sway, but only for a moment.

"Rock and roll," I thought. "Here we go." So I sat down on my couch to wait it out, which is what I usually do when a quake strikes. But it kept getting stronger. The lurching started to get violent, and my windows began vibrating, and the TV started swaying and shimmying towards the edge of the sideboard. The light fixture above my head swung about. The quake kept getting more and more intense, and I wondered vaguely if I should get under the table. By then, the adrenaline had kicked in, and I felt like I was in a dream—yet the motion was all too real. Time seemed to stand still yet rush forward all at once. And I kept thinking, "This is getting weird, it's lasting way too long."

Another big lurch made up my mind for me. I yanked out a chair and crawled under. I started saying the Lord's prayer and hoping the quake would stop.

Once it was over, I realized it was time to get my son's baseball uniform to the school. As I went outside, I saw another mom rushing out with gear in hand. We piled into the van. The sound of sirens filled the air, and the firetrucks and ambulances were rushing madly about. At the school our sons were huddled in the van of another baseball mom. They charged out once they saw us, clearly high on an adrenaline rush of their own. But the school looked different. The principal was out on the grounds and teams of teachers are rushing about checking for damage. The yard was strangely bereft of students—usually some are playing after school. I sensed the principal wanted to talk to me, but there's a language barrier so we just looked at each other. The other mom was telling the boys to hurry up and change. The principal continued to frown at us.

A little after 4 p.m. the head coach arrived. He was clearly on edge in addition to his usual drill-sergeant demeanor. "Sugoi jishin! (Huge quake!)" he barked at me. I responded, "Kowai! (It was scary!)" Finally the principal decided to cancel baseball practice.

Little did we know about the tragedy that befell the northern region at that time. In Tochigi, the earthquake rated a 6. No major damage—just a broken cup in the sink and a stack of books that fell off my shelf. I didn't realize that the epicenter was up north, and that we'd only experienced the outer ripples. Yet in Tohoku, the truly "huge quake" unleashed a huge, destructive tsunami that wiped out entire towns.

Close, but not that close. Far, but not all that far. There, but for the grace of God...

Debora K Ohnishi
Utsunomiya, Tochigi

遠すぎず、近すぎず

私は日本人の夫と結婚し、日本に暮らすハンガリー系アメリカ人です。ロサンゼルスで育った私にとって、地震は特別珍しいものではありませんでした。しかし、今となっては、今後地震を軽率に考えることは二度とないと思います。

3月11日金曜日、午後2時40分ごろ、私は（東京の北、仙台の南に位置する）栃木県宇都宮市の自宅マンションにいました。大急ぎで息子の野球の練習用荷物を準備しているところでした。最初にかすかに感じた揺れは午後2時46分。時差ぼけのときに感じるような感覚で、一瞬だけあたりが揺れました。

「ロックンロールだわ」なんて思いつつ「よいしょっ」とソファに腰を下ろし、揺れがやむのを待ちました。地震が来たときのいつもの過ごし方です。しかし、揺れはやむどころか、ますます強くなっていきました。揺れはさらに激しさを増し、窓がガタガタと鳴りはじめ、テレビは肩を揺らしながらサイドボードの端へと動いていきます。頭上の天井照明はぶらぶら揺れています。揺れの衝撃は激しくなる一方で、私は漠然と机の下にもぐるべきか考えていました。そのころになると、アドレナリンが出はじめ、夢を見ているような心地になっていました。揺れは現実に起きているにもかかわらずです。時間は止まっているようでいて、すべてが一気に突き進んでいるように思えました。私は考えていました。「おかしい、揺れが長すぎる」

次に来た大きな揺れで、心は決まりました。椅子を引っ張り出し、下に潜り込みます。主の祈りを唱えながら、地震が収まることを願いました。

揺れがやむと、息子の野球着を学校へ届ける時間だと気づきました。外に出ると、野球着一式を手に急ぐ息子のチームメイトの母親の姿がありました。2人でバンに乗り込みます。あたりはサイレンの音が鳴りやまず、救急車や消防車が狂ったように行き交っていました。学校へ着くと、息子たちが別のチームメイトの母親が運転してきたバンの中に身を寄せていました。私たちを見るなり飛び出してきます。見るからにアド

レナリンが出て、かなり興奮しているようでした。学校はいつもと違う様子でした。校長も校庭に出ていて、先生たちがいくつかのグループに分かれて被害確認に走り回っています。いつもなら生徒たちが放課後遊んでいる校庭に、その姿はありません。校長先生が私に話しかけたそうにしているのがわかりましたが、言葉の壁があり、私たちはただ見つめ合うだけでした。一緒に来た母親は子どもたちに早く着替えるように言っています。校長先生は険しい顔で私たちを見つめていました。

　午後4時を回ったころ、野球部の監督が到着しました。彼はいつもの鬼教官のような態度に加えて、明らかにいらいらしている様子です。「すごい地震！」と吠えるように私に言い、私も「怖い！」と返しました。校長先生はようやく野球部の練習を中止にすることにしました。

　この時点では、東北地方を襲った悲劇については知る由もありませんでした。栃木での震度は6。大きな被害はありませんでしたが、シンクにあったカップが割れ、本棚から本が崩れ落ちていました。震源地はずっと北で、私たちは震源から遠く離れた場所で起こった余波を体験したにすぎないなどとは、そのときは思いもしませんでした。東北地方で起きた本当の「大地震」は破壊的な大津波をもたらし、いくつもの町を根こそぎ洗い流したのです。

　近いながらも、近すぎず。遠いながらも、遠すぎず。神の慈悲の心により……。

Debora K Ohnishi
栃木県　宇都宮市

Contrast

Big contrast: While the foreign media is obsessed with Apocalypses, the Japanese people are already talking of rebuilding.

Aurelio Asiasin
Kyoto

温度差

際立つ温度差—欧米メディアは終末論報道にやっきになっているが、日本人はもう、復興の話をしている。

Aurelio Asiasin
京都府

Conversation

Living safely in the bosom of central Japan, I've only been able to sit and watch in horror from afar. My struggle has been not from the direct effects of the triple disaster, but the spread of information in the media.

On March 11th at 2:46 p.m. the six-storey building where I work began to quiver. After a few minutes, the tremors subsided and everyone in my office went back to work. Twitter, however, was buzzing. My friends in Tokyo were tweeting in shock—the quake had been huge. With no television or radio in the office, I relied on the internet for updates. People pointed cameras at TVs and began live streaming the news. Cell phone pictures of fires began to leak out.

And then the tsunami came. I watched pictures on my monitor of the land turning black as seawater rushed in, crumpling burning houses and swallowing cars. I rushed home to put the television on as soon as I could. Report after report poured in on the worsening situation and Twitter was alive with new, informed people spreading all sorts of news. I decided to start collecting it together—at the very least I thought it might prove helpful for people looking for information on the quake. Before long, it was the wee hours of morning and my article was pages long. But the onslaught of information didn't stop.

The Japanese news channels had set up live streams online and several other blogs had begun disaster information pages. These provided basic survival information, ways to check the phone numbers of friends and relatives, and pages showing all recent earthquakes and places to donate.

The situation continued deteriorating over the following days, particularly at the Fukushima Daiichi Nuclear Power Plant. The foreign press was scrambling, plastering the headlines with alarming words and shocking pictures. Fear mongering over the possibility of another Chernobyl was rampant as was doom-saying about nuclear fallout over Tokyo, which is 200 km south of the affected area.

Misinformation about radiation spread, overshadowing the plight of the people in the stricken areas of northern Japan. Even previously respectable newspapers seemed to be gripped by sensationalism and were not reporting the basic necessary, objective facts.

But something amazing happened on Twitter. Those of us in Japan and able to understand Japanese noticed a stark contrast between the relatively calm Japanese media and the foreign press. We began translating live press conferences of the Chief Cabinet Secretary and linking to official radiation readings posted by the Tokyo Electric Power Company (TEPCO). People with an understanding of nuclear radiation pitched in and started clarifying out our knowledge on the subject. A team of citizen journalists had self-assembled and started disseminating information that was factually correct, balanced, and peer-reviewed. This was a far cry from the reporting by many professional journalists—reporting that was exaggerated and, in some cases, almost bordered on unethical.

I don't claim that the amateur journalists on Twitter were free from bias or ulterior motives. It is easy to imagine ordinary people being driven by heightened ego and a sense of self-fulfillment, or perhaps a desire to rip down the traditional forms of media. I'm sure my own actions as a blogger are not completely selfless. I wonder deep down how much of my motivation came from a true sense of altruism and how much of it from the growing encouragement and acceptance I found in my peers. I'd like to think that the terrible situation unfolding helped us all to move beyond personal interest.

But what this all proved to me is this: Sometimes what starts as a conversation between a few people about a shocking event can flourish into a service truly useful to many.

Michael Gakuran
Nagoya

小さなつぶやき

被災地から離れた愛知県で、テレビから映し出される大災害のすさまじい映像をただ見つめることしかできなかった僕。地震・津波・原発という3つの災害から直接の被害は受けなかったが、僕には別の葛藤があった。それはメディアが拡散する情報だ。

平成23年3月11日、午後2時46分、僕の働いている6階建てのビルが揺れ始めた。少したってから揺れが収まり、何もなかったかのように周りの同僚は平常の仕事に戻っていった。だが、ツイッターは動き始めていた。地震の大きさにショックを受け、次々とツイッターの中でつぶやく人が増えてきた。関東に住む友人のつぶやきも多くあり、予想以上の巨大な地震だったことを再確認した。テレビもラジオもないオフィスの中では、インターネットからの情報だけが頼りだった。ツイッターでは、だれかがテレビの映像をビデオカメラに写し、NHKのニュースをインターネットを通してライブストリーミングし始め、一般の人々が携帯電話で撮った被災の写真も徐々にアップロードされた。

そして津波が襲った。小さなパソコンの画面の中で、真っ黒に染まった海に呑み込まれる建物や車の映像を何度も見た。自宅に戻るとすぐにテレビの電源を入れた。災害の報告が次々と入り、ツイッター上でも新たな情報があふれている。ブロガーとして僕は散乱する多くの情報を収集し、ひとつにまとめることにした。少しでも情報を必要とする人の手助けになるのではないかと考えたのだ。しかし、あまりの情報の多さに、収拾がつかないまま朝を迎えた。

日本のメディアもようやくライブストリーミングを始め、他のブロガーたちも災害情報ページを作成し、安否確認、チャリティーへの寄付の方法などの基本情報を提供した。

その後も、災害の状況はさらに悪化し続けた。特に海外メディアが注目したのは福島第一原子力発電所の事態であった。恐怖感を生み出す言葉や衝撃的な写真と見出しを使い、混乱した状態で報告した外国の報道機関。「第二のチェルノブイリだ」と大げさに言い、災害地から南200キロほどにある東京に「放射線降下物が降る」などの情報をばらまいた。

それに加えて、放射線についての誤報も広がり、原発の問題が重視され、被災者に暗い影を落とした。以前は信頼できた新聞も扇動的な情報にとらわれ、基本的な事実さえ報告できていなかった。

一方、ツイッターでは革命が起きていた。日本に滞在して日本語を理解する人が、冷静な日本メディアと海外メディアとの際立った違いに気づいていた。そして僕らは、内閣官房長官の記者会見をライブで翻訳しはじめ、東京電力がモニタリングを行った放射線の計測状況へのリンクを載せることや、放射線知識のあ

る人がさまざまな事実を明らかにした。つまり、インターネット上で市民ジャーナリストが集まり、バランスのとれた、お互いに評価された情報を広めていった。これまでの誇張された、ときに倫理にもとるようなプロのジャーナリズムと違い、正反対の報道となった。

そうはいっても、ツイッターでの市民ジャーナリストには偏見がないとは思っていない。自尊心が強くなり、自己満足で活動する人もいるし、伝統的なメディアを打ち壊す考えを抱く人もいるだろう。ブロガーとしての自分自身の活動も、無欲から始まったものではないかもしれない。自分の行動は利他主義からなのか、人助けや仲間の共感で得た満足感からなのか、自問自答している。ただ、僕が信じたいのは、この大災害を通して人々が個人の利害を超えて行動したこと。

そして何よりはっきりしたことがある。小さなつぶやきが、大きな役割を果たすサービスとして活用されることもあるのだ。

Michael Gakuran
愛知県　名古屋市
(日本語訳も本人)

Cushions

I was teaching my elementary school class when I was interrupted by the ground shaking and an announcement over the PA system telling the kids to get under their desks. The kids did this pretty quickly, though a couple paused for a chat before getting shouted down by the homeroom teacher. This process had happened a couple of times before, one time for a minor quake and another time for a drill, so I didn't think too much of it. But after about a minute, I thought it was a good time to dive under the desk myself at the front of the class.

I'm not sure how long I spent under there. But as the stuff hanging from the walls began to fall around me and the kids gave panicked shouts, all I could think of was the accuracy of the earthquake simulation machine in London's Natural History Museum.

When the quake died down, the kids got up from under their desks and put their seat cushions on their heads. Everyone filed to the playground. The whole thing felt like a fire drill from my own school days. All the classes lined up while teachers took the register. What shocked me was that the kids were so calm about it all. I guess they are well prepared. However, just as we were let back into the school and were walking down the hall, the first of many aftershocks hit.

All the kids sat on the floor quietly. For some reason, there was a fish tank on a desk in the hall. I thought it best to hold on to it to stop it from falling. Parents had begun to gather at the school gate to take the kids home. School was now officially finished for the day.

I returned to the staff room and began to watch the footage of the tsunami on TV. Watching these horrible scenes, I understood that the quiet surreality of my

Philipp Christoph Tautz

classroom experience was a part of something bigger, something tragically real.

Shaun Hickox
Tokyo

座布団

小学校で授業をしている最中に地面が揺れはじめた。机の下に潜るようにとの校内アナウンスで授業は中断した。ほとんどの児童はすぐ言われた通りにしたが、ちょっと立ち止まっておしゃべりしていた2人が担任の先生に一喝された。こういった事態は過去にも2度経験している。あるときは小さな地震だったし、あるときは避難訓練だった。だから、今回もあまり心配していなかった。だが、1分ほどして、さすがの私も教壇の机の下に潜り込んだ。

そこにどれくらいの時間いたかはわからない。ただ、壁に掛かっていたものが次々と私の周りで落ちはじめ、パニックになった子どもたちが悲鳴を上げるようになると、ロンドンにある自然史博物館で体験した地震シミュレーターがいかに正確に地震を再現していたか、そのことしか考えられなかった。

揺れが収まると、児童たちは机の下から這い出して、各自の席にある座布団を頭に載せた。そして全員、校庭に出た。何もかもが、昔学校で経験した避難訓練のようだった。担任が点呼を取っている間に、全生徒がクラス別に整列した。驚いたのは子どもたちがあまりにも落ち着いていたことだ。心構えができているのだろう。しかし、ようやく教室に戻ることを許され、廊下を歩いていると、数多く襲ってくることになる余震の一撃目がやってきた。

児童たちは全員、静かに床に腰をおろした。どういうわけか、廊下の机の上に水槽が置いてあった。それが落ちないよう、私は手で押さえていた。すでに親たちが子どもを迎えに校門に集まってきた。その時点で正式に休校となった。

職員室に戻り、テレビで津波の映像を見た。恐ろしい光景を目の当たりにして、教室でのあの非現実的な静けさが、もっと大きな、もっと悲劇的な現実の一部でしかなかったことを私は理解した。

Shaun Hickox
東京都

Dark

Family and friends ask me if things have changed in Kyoto since the quake. Well, cafe lights go dark and convenience store shelves are empty. But what hurts is the idea that the earthquakes were like seeing a loved one getting beaten and being unable to stop it. One of the things Kyoto dwellers most look forward to is the "Higashiyama Hanatoro," a long procession of electric lanterns illuminating the streets of Kyoto's eastern area. Every spring, lovers, friends and families bustle excitedly through glowing alleyways.

Except this year.

This year was different. In Kyoto in March there is snow, wind and rain. There are no cherry blossoms. There are lanterns lining the paths and alleys, but they are not lit.

Kyoto is on a different electricity grid than eastern Japan, so the city is not so much saving electricity as it is saving money to donate to the recovery. This is largely a symbolic gesture, but its power cannot be underestimated. Tourists and residents alike are struck by the forlorn nature of the Hanatoro this year. There is little romance or celebration. The dark streets and alleys are a mournful sight that tells you Japan is hurting.

Volunteers stand out in the cold for hours, soliciting donations from the few people passing by in the snow. People are smiling and embracing less than usual. Our stoic faces all say we know this is the right thing to do, but in the streets there is a pervasive, palpable sense of loss.

Andy Heather
Kyoto

暗闇

地震以来、家族や友人が京都で変わったことはあるかと聞く。それはまあ、カフェの電気が暗くなり、コンビニの棚は空になっている。しかし、つらいのは、地震がまるで、愛する人が打ちのめされるのをただ見ているだけで止められないような気持ちにさせることだ。京都の住民が最も楽しみにしていることのひとつが、長くつらなる電気灯籠が街路を照らす京都東部の東山花灯路だ。毎年春になると、恋人たち、友人、家族は光輝く路地をはしゃぎながら行き交う。

今年を除いては。

今年は違った。3月の京都にあるのは雪と風と雨。桜はない。歩道や小道には灯籠が並んでいるが、明りは灯っていない。京都は東日本とは別の配電網にあり、町は節電しているのではなく、復興募金のために節約している。これは大いに象徴的な行為だが、その影響力を軽んじることはできない。観光客も住民も、今年の花灯路のわびしい姿にショックを受けた。ロマンスもお祝い気分もほとんど見られない。暗い通りや路地は、日本の痛みを物語るように、悲しみに沈んでいる。

ボランティアは寒い戸外に何時間も立ち、雪の中を行く数少ない通行人に募金を呼びかけている。人々の間で交わされる笑顔と抱擁はいつもより少ない。私たちのストイックな表情は皆、これが正しい行いだと語っているが、通りには明らかに喪失感が蔓延している。

Andy Heather
京都府

Debris

As I rode on my bicycle eastward from my home in Taihaku Ward, the scenery grew progressively worse. Near my house, the only damage that could be seen was small cracks in the houses and people waiting patiently for food at convenience stores or groceries. But soon I started to see dirt on the ground, and then I noticed that things were muddy, and then houses with flood damage.

Before long, I hit areas which had been swept away. Huge trees were uprooted, some fallen onto cars, smashing them to bits. I saw cars stacked on other cars. A house in the middle of the street.

Perhaps if I'd gone further, I would have seen more rescue workers. What once was farmland and small communities was now waterlogged and loaded with trash. There were broken houses strewn around me. Rice cookers and hot water kettles half-filled with mud next to brightly colored futons mixed with the debris of broken trees.

I don't know how it's going to be cleaned up. I can't imagine how any of this will ever return to the normal that I remember seeing just a few months ago. Eventually I had to turn around and go home. In just twenty minutes I was in a bustling city center, able to buy a hot water kettle of my own as other residents crowded into the electronics store, all of us trying to replace what was lost.

Greg Harbin
Taihaku, Sendai

Greg Harbin

瓦礫

太白区（仙台市）の自宅から東に自転車を走らせると、景色は次第にひどくなっていった。家の近くで目にする被害といえば、住居に入った亀裂や、コンビニやスーパーに食べ物を求めて辛抱強く並ぶ人の列くらいだった。でも、やがて地面に泥が見えはじめ、ものは泥にまみれ、家は浸水被害にあっていることに気づいた。

ほどなくして、津波で流された地域に行き着いた。大きな木々が根こそぎ倒れ、何本かは車上に倒れて車を押しつぶしていた。車が積み重なっているのも見えた。道路の真ん中に家があった。

もう少し先まで行っていたら、もっと救助隊を見かけただろう。かつて田畑であり小さい集落であったところは今や水につかり、ゴミであふれ返っていた。周囲はあちこちで家が倒壊していた。半分泥が詰まった炊飯器やら湯沸しポットやらが鮮やかな色の布団のそばに転がり、木の破片といっしょくたになっていた。

これからどうやって片づけられていくのだろう。この場所がつい数か月前に見たいつもの景色に戻ることはあるのか、想像もつかない。結局、私は引き返して家へ向かった。20分もすると、ざわついた街の中心部にいて、他の住民たちと同じように家電量販店に群がり、自分の電気ポットを買うことができた。みんな失ったものを取り戻そうとしていた。

Greg Harbin
宮城県　仙台市　太白区

Decisions

I awoke before dawn to get to my early morning yoga class. I swallowed a splash of coffee to fully awaken, then checked my email. A message from my sister asked if my wife's family was OK. I didn't have time then to check the news, but the message made it difficult to concentrate on teaching yoga that morning.

Later that day, I saw the videos of the tsunami rushing in. I watched one video after another, somehow not quite believing the disaster was real. I monitored Facebook updates from friends, because cell phone reception was down and the internet was the only reliable means of communication.

It was unsettling reading friends' posts that said things like, "Where are you? Did you get the kids?" and, "Trains stopped. Walking home. I should be home in seven hours." I imagined my friends walking helplessly through the cold night. At bedtime, I had a hard time falling sleep. When I did, my dreams were filled with images of walls of moving black water.

The next morning, people I cared about were having a rough time. I went to work, but couldn't keep my concentration. My co-workers could see I was upset. I work retail, and that morning my job just seemed so meaningless. My manager let me go home early. By Sunday, we needed to turn off the laptops and go for a walk. The news was becoming less objective and more sensationalistic. I started to rely more on Facebook and Twitter than any media source. The foreign press sickened me. They were playing up stories of fleeing foreigners that drew attention away from the suffering in Fukushima and further north.

As the week went on, our worries shifted to the reactors in Fukushima. At first, the Japanese media said people in Tokyo were slowly losing their minds worrying about radioactivity while they were jolted by aftershock after aftershock. Yet by the following weekend the Japanese media started reporting more mundane things, and in the international media Japan dropped out of the top headlines.

Now, two weeks later, I still sleep disturbed sleep, and occasionally break down in tears. I lived in Japan for 15 years and I am still very emotionally attached to the country. My wife and I want to move back to raise our new baby when he's born, but I am still seriously trying to consider where to live the rest of my life.

Ted Taylor
Santa Fe, New Mexico

決断

早朝ヨガのクラスを教えるため、夜明け前から起きていた。しっかりと目を覚ましたくてコーヒーを一口飲み、メールに目を通す。妹から妻の実家の安否を気遣うメッセージが届いていた。ニュースを見る暇がなかったが、メッセージが気になってヨガのクラスに集中できなかった。

午後になって、津波に呑み込まれる町の映像をいくつか見た。被災地の映像を次から次へと見たが、現実に起きた災害とはどうも信じられなかった。フェイスブックの友人たちの書き込みをチェックした。携帯電話が使えないので、インターネットだけが信頼できる通信手段だ。

友人の投稿を読みながら胸が苦しくなった。「今どこ？　子どもたちを迎えに行けた？」「電車が運休。歩いて帰る。7時間で着くはず」寒い夜を不安に歩いて帰る友人たちの姿が目に浮かぶ。夜、なかなか寝付けなかった。ようやく眠りにつくと、夢の中で黒い海水の壁が次々と現れた。

翌朝、私が気にかけていた人たちはつらそうだった。仕事に行ったが集中できない。同僚たちにも私が精神的に参っていることは一目瞭然だった。販売の仕事をしているが、その日は自分の仕事が無意味なものに思えた。上司は早退させてくれた。日曜日になると、ラップトップの電源を切って気分転換に散歩することが必要になった。テレビのニュースは客観性を失い、煽り立てるようになっている。メディアではなく、フェイスブックやツイッターから情報を得ることにした。外国のメディアにはうんざりした。日本から逃げる外国人の話ばかり取り上げ、福島以北にいる被災者たちの苦しみから関心を奪ってしまう。

1週間経って、私たちの心配は福島の原子炉事故に移った。容赦なく襲ってくる余震に加え、今度は放射能の問題に対する不安から、東京に住む人たちにも精神的な疲れが見え始めている、と日本のメディアは当初伝えていた。ところが翌週の終わりには、もっと日常的な話題を報じるようになり、日本のニュースは国際メディアのヘッドラインからも消えてしまった。

2週間が過ぎた今も睡眠を妨げられ、感情を抑えられず泣くこともある。日本には15年暮らし、今もこの国には特別な思い入れがある。もうすぐ子どもが生まれたら、育てるために日本に戻りたいと夫婦で思っている。しかし、自分たちが今後の人生をどこで送りたいのか今も真剣に悩んでいる。

Ted Taylor
米国　ニューメキシコ州　サンタフェ

Determination

The Hiroshima Peace Memorial Museum is a shrine to the victims of the August 6, 1945 atomic bombing of the city. One of the museum's simplest yet most powerful exhibits is the large "before and after" models of the city, from a bustling regional capital to ashes.

The Google Earth shots of towns and villages in the Tohoku region before and after the cataclysmic quake and tsunami reminded me of this blackest of days in human history.

The only difference is that the devastation of Hiroshima was at the dirty hands of mankind, while the obliteration of those vast swathes of northeastern Japan was caused by the immeasurable force of Mother Nature.

There was nothing local residents could do to prevent the indiscriminate destruction in either case. As it did in Hiroshima and Nagasaki, it will take many years to restore these areas back to any semblance of normalcy. It will also require immense resources and huge reserves of determination.

But people, especially hardy northerners inured to bitterly cold winters, have an inbuilt resilience in times of trouble. Like the victims of the A-bomb, they will form tighter bonds, dig deeper and come through stronger. Before the disaster up north, people just carried on with their lives. In its aftermath, they will strive to build better ones.

Andy Sharp
Yokohama

決意

広島平和記念資料館は、1945年8月6日の原爆投下による被爆者を祀っている。この資料館の中で最もシンプルだが、ひときわ力強い展示のひとつは、活気ある地方都市から灰へと一変した「被爆前と被爆後」のジオラマ模型だ。

壊滅的な被害をもたらした地震と津波が襲う前とその後の東北地方の町や村を写したグーグルアースの写真を見て、原爆投下という人類史上最悪の災いとなった日々を思い出した。

ただひとつ違うことがある。広島は人類の汚れた手によって壊滅された。これに対し、東日本の広範囲は、母なる自然の計り知れない力によって壊滅されたのだ。

どちらの場合も、無差別破壊を防ぐ手だては現地の人々にはなかった。広島と長崎がそうであったように、今回の被災地をいくらかでも通常に近い状態へと復旧するには何年もかかるだろう。また、それには膨大な支援と強い決意が必要となるだろう。

それでも人間は、特に厳しい冬を耐え抜く東北の人たちは、困難な時をしのいで立ち直る力を備えている。被爆者のように、彼らはさらに絆を強め、いっそうの努力をし、より強くなってこれを耐え抜くだろう。被災前、北国の人々はいつも通りの生活を続けていた。この災害の余波の中で、さらによい生活を築くために彼らは奮闘するだろう。

Andy Sharp
神奈川県　横浜市

Brighid Rader

Disappeared

My friend Mari and her 15 year old daughter Haruko were in Kesennuma, Miyagi prefecture, when the tsunami hit. They managed to stay safe on a building, but they were trapped as the water rushed into the city. When I finally got in contact with Mari two days ago, she told me how they witnessed a neighbor try to hold onto a post to stop from being swept away. The post broke, and the woman disappeared in the water. She hasn't been found yet.

Brighid Rader
Kentucky, USA

消えてしまった

津波が襲ってきたとき、友だちのマリと、彼女の15歳の娘ハルコは宮城県の気仙沼にいました。ビルに留まっていたので難を逃れましたが、町中に津波が押し寄せてきて身動きが取れなくなりました。ようやくマリと連絡を取れたのは2日前で、そのとき彼女は、近所の人が津波に押し流されないように柱にしがみついていた様子を話してくれました。その柱は壊れ、女性は水の中に消えました。女性はまだ見つかっていません。

Brighid Rader
米国　ケンタッキー州

Distance

I lived in Fukushima City from August 2006 to August 2010, where I worked as an Assistant Language Teacher on the JET Programme. I have since relocated to Ottawa, Ontario.

When I first heard the news of the earthquake and subsequent tsunami I got on Skype and contacted every single person I knew in Japan that I could and asked about their situation: Did they have water, food, gas in their cars? I feared for my friends scattered throughout Fukushima prefecture. I began reading news reports and quickly realized that the situation was indeed dire. Predictions of a nuclear meltdown and references to Chernobyl scared me. I urged all of my friends to leave, regardless of how close or not they were to the Daiichi power plant. They were getting similar urgings from their own family members and loved ones.

In Ottawa, I further immersed myself in coverage of the events in Fukushima, almost completely dropping out of society and spending over 16 hours a day online. I posted things to Facebook so people there could see what I was reading. My friends throughout Fukushima had mixed emotions: some feared for their lives and fled, others were scared but rational and calm. I think the people who stayed calm and positive had the correct approach. Initial reports of impending doom were sensationalist, scaring people in an already stressful situation. And it turns out the sensationalist media reports of instant death were completely contradictory to what nuclear experts were saying.

From NHK and BBC news, I posted Facebook and Twitter updates for the people in Fukushima about the status of gasoline, trains, roads, and the weather. I also posted reactor conditions and articles about the situation, keeping things objective and avoiding the doom-and-gloom of major news outlets. It was incredible to watch how current and former residents of Fukushima helped each other get the information they needed.

By now, some friends have left Fukushima and some are still nearby volunteering and helping. All vow to return. Through Facebook and Twitter, I am grateful I could help the Fukushima community through this difficult time.

Brent Stirling
Ottawa, Ontario

遠方より

私は2006年8月から2010年8月まで、JETプログラムの外国語指導助手(ALT)として福島市に派遣されていた。その後、オンタリオ州のオタワに戻っている。

最初に地震と津波のニュースを聞いたとき、私はスカイプにログインし、日本にいて連絡先がわかっている知人全員に連絡を取り、状況を尋ねた。水はあるのか、食べ物はあるのか、車のガソリンはあるのかと。福島県のあちこちにいる友人のことが心配だ。ニュースを読みはじめて、すぐに事態が深刻であることに気づいた。原発のメルトダウンが予測され、チェルノブイリが引き合いに出され、恐ろしい。第一原発の近くにいようがいまいが、私は友人たちに逃げるよう強く勧めた。みんな、家族や愛する人たちから同じように求められている。

オタワにいても、私は福島についての報道に没頭した。世間からほとんど離れ、一日16時間をインターネットに費やす。フェイスブックに書き込み、福島のみんなと情報を共有できるようにした。福島にいる友人たちの思いはさまざまだ。命の危険を感じて逃げた人もいれば、恐怖を抱きながらも冷静で落ち着いている人もいる。冷静で前向きな行動をとった人たちは正しく対処したと思う。今にも破滅が迫っているかのような当初の報道は煽りたてるようで、すでにストレス状態にある人々の恐怖をかきたてるものだった。すぐにも死が迫っているかのような煽動報道は、原子力の専門家が言っていることとまったく矛盾していた。

NHKとBBCニュース経由で、福島に住んでいる人たちのために、ガソリン、電車、道路の状況、そして天気についての更新情報をフェイスブックやツイッターに投稿した。原子炉の状態や事態に関する報道記事も投稿した。物事を客観的に捉えたものを選び、大手報道機関による悲観的な見通しのものは避ける。福島に現在住んでいる人たちと、かつて福島に住んでいた人たちが互いに助け合って必要な情報を得る姿を見て心打たれた。

友人の中にはすでに福島を離れた人もいれば、いまだに近くでボランティアと支援活動を行っている人もいる。全員がこの地に戻ってくることを誓っている。フェイスブックやツイッターを通じて、福島の人たちがこの困難な時を乗り越える手助けができることに感謝している。

Brent Stirling
カナダ　オンタリオ州　オタワ

Encouragement

It's been a nightmare of a week. I pray that everyone afflicted in this terrible disaster will soon wake up from this bad dream, but I don't have any words of comfort. As an old man with an old wife, I've put up with a lot this week. But it's nothing compared with the lives of those staying in shelters. Now things have settled down a little, I will attempt to convey the thoughts of the many other elderly people I have spoken with.

For us old folk confused by the scarcity of information, the radio has been our most reliable source of news. Many of us oldies are familiar with the radio and listen to late night broadcasts, with batteries that last a surprisingly long time. While we can use ordinary mobile phone functions, we've barely been able to operate emergency functions. Batteries run out as we fumble with our phones and the vast majority of us have given up trying to use them.

Very few people of my generation use the internet in the first place, and as power is needed to get online, we haven't been able to use it during power cuts. Even if we connect to the net, we're poor at finding the information we want. Naturally, we can't watch television during blackouts.

While we have inadequate access to information, we can ask net-savvy people living near us to get this information for us. For this reason, we are grateful that mobile phones and the Internet provide information. We rely on one company to provide our home with television, internet and telephone services. While we feared that the infrastructure might have collapsed, the services were quickly recovered. We are thankful for this.

The strength of our generation is our experience. While this disaster is unprecedented, similar experiences such as post-war chaos, oil shocks and the 2005 Miyagi earthquake have kept us prepared. Many people also had stocks of emergency supplies.

I pray that old people who are sick or weak can quickly receive medical attention. But rather then telling healthy old folk that you will support them, it would cheer them more to say that you'll strive to get through this together.

To be honest, it has not been comfortable for people aged over 80. Lining up for hours to get water or do some shopping chills us from the tips of our toes up and gives us back pains. But seeing young mothers of small children patiently waiting for their turn and the impressive qualities of young women who use just a calculator to total up the bills for many customers' shopping, gives me the strong conviction that this country will not break under these circumstances.

It's been a while since my wife and I shared activities and fulfilled our respective roles. Our children have encouraged us and this has led to a reconfirmation of our family bonds. We've also received much encouragement from unexpected people.

I've lived for many years. Night has always turned to day and rain has never failed to cease. Conditions have greatly improved during this week, and will get even better next week. It's time to show everyone what the prewar generation is made of. We need to stay strong.

Grandfather Hibiki
Sendai

鼓舞

悪夢のような1週間が過ぎました。深刻な被害を受けられた皆さんは、夢なら覚めよと念じてこられたと思います。慰めの言葉もありません。爺のところも年寄り夫婦で何とか耐えてきました。避難所でお暮らしの皆さんから見れば、さしたることではありませんが、少し落ち着いたところで、同年配の年寄の皆さんと話し合ったりした震災の感想を書いてみます。

我々の年代では、情報不足で混乱する中で役に立ったのはラジオでした。我々の年代は深夜放送のファンも多く、ラジオは身近にあり、電源も乾電池は意外に保つことを体験しました。ケータイは、何とか通常の操作はできても、緊急時の操作などはほとんどできませんでした。モタモタしているうちにバッテリーが切れておしまい、というケースがほとんどです。

ネットは、そもそもこの年代はネットを利用している人が少ないうえに、ほとんどは電源がなければ繋がらない環境ですから、停電の間は使えませんでした。繋がっても、欲しい情報のありかを探すのも未熟です。テレビは、当然停電の間は使えませんでした。我々は、やはり情報弱者ではありますが、でも、強者が回りにいてくれれば、そこから情報は教えてもらえるわけです。その意味では、ケータイやネットでさまざまな情報提供がなされるのはありがたいことです。

爺の自宅は、テレビもネットも電話も有線の一社に依存していて、インフラ総崩れを懸念していましたが、復旧が遅れることはありませんでした。ありがたいことです。この年代の強みは、やはり経験だと思います。今回のことは未曽有の災害ではありますが、それでも、戦争と戦後の混乱、オイルショック、仙台沖地震、とさまざまな類似体験を切り抜けた経験は大きな心の支えですし、現実にも、緊急用物資のストックがあったところも多いようです。

病気や体の弱っておられるお年寄りに、一刻も早く医療の手が差し伸べられることを祈りますが、もし元気なお年寄りがおられたら、「支える」という言い方よりも、「一緒に頑張りましょう」と声掛けしてもらったほうが元気が出そうです。

正直なところ、80過ぎの老人には、給水や買い物に何時間も並ぶのは、足先からじんじん冷えてきて、腰は痛むし、楽ではありませんでした。でも、小さいお子さん連れの若いお母さんが辛抱強く順番待ちしている姿を見たり、電卓だけでたくさんの客の買い物金額を計算してくれる若い女性のレベルの高さを思うと、この国はこんなことで決して参りはしないと強く思えてきます。

こんなに夫婦で行動を共にし、それぞれの役割を果たしたのも久しぶりだし、子どもたちからの激励に、家族の絆を再認識もしました。まったく思いもかけない人からもたくさん激励されました。

爺は長いこと生きてきましたが、明けない夜はなく、やまない雨もありませんでした。この1週間で、状況はかなり良くなりました。次の1週間はもっとよくなるでしょう。

昭和一桁のド根性の見せどころです。頑張りましょう。

響爺
宮城県　仙台市

Engage

People keep asking me what they can do to help Japan. And while I am all about donations, spreading the word, organizing charity events and the like, I realize not everyone has money to give—and no one seems to have the power to stop the media from sensationalizing the stories while ignoring the victims.

To support Japan, what I would say is this: Simply do what you do every day, but do it better. Go to school or to work but with passion and energy. Engage your neighbors or community but with more sympathy and compassion than you ever have. Let these historic moments move you, inspire you and invigorate you for as long as the feeling lasts because, believe me, that initial adrenaline and humanitarian solidarity will wear off. Ride it as long as you can. Let it make you be a better person, and let it wake you up from the complacency in your life.

Tokyo Twilighter
Tokyo

関わり方

周りの人から日本のために何ができるかと何度も聞かれている。ひたすら、募金や、現状を周囲に知らせること、チャリティーイベントを開催することと思ってきたけれど、あるとき、みんながみんな募金できるわけではないことに気づいた。被災者を無視したマスコミの煽るような報道を止める力は、だれにもないだろうということもわかった。

日本のためにできること、それは、こういうことだと思う。普段やっていることをやる。ただし、今まで以上にうまくやる。学校に行く、あるいは仕事に行くなら、いつもより明るく、元気に行く。近所の人たち、または地域と関わるなら、今までにないくらいの思いやりと温かい心で接する。震災がもたらしたこの歴史的な瞬間によって心動かされ、奮い立ち、気持ちを高め、その気持ちをできるだけ長く持続できる自分でいよう。なぜなら、当初の意欲や結束は長続きしないものだから。できるかぎり、それを長く維持し続けていこう。震災を機に、より良い人となり、現状に満足しきっていた自分からめざめよう。

Tokyo Twilighter
東京都

Escape

I'm in the Benimaru supermarket, just reading a message from Aki about what I should buy for dinner. The phone alarm rings as it always does when a large earthquake occurs, but I don't notice it over the noise in the supermarket. The floor starts shaking a little, and everyone stops and waits. It shakes harder, and everyone starts to panic. The workers calmly gather people around, but the force makes it hard to stand and I pull my phone out to mail Aki, fearing this could seem like a movie, but is in fact real.

The ceiling breaks, glasses break, food stands fall, and all I can think of is how not to die. "Don't die here, James, don't die," I say to myself. I hurried outside toward my school to catch my breath, and suddenly the wind blew and snow started to fall. I felt cold, a cold that chilled my heart. My classroom was a mess and strong aftershocks were regularly warning people that this quake wasn't simple. I must have been stupid to think there was a chance I would be going back to work that day. I gathered myself and started walking home for an hour to find Aki.

I was worried. I couldn't reach her because my phone's battery had run out. It turned out she was home trying to clean up our place, which looked as if it had been robbed. When I got there, we gave each other a big hug without saying anything. We tried to clean, but aftershocks left us no choice but to grab the essentials and leave the apartment. Our apartment had cracks everywhere, so we developed a routine of going to the refuge center at night and back home during the day.

After two days, cell phones began to work again, but only barely. Everywhere you went, there were long lines of people trying to gather any food and water they could find. Things in our neighborhood were getting harder while the situation at the Fukushima nuclear power plant deteriorated. We were still not aware of how bad the situation really was, since the government wasn't providing much information. To add insult to injury, we also found out that our company stopped paying us the day the quake hit.

So, acting on our instincts, we decided to leave the prefecture. We had heard that some of our "friends" had left already without deciding to tell us. We booked a taxi, knowing the fare to where we were going would be ridiculous, but we didn't care. We packed very little since we didn't have much time to think and took our cab to Nasushiobara station in Tochigi Prefecture. This was the closest Shinkansen station to Tohoku.

So began our escape from the Tohoku region. And we left without knowing when, or if, we would ever return.

James Hou
Koriyama, Fukushima

逃避

そのとき私は、スーパーマーケットのヨークベニマルにいて、アキから送られてきた夕飯の買い出しメールを読んでいた。大きな地震の発生を知らせる携帯電話のアラームが鳴ったようだが、スーパーの雑音で気がつかなかった。床が少し揺れはじめ、だれもが立ち止まって様子をうかがっている。揺れが激しくなるにつれ、パニック状態になってきた。従業員たちが冷静に客をまとめはじめたが、立っているのがやっとという状態だ。私はアキにメールを送るために携帯を取り出しながら、映画のようだけれどこれは現実なんだ、と恐ろしかった。

天井が崩れ落ち、ガラスが割れ、食品棚はなぎ倒され、頭の中は生き残るにはどうしたら良いか、という

考えでいっぱいになった。「ここでは死ねない、ジェームズ、死なないぞ」と自分に言い聞かせた。学校へ向かうために急いで外へ出て息を整えようとしたが、突然、冷たい風が吹き、雪が降りはじめた。寒かった。心まで凍えそうだった。私の教室はめちゃくちゃになっていて、強い余震が、この地震はただごとではないと伝えているようだった。今思うと、その日のうちに仕事へ戻れると思っていた自分が愚かに思える。落ち着きを取り戻してから、1時間かけてアキのいる家へと向かった。

アキが心配だった。携帯のバッテリが切れてしまい、彼女とは連絡が取れない。後になってわかったのだが、彼女は家にいて、まるで泥棒にでも入られたかのように散らかった家の中を片づけていたらしい。家に着くと、無言で抱きしめ合った。片づけに取りかかろうとしたが、余震が続くので、必需品を持って家を出るしかなかった。住んでいたアパートにはあちこちに亀裂が入ってしまい、夜は避難所に泊まり、日中は家に戻ることにした。

2日後、携帯電話がどうにか使える状態になった。どこへ行っても、食べ物や水を求める人々が長蛇の列を作っている。福島原子力発電所の状況が悪化するにつれ、私たちの近所でも生活が厳しくなっていった。政府からの乏しい情報だけでは、どれほどの危険や害があるのか把握できない。さらに悪いことに、私たちの勤務する会社が震災当日から給料の支払いを停止したことを知った。

心の命じるままに、福島県を去ることにした。仲が良いと思っていた何人かが、私たちに一言も言わずに、すでに避難したと聞いていた。目的地までの運賃がばか高くなることなど気にせず、タクシーを予約する。そもそも時間がなく、まともに荷造りはできなかった。タクシーで栃木県の那須塩原駅へと向かった。それは東北から最も近い新幹線の駅だった。

こうして、私たちの東北からの避難劇は始まった。いつ帰れるのか、いや帰れるかどうかもわからないままに。

James Hou
福島県　郡山市

Evacuated

I wasn't able to continue writing since my battery died, but I got an adapter at the Apple Store after arriving in Osaka. Yes, we have evacuated.

Yesterday morning I woke up my son early and told him, "We've decided to leave Sendai. Please know that you might not be able to return to this house again. It will be at least a week, maybe a month, or a year before we return. Or maybe never. Start packing your clothes in the school bag. You will not need any of the first grade textbooks nor your notebooks because there will be no more school in March. You can take your baseball gloves with you, but will have to leave behind the bat."

The primary reason for evacuation is our concern over the effects of the radiation exposure on small children, in the event of meltdown at the Fukushima Nuclear Power Plant. I, of course, feel guilty about leaving when I think of our friends who are left behind in Sendai. However, I thought I have to be responsible about my child's future, and not allow him to be exposed by choosing not to evacuate when means are available, not to mention how much I might regret it.

In addition, small children must be prioritized for care and assistance in a disaster area. Parents with small children, therefore, are not able to do much while just being a

Linda Yuki Nakanishi

recipient of the relief aid. For this reason, we also concluded that a family such as ours must evacuate as soon as possible.

When the first explosion happened at the Fukushima Plant, we decided to leave for at least a week and then monitor the situation. However, Sendai is in complete isolation, with no prospect of reinstatement of the train service at Sendai Station, the airport is completely destroyed, and access to highways is restricted to emergency vehicles only. The only escape route is via Yamagata airport in Yamagata Prefecture and accessible on the regular road. Yesterday on the way to Yamagata, we heard the news of the second explosion on the car radio. We told our son, "We don't think you'll ever be able to go back to Sendai."

Crossing the border into Yamagata, we were shocked to see a different world: traffic lights working and shops open normally. Why was nothing coming into Sendai when there were food and electricity only an hour away, and no access restriction to the regular roads?

In Yamagata, Mayo, my partner, chose to return to Sendai with food, medicine, and other essential supplies. She had been torn, up until our departure, about evacuating while others were left behind. She now strongly insisted on going back. "We don't need two adults for evacuating one child. I know how to drive back. I have so many friends and I'm concerned about their whereabouts. We have just enough gas for driving back to Sendai."

We then called a friend of ours with experience in disaster relief from the Kobe Earthquake, and asked about practical needs at evacuation shelters. So Mayo drove back to Sendai, with our car piled up with various medications, female sanitary goods, heating supplies, and food items that are easy to share and distribute. It has been a difficult, painful separation for me, accompanied by a deep sense of regret as we have gone our own ways.

In fact, upon deciding to leave Sendai, we took all that was left in our home (vegetables, eggs, diesel fuel, etc.) to the nearby evacuation shelter at our son's school. We were told then that no aid had arrived, and saw the profound need for relief goods and supplies. Was I right to just leave when those much-needed goods were right in front of me and I had the ability to transport them to Sendai? I struggle with these questions. And was I right in allowing Mayo to turn back when the situation was going from bad to worse and the evacuation was becoming more difficult with each passing day? Should I also have gone back?

My son and I remained at Yamagata airport and tried to get on a waiting list for one of the emergency flights. But it was extremely crowded (mostly with those returning from business or sightseeing trips in the area) with a long line of people trying to get a number just to be on the waiting list. While standing in the line we were told that all flights were full for the day, and that we needed to come back in the morning to start waiting in the line again for tomorrow's flights. I just prayed that we would be called today and kept staring at our number. Fortunately, we were called at the very last minute for the last flight of the day, and were able to arrive in Osaka that night.

Arriving in Osaka, what we saw from our bus to the city was another world. At

Shin-Osaka Station, I felt confused. Did the earthquake happen in the same country? But I was finally able to watch the TV at our hotel, and saw the graphic images of roaring floods and the explosion at the power plant, something I hadn't been able to see under the blackout in Sendai. And I was truly glad at the timing of my son's evacuation when I heard the news of the third reactor in crisis.

At the same time, my thoughts went out to the many children still remaining in Sendai, including our son's classmates, and I was horrified at the worsening situation with no end in sight.

I woke up this morning to the news that things had become even worse and resolved not to return my son to Sendai. It became clear to me that we must help people evacuate from Sendai as quickly as possible, especially families with small children.

Mayo and I are now working to arrange the evacuation for families based on our own experience. We're also exploring options for places to stay in Osaka. Mayo will be traveling to the Kansai area and bringing some families with her.

Mari Kurisato

I have a request for all of you. If you know of any families with small children in Sendai, please urge them to leave. I'll write more if I have energy left, but I'd like to consult my friends in the Kansai area about our evacuation and temporary housing plans. I really appreciate your help.

(Takanori and Mayo have managed to arrange the evacuation for 30 people by chartering two mini-buses. They were to leave Sendai tomorrow.)

Takanori Hayao
Osaka

避難

バッテリの残量がなくなって続きが書けませんでしたが、大阪に来てアップルストアで電源アダプタを入手することができました。そういうことで、現在大阪に避難してきています。

昨日の朝早く、子どもを起こし、仙台を離れることにしました。「キミはもうこのおうちには戻れないかもしれないことを頭においていてほしい。最低1週間、もしかすると1か月か1年かかるかもしれないけれど、二度と戻れないかもしれない。すぐに着替えをランドセルに詰めなさい。3年生の教科書とノートは全部いらない。もう3月中は、学校はない。グローブは持っていっていいけど、バットはあきらめるように」そう言いました。

避難の第一の理由は、福島第一原発のメルトダウンなどによる、小さな子どもの体内被曝への影響です。当然ながら、仙台を脱出することについては、まだ残っている友人らのことを考えると、後ろめたさがあります。しかし、脱出する手段があったはずなのに、その選択を自分がしなかったことで、もし子どもを被曝させてしまったとしたら、それで自分が後悔するだけでなく、子どもの将来に対する責任について取り返しのつかないことになると思いました。

付随的には、小さな子どもは被災地にいるだけで、いろいろ優先してケアすべき対象となります。同時に、小さな子どもがいる親は、それだけで十分に動くことができないのに、ひとり分の救援物資を必要とします。そういう家族はできるだけ早く離れるほうがよいと判断しました。

福島原発で1機目の爆発が起こった段階では、様子を見ながら最低でも1週間はと考えて出る決断をしました。しかし仙台では、仙台駅は復旧の見通しなし、空港は完全に壊滅、高速道路は緊急車両のみという封鎖状況にあるため、一般道から山形に出て、山形空港から出発するしかありません。昨日、その山形に向かう途中のラジオで2機目の爆発を知り、子どもには「たぶんキミはもう仙台に戻ることはないと思う」と言いました。

山形県境を越えると、信号も動いており、お店も普通に開いており、仙台から車でわずか1時間ほどなのに別世界であることに驚きました。1時間離れたところに食べ物も電気もあるのに、なぜ仙台には入ってこないのか。一般道には規制もないのに。

そこで、連れの皆川は、ひとりで食料や医薬品や生活物資を積んで仙台に戻ることを選びました。出発前から、自分だけが離れていいのかと悩んでいましたが、「子どもを脱出させたいという目的であれば、大人がふたりも出る必要はない。自分は運転ができるし、安否が気になる友人もたくさんいる。幸いガソリンは、仙台に戻る分ぐらいはギリギリ残っている」と言って、断固として戻ると言い張りました。

その時点で、阪神大震災のときの支援活動経験者に、本当に避難所で必要になるものは何か電話で問い合わせ、さまざまな医薬品、女性用品、暖を取るもの、分配しやすい食品など、自動車いっぱい積み込んで仙台に戻っていきました。僕にとっても非常につらく、後悔が募る別行動となってしまいました。

実は、3人で仙台を離れる決断をしたときに、自宅に残っていた一切の食料（野菜・卵）や灯油などを近くの避難所（私の子どもの小学校）に置いてきました。そのときに、まだ何も入ってきていないということを言われ、支援物資の必要性を感じていました。その物資が目の前に並んでいるのに、それを買って届ける能力が自分にはあるのに、それをしないで仙台を離れていいのか、という思いは、もちろん僕にもあります。しかし、どんどんと状況が悪化していく中で、一日一日と脱出が困難になっていくのが明白なのに、山形から引き返すのを許してしまっていいのか。あるいは僕も戻るべきだったのか……。

　僕と子どもで山形空港に残り、臨時便のキャンセル待ちをすることにしました。しかし、たいへんな混雑で（とはいえ、まだ大半が東北地方に旅行中か出張中の人という段階）、キャンセル待ちのための整理券をもらうところから行列するという状態。並んでいるときに「基本的に全便満席状態。今日の便に乗れるかはわからない。明日の便についてはまた明日朝から並ぶしかない」そう係員から言われ、とにかく整理券の番号を見つめながら、今日のうちに呼ばれることを祈りました。幸運なことに、臨時便の最終便の最後のほうに滑り込み、夜に大阪に着くことができました。

　大阪に着き、空港から市内へのバスの中から見えたのは、さらなる別世界。新大阪駅では、大震災とはどこの国の出来事か、という感じで、頭が混乱しました。しかし、ホテルでようやくテレビを見ることができ、停電下の仙台では見られなかった生々しい津波の映像と、原発の爆発の映像を目にしました。そして、3機目が危機的状況にあるというニュースに接し、昨日のタイミングで仙台から子どもを出せてほんとうに良かったと思いました。

　同時に、まだ仙台にいる多くの子どもたち、私の子どもの同級生たちのことが頭をよぎり、また、とめどなく悪化していく原発の状況に恐怖感が募りました。

　事態がさらに悪化しているというニュースとともに朝を迎え、私は、子どもを仙台に戻さないことを決心しました。それと同時に、一刻も早く他の人たち、とりわけ小さな子どものいる家族を、仙台から脱出させる手助けをしなければならないということも明白になりました。

　仙台に残った皆川とともに連絡を取り合い、自分たちの経験を参考に、具体的にいくつかの家族の脱出の手配をしているところです。また、大阪での受け入れの可能性も探っています。マヨは何組かの家族を連れて関西方面に来ることになると思います。

　皆さんにもお願いです。とくに小さな子どもがいる家族を仙台でご存じの方々は、退避を呼びかけてください。また余力があれば書きますが、その前に、関西在住の方数人には直接メールか電話をして、上記の脱出と受け入れの計画をさらに進めるためにご相談したいと思います。ご協力、よろしくお願いします。

（早尾夫妻は、貸し切りバス2台で約30人を仙台から避難させることに成功し、明日仙台を発つことになっていました）

早尾貴紀
大阪府

Exactly

The hardest thing for me, as a father, was that we were all separated when it hit. My wife was at her office, and my two boys were at their schools on opposite sides of the city. That's always the big fear, that we won't be together when the big one comes. I couldn't get through on the phone, so I sent my wife an email and turned on NHK, keeping one eye on my Twitter feed. My older boy arrived home last, after walking the

13 kilometers from his high school. It was only around 8 p.m., but it felt like we'd waited an eternity for him, especially since by then the TV was showing some truly scary footage.

People here in Nihonbashi are calm and pulling together, despite minor inconveniences like limited train service, rolling blackouts, continuing aftershocks, and some bare shelves in the shops. I can't complain, compared to the unimaginable suffering of the survivors and evacuees up north.

I see that I have finished writing this exactly one week after the earthquake hit, at 2:46 on a Friday afternoon.

Mark Rende
Tokyo

きっかり

父親として最もつらかったのは、地震が来て家族がみな離れ離れだったことだ。妻は会社に、ふたりの息子は町の反対側にある学校にいた。大地震が来たら一緒にいられないだろうと、ずっと不安に思ってきた。電話がつながらなかったので、妻にメールを送り、テレビをつけてNHKに合わせ、ツイッターから目を離さなかった。長男が高校から13キロ歩いてやっと帰ってきたのは、まだ午後8時くらいだったが、特にテレビで恐ろしい場面が流れはじめてから後の時間は、私たちには果てしなく長く感じられた。

ここ日本橋の人々は冷静で、落ち着いている。電車の運行が制限されたり、計画停電が行われたり、余震が続いていたり、店の棚が空になっていたりという小さな不便など気にしていない。東北の被災者や避難民の方々の想像を絶する苦しみを思えば、文句など言えない。

今、この文章を書き終えて時計を見た。あの地震からちょうど1週間が過ぎた、金曜日の午後2時46分だった。

Mark Rende
東京都

Mark Rende

Expectations

The great earthquake on March 11th has caused devastation in the Tohoku and Kanto regions, the likes of which has never been seen before. First, I send my condolences to those who have died and to the survivors. I thank the workers fighting hard to minimize the effects of the disaster despite the risk to their own lives, and I wish them a safe return to their families.

In my hometown of Abiko in Chiba prefecture, a quake of grade low-5 on the Japanese scale was recorded, far smaller than near the epicenter. Because we are inland, we did not get any tsunami effect. Nonetheless, it was the biggest earthquake I have ever experienced, and we have suffered greatly. I am a mother of two small children and the innumerable aftershocks worry me. But, above all, my greatest anxiety is caused by the radiation leak from the Fukushima Daiichi nuclear plant.

I think the biggest problem has been in the transfer of information. The only thing I can praise the Tokyo Electric Power Company for is the rapidity and accuracy of reporting radiation levels to the public.

They said at their press conferences that the radiation level was only a few microsieverts per hour. When they explained that amount to the public, they compared their figures with the amounts we're exposed to naturally every year, or the strength of an x-ray. Surely these figures are not comparable because the radiation exposure times are very different? These comparisons have only served to confuse the public and have made the explanations difficult to understand.

Also, we're told that people living over 30 km from the radiation area of the nuclear plant should not be concerned. I don't need to be told the same story over and over again in news reports because I know I am not getting sick here.

What I really want to know is, if the situation worsens, what happens? How is the condition of the nuclear plant going to affect us, how far is the risk going to spread, and what is the possibility of this happening? We need to know this kind of information but almost nobody has told us anything. If we had that info, everyone could consider all the options and be prepared for action, and public panic could be avoided if a worst-case scenario happened. But because we lack information, people evacuated the capital unnecessarily.

Why did we not get any information about the risks? I suspect that there has not been sufficient research into the risks posed by nuclear plants because, in the past, everyone believed the pipe dream that all Japanese nuclear plants are completely safe. Perhaps, as a result, nobody had information about the risks involved until an actual accident happened.

Japan is the earthquake capital of the world and, in this country, it is impossible to think that any construction is completely safe. In describing this earthquake we frequently use the word "unprecedented", but when they designed the nuclear plants, they should have expected the unexpected and built beyond basic specifications.

The tsunami that hit the Fukushima plant may have reached over 14 meters. That is over three times bigger than their specs allowed for.

Records from 1896 show that a tsunami of 38.2 meters hit the Tohoku region after the Meiji-Sanriku earthquake. Following the Showa-Sanriku earthquake in 1933, a tsunami of 28.7 meters was recorded. Considering these figures, the "expectations" for the highest safety standards at the Fukushima nuclear plant were not at all enough.

My wish is that all the electric power companies will learn from this accident and do their utmost to prevent future risks. This accident has given us a good opportunity to take stock of the expansion of the nuclear power plants we Japanese have embraced as a solution to global warming. I hope that, in the future, renewable power sources will supply the bulk of our electricity and we won't depend on nuclear power.

Miho Nishihiro
Abiko, Chiba

これからのこと

3月11日に発生した大地震は、東北および関東地方に未曾有の被害をもたらした。まずは、亡くなられた方々のご冥福をお祈りするとともに、被災された方々に心からお見舞い申し上げる。自分の身の危険も省みず、被害を最小に食い止めようと懸命に働く作業員の方々には感謝するとともに、皆さんがご家族のもとに無事にお戻りになることを願っている。

私の住む千葉県我孫子市も震度5弱を記録した。その揺れは震源地付近に比べれば小さいものであったろうし、内陸のため津波の被害もなかった。しかし、私にとっては生まれて初めての大きい揺れであり、実際に被害を受けた地震であった。また、幼い2人の子どもを守る母親として、地震発生当初は度重なる余震に不安を覚えた。しかし、今回の地震で最大の不安をもたらしたのは、福島第一原子力発電所の放射線漏れ事故である。

今回、この事故における情報伝達に最大の問題があったと思う。東京電力について唯一評価できるのは、放射線量の観測値を迅速かつ正確に公表したことである。

東京電力は記者会見で、毎時数マイクロシーベルトにすぎないと発表した。しかし、その値を解説する際に彼らが比較に用いたのは、自然界において私たちが1年間に浴びる放射線量であったり、X線の強さであった。これらの数字は比較にならない。放射線を浴びる時間がまったく異なるからだ。こうした比較は人々を混乱させ、東京電力の説明をきわめてわかりにくいものにしただけだった。

また、放射線漏れを起こしている原発の周囲30キロメートル以遠に暮らす人々は心配する必要はないと言われた。そんなことは、ニュースで繰り返し言われなくてもわかっている。なぜなら、私は今どこも不調をきたしていないのだから。

本当に知りたいのは、さらに事態が悪化した場合はどうなるのかということである。原子力発電所の状況はどのように私たちに影響を及ぼすのか。危険はどの範囲にまで広がるのか。このような事故はどれくらいの確率で起こるのか。こうした情報を知りたいのだが、だれも教えてくれない。情報さえあれば、あらゆる選択肢を考慮に入れて、取るべき行動の準備ができる。最悪のシナリオが現実になったときにも、パニックを回避できるだろう。しかし、情報がないために、人々は必要もなく東京から避難したのだ。

今回、リスクに関する情報がまったくなかったのはなぜか。原子力発電所がもたらすリスクについて十分な調査が行われてこなかったのではないか。それは、過去において、日本の原発は絶対に安全である、という神話を信じたためだ。結果として、事故が現実となるまで、だれもリスクに関する情報を手にしていな

かったのだ。
　日本は世界有数の地震国である。この国においては、建造物が絶対に安全であることはない。今回の地震では「未曾有の」という表現が頻繁に使われているが、原子力発電所の設計段階においては、未曾有の事態を想定して、基本設計以上のものを建設すべきだったのである。
　福島原発を襲った津波は14メートルを越えるものだった可能性がある。それは、原発設計仕様の3倍以上の高さである。
　1896年の明治三陸地震では38.2メートル、1933年の昭和三陸地震では28.7メートルの津波が記録された。この数字を考えると、福島原発のもっとも厳しい安全基準ですら、とても十分だったとは言えない。
　電力会社は今回の事故を教訓にして、今後のリスク管理に最善を尽くしてほしい。今回の事故は、私たち日本人が地球温暖化の解決策と考えてきた原子力発電所を拡大していくことについて改めて考えるきっかけとなる。今後は再生可能エネルギーが電力の中心となり、原子力に依存しない方向に進むことを私は願っている。

西廣美穂
千葉県　我孫子市

Experience

On March 11th at around 2:50 p.m., I was waiting for my boss to join me before heading to a branch office of our company in Tokyo. I'm nearly 40 years old. All my life, whenever an earthquake came I'd always tell myself, "It's no big deal, it'll be over soon."

But this quake was stronger than any I'd experienced before. I began to question reality itself.

I was on the 8th floor of our building, which swayed so violently I couldn't stand up. The decorative plants around the office toppled over. Computers tumbled from desktops. My gut told me that this wasn't a typical quake. I turned on the TV and saw the number "7" (the highest on the Japanese seismic scale) and the word "Miyagi" and cancelled our trip to the branch office. In accordance with company procedures we rushed to the disaster prevention room.

Since I work for a certain telecommunications company, we knew right away that communication systems were badly affected, but since we were far from the epicenter we weren't immediately certain of the entire extent of the damage.

Two days after the quake, the news was filled with images of terrible destruction. We sent dozens of staff members to the hardest hit areas, along with dozens of vans equipped with satellite communication systems.

According to a colleague at the scene, the support crews were working around the clock to restore service. These workers had family members that were missing, yet they threw themselves into their work. Just hearing about their sense of purpose moved me beyond words.

Countless people died in the tsunami.

Several days after the quake, the telecom systems are back up and running. But I'm sure it'll take many years for the areas directly affected by the quake and tsunami to recover. It'll be far longer for the spirits of the survivors who lost their homes and families to fully recover. I'm not sure that this is appropriate to say right now, but this terribly sad and devastating earthquake that has made us reconsider our normally tranquil day-to-day lives was like a warning from Mother Nature.

This disaster has made us appreciate the importance of life, of things, the bonds of family, the things we take for granted in our daily routines. To the victims—I know you're in dire straits, but keep your hopes up! Keep moving forward! If you're alive, you'll experience wonderful things! We're here for you.

Kosuke Ishihara
Abiko, Chiba

Mari Kurisato

良い機会

3月11日（金）午後2時50分ごろ、ちょうど、都内の自社から都内の事業所に向かうため上司を待っているところだった。生まれて40年近くなるが、地震に対する感覚は「すぐに収まる」「たいしたことない」というのが当たり前だった。

ところが、今回の地震は、今までに感じたことのない感覚と、現実を疑うかのような光景だった。

自社の8階にいたこともあって、まず立っていられない、めまいがするくらいの揺れ、フロアにおいてあった観賞用の木が横倒しになり、机の上のパソコンのほとんどが散乱し、直感でただならぬ事態だと感じた。すぐにテレビをつけると、宮城エリアで震度7の文字、すぐに外出を取りやめ、業務規定に則り災害対策室に駆け込んだ。

職場は電気通信会社であるため、すぐに通信サービスへの被害や影響の把握を行ったが、遠隔地からでは思うように状況がつかめないのが実態だった。

発生から2日経過したころには、現地の惨状がテレビニュースで次々入ってきた。会社からも現地支援のため、数十人が送り込まれた。また衛星通信車も数十台の支援をもらい、現地に向かってもらった。

現地支援に行った同僚からの連絡では、不眠不休で支援や通信サービスの復旧に努める社員、家族が行方不明なのに仕事に徹する社員の使命感の強さを耳にし、言葉では言い表せないものを感じた。

現地の話を聞くと、津波では亡くなった人が数えきれないくらいほどだという。

今日で発生から数日経過し、通信サービスも回復してきたところだが、被災した現地の復旧には数年かかるだろう。また家族を失った方々の心が癒されるのにも数年以上かかるだろう。適切な表現ではないかもしれないが、今回の震災はたいへん悲しい出来事であったと同時に、我々の安穏とした日々の生活を見直す、自然界からの警告だと私は思った。

この震災は、命の大切さ、ものの大切さ、家族との絆、当たり前の生活の大切さを考えさせる機会を与えてくれた。被災者の方、何もできませんが、元気を出して、前に進みましょう！　生きていればまた、よいことが必ず来ます。応援しています。

石原浩輔
千葉県　我孫子市

Facebook

My first thought was to update my status on Facebook. I wrote, "Mom-in-law & I are OK; house is trashed. Piano was shifted three feet, aquarium is just...gone. Neighbor kids are scared witless and the local construction workers shrugged it off & went back to work. No phones & no power yet. Hope everyone else is OK."

And that was the end of it. I tried to call my wife but couldn't get through. I shrugged it off and went on cleaning, knowing she would get in touch with me as soon as she could.

My phone beeped and I checked it, thinking it would be from my wife. Instead, it was a half-dozen posts from friends on Facebook in Japan relaying either their own "shaken-but-OK" statuses, or worried posts from the United States wanting details. Soon, info began to filter in through Facebook and Twitter and Google news about the earthquake and the following tsunami.

More friends checked in while the earthquake was upgraded from 8.8 to 8.9 and the tsunami was reported as ten meters high in places. Just numbers on a phone screen.

Joel David Neff
Takanezawa, Tochigi

フェイスブック

私が最初に思いついたのは、フェイスブックを使って私の状況を知らせることでした。私は次のように書き込みました。「義母も私も無事です。家は倒壊し、ピアノは1メートルぐらい移動、水槽は……どこかへ行ってしまいました。近所の子どもたちはとても怖がっていたけれど、地元の建設作業員は気にせず仕事に戻っていました。電話も電気も通じません。みんなが無事でありますように」

これで終わりです。妻に電話をしようとしましたが、つながりませんでした。電話が通じるようになれば妻は連絡をくれると思ったので、気にかけずに片づけに行きました。

電話が鳴ったとき、妻からだと思って確認したところ、フェイスブックの友人からの6件の書き込みでした。「揺れたけど無事でした」という国内の友人からの報告や、心配しているので詳しく教えてほしいという米国からの書き込みです。まもなく、フェイスブックやツイッター、グーグルニュースを通して地震や津波についての情報が入りはじめました。

マグニチュードが8.8から8.9に訂正され、津波が10メートルにも達したことが報告される間に、さらに多くの友人が書き込んできました。多くの電話番号が携帯電話の画面に並んでいました。

Joel David Neff
栃木県　高根沢町

HLP JPN

Gavin Strange

Faculty

"Earthquake," I said quietly. Nobody noticed. Kei kept on talking. Even I wasn't completely sure at first, and I'm pretty quick to pick up on them. "Earthquake, we're having an earthquake," I said, a little louder.

Kei said, "Earthquake?...You're right..." Osamu said "Earthquake? Really?" By this time, we had already been swaying for several seconds.

I was in a faculty meeting, in the newest, most shock-proof building on campus. In Yokohama, we were far from the epicenter, and the building insulated us well from even the worst local shaking. We would not know how serious the devastation was for some time.

"It's getting bigger," someone said. Kusumoto got up, walked across the room and peeked through the blinds. "Electric poles are swaying," he said. I got up and walked across the room to join him.

"It's getting even worse," someone said. "Better get away from the windows." For a group of technical faculty members all accustomed to earthquakes, it was at first a curiosity, never frightening.

"Wow, it's big. This is far away and big..." Comments like that continued for what seemed like several minutes before it calmed down, though such a building sways for a long time and, in your mind, for even longer.

The electricity went out. Then the announcement came to evacuate the building, so we grabbed our jackets and went out. Several of us helped a man in an electric wheelchair, lifting him down the stairs. The building includes a gym and pool, so dozens of kids in Speedos and goggles were forced out into the cold. I handed out a shirt and a fleece I was carrying. They haven't been returned, but if that's my biggest loss, I'm fine.

Only once outside, as aftershocks hit and the first reports filtered in through both official news and those arriving on foot from other parts of campus, did we become aware of how enormous and frightening it had been even in Yokohama, let alone the Tohoku area.

About fifteen minutes after the first shock, I got an email on my cell phone from my wife, letting me know that she was okay, that she had one of our daughters and was getting the other. It would be fifteen hours before we would be able to connect via voice or SMS, but DoCoMo's mail and internet operated sporadically from the beginning. I was able to access Gmail, Facebook and Twitter from my smartphone, enough to get a message to friends who relayed it to my parents in the U.S. Internet connectivity, even if imperfect, proved to be a key lifeline for many people. Several people around me had cell phones capable of receiving low-resolution TV broadcasts, which gave enough information to be scary but did not provide a lot of detail.

I spent a frightening night on a chilly classroom floor, terrified that each new shock might bring a tsunami to the coastline where we live. If so, would my wife and girls have time to escape? Our house would have been swept away if a tsunami hit Kamakura. We are closer to the beach than the thirteenth-century Great Buddha, who sits outside in the weather because his wooden temple was swept away in a tsunami several centuries ago.

Ultimately, I arrived home about twenty hours after the initial shock. I found that many friends and colleagues had taken off on foot right after the quake, arriving at their homes after walking as much as ten hours, then waiting even more for trains and buses to resume. Some of them ended up standing out in the cold overnight. In the end, our story is one of distress, but is nothing compared to the ongoing suffering of those in the Tohoku area. Our thoughts are with them.

Rodney Van Meter
Yokohama

教員

「地震だ……」私は静かに言った。だれも気づかなかった。ケイは、しゃべり続けている。地震に敏感な私でさえ、最初は確信が持てなかった。「地震だ、これは地震だよ」今度は少し大きな声で言った。

ケイが言う。「地震？……ほんとだ……」そして、オサムも。「地震？　本当に？」その頃には、私たちの体は、数秒間揺れていた。

そのとき私は教員会議に出ていた。場所はキャンパス内の一番新しい、頑丈な建物の中。横浜にあるキャンパスは震源地からは離れており、過去に近場で発生した大きな地震のときも私たちを守ってくれた。今回の被害の大きさは、だいぶ後になってからでないとわからなかった。

「揺れが大きくなってる」とだれかが言った。クスモトは立ち上がると、部屋を横切り、窓のブラインドの間から外をのぞいた。「電信柱が波打ってる」と彼は言った。私も立ち上がって彼の横に立つ。「どんどん、ひどくなってる」と、まただれかが言った。「窓から離れたほうがいい」そこにいたのは地震に慣れている研究者ばかりで、最初のうちは好奇心があったとしても、恐怖心はまったくなかった。

「これ、結構大きいよ。震源地は遠くて、かなり大きい…」こんな会話が数分交わされたのち、地震はようやく落ち着いてきた。だが、耐震構造の建物は長い間揺れるので、時間はもっと長く感じられた。

そして停電になった。そのあと「建物から避難するように」との校内アナウンスで、全員上着を持って部屋を出た。私たちの何人かは、電動車椅子の男性を抱え上げて、階段を下りるのを手伝った。建物内には体育館、プールなどの設備があり、競泳用の水着姿でゴーグルをつけた学生たちも、寒い中、外に出された。私は持っていたＴシャツとフリースを差し出した。まだ返してもらっていないが、それが今回最大の損失なら大したことはない。

次々に襲ってくる余震、キャンパスのあちこちから歩いてきた人たちから聞く話、ニュースなどで入ってきた地震の第一報。外に出て、初めて私たちは東北で起きた地震のすさまじさ、恐ろしさ、そして横浜でも被害が出たことを知る。

地震が発生して15分くらいして、妻が携帯メールで無事を知らせてきた。娘のひとりと一緒で、これからもうひとりの娘を迎えにいくとのことだった。通話やショートメールが使えるようになるまでには15時間かかった。だが、ドコモの携帯メールとインターネットは、単発的な障害を除いては最初から使用可能だった。スマートフォンでＧメール、フェイスブックとツイッターにもアクセスできた。私たちの安否を友人たちに伝えるには充分で、彼らは米国にいる私の両親にも私たちの無事を知らせてくれていた。インターネット接続は完璧とは言えないまでも、今回の地震では重要なライフラインとして、大勢の人の役に立ったことは間違いない。周囲でワンセグを見ている人もいたが、不安にさせるような情報はいくらもあるが、詳しい情報を得ることはできなかった。

私は冷たい教室の床で不安な一夜を過ごした。余震が来るたびに、海岸に近いわが家が津波に襲われ

やしないか心配でたまらなかった。もし津波が来たら、妻と娘たちは避難する時間があるだろうか？　もし津波が鎌倉に到達したら、家は流されてしまう。わが家は13世紀に建立された鎌倉の大仏よりも、海に近い場所にあるのだ。現在、大仏が露座になっているのも、数世紀前に殿舎が津波で流されてしまったからだ。

　最終的に家に着いたのは地震が発生してからおよそ20時間後。多くの友人や同僚は地震直後に歩いて帰宅を始め、中には10時間歩きっぱなしの者もいたし、電車やバスが動きだすまで、もっと長い時間待ち続けた者もいた。寒い中、一晩中外にいた者もいる。結局、ひどい災難に見舞われたが、今もなお、困難な生活を強いられている東北地方の被災者たちの苦難とは比べものにならない。私たちの思いは被災者たちと共にある。

Rodney Van Meter
神奈川県　横浜市

Fernando Ramos

Forget

This is a country of earthquakes but this old woman was surprised. Some aftershocks haven't calmed down yet. We don't know what will happen next with radiation issues. I'm old enough to not have to worry about any radiation effects, but that's not true for young children who have a bright future. I was talking to myself and shook my head. I just could not stop thinking about all the victims from Nagasaki, Hiroshima and Chernobyl.

　I gave birth 42 years ago. A couple of days after, there was the big Tokachi earthquake in Hokkaido. It was about 7.8 magnitude, if my memory serves. The shaking didn't stop even when I was breast feeding. I picked up my baby and ran outside from the second floor of my apartment. I remember clearly that I ran under the table and couldn't stop shaking, holding my baby in the middle of the night when the earthquakes started. I told myself every time I felt the shakes that I didn't want to lose my child—I couldn't.

All I could do was hold my child in my arms and cry.

The aftershocks then continued for a month or so. When I saw a picture in the newspaper in which some university's buildings in Hakodate had collapsed from the quake, I just couldn't believe it. Can nobody do anything to stop natural disasters? Every time we face a horrible natural disaster, it makes me think that the land, sky, seas, and mountains are exploding in anger. Tsunamis swallowed houses, cars, electric poles, schools, buildings, parents, grandparents, and children so quickly.

I can't express how I feel for the victims and their family. Did they have a happy life? How cruel to lose something so precious to a tsunami. They could not even say goodbye to those they loved. I only hope at least all the bodies can go back to their waiting families.

Is there a God or Buddha? Did all humans rush off in the wrong direction? I wonder if we've been neglecting to love our parents and children and to love nature, and that's why nature is destroying us.

We hear so much sad news of the killing of our own children, own parents, and massacres, it's like a horror movie. Why? What went so wrong? More than ten thousand people's lives were taken. Can't the super technologies we created in this modern world prevent a disaster?

A fisherman I know had a minor tsunami experience in Choshi, Chiba, and he said, "You just can't imagine how beautiful the sea is after the tsunami!" I can't forget his comment.

Michiko Segawa
Chiba

Lee Chapman

置き忘れたもの

　いくら地震大国日本といえども、老婆は驚いた。余震はいまだ終りそうもない。放射線の恐れもある。私はこの年齢まで何とか生きてこられた。でも「これからの子どもたちには絶対ダメよ」とひとりごとを言い、頭を振っていた。頭に広島、長崎の原爆、チェルノブイリのことが思い浮かんで消えなかった。

　42年前、子どもを出産し、数日後、北海道十勝沖地震が起きた。あのときも確かマグニチュード7.8だったと思う。日に何回も揺れるたびに子どもを抱いて2階のアパートから外に出た。授乳中でも急いで子どもを抱いて逃げ、震えていたのを思い出した。夜は、揺れるたびに赤子を抱いて、机の下、押し入れに入り、震えていた。そのとき思った。「わが子を死なせたくない。この子だけは絶対にだめ」と。

　十勝沖の余震も長く続いたし、函館の大学が真ん中から潰れてしまった写真が新聞に載っていた。目を疑うような光景だった。自然には、何者も勝つことができないのか。毎年災害が発生するたびに私は思う。何か、天が、地が、海が、山が、怒り狂ったように思えた。津波は、家、車、電柱、学校、ビル、親、兄弟、祖父母、夫婦、子ども、選ぶことなく皆流してしまった。

　その犠牲になった1万人以上の人たちは、幸せなことがあっただろうか？　だれにもさよならも言えず、気の毒で言葉が見つからない。せめて、体だけでも身内の元に返して欲しいと思う。

　本当に神や仏がいるのか疑問である。人間は、急ぎ、走りすぎたのではないか。何に向かって、そんなに急ぎ、走りすぎたのか。親子の愛や、自然に目をやることも、段々と人間がどこかに置き忘れてきてはいないだろうか。そういったことが自然界を怒らせてしまったのではないか。

　子殺し、親殺し、他人殺しと、まるで、昔ならホラー映画のような事件が頻繁に起きているのはなぜなのか。何かが狂ってしまったのか。1万人以上の人命が奪われた。このハイテク時代といわれる世の中で、大惨事を防ぐことができなかったのか。

　津波が荒れ狂った後、銚子で海を見て呟いた漁師の一言が心に染みた。「津波のあとの海のきれいさ、あんなにきれいで美しい海を見たことがない」

瀬川道子
千葉県

Andrew Woolner

Forward

What will tabloid editors do when the apocalypse doesn't arrive? Each day they conjure new horrors to visit upon Japan and television pundits evoke historic disasters. But each day we can see Japan moving resolutely forward, and so they lose traction. At least for Japan, the apocalypse is definitely not in sight.

Maxamillian John
London

前へ

結局この世の終わりではないことが明らかになったところで、タブロイド紙の編集者はどうするのだろうか。彼らは、日本を打ちのめすような新しい恐怖の種を毎日あげつらい、テレビに出る批評家たちは歴史的災害を言い連ねる。しかし、私たちには、日本が日々しっかりと前進しているのがわかるし、それにより、メディアは勢いを失っていく。少なくとも日本には、終末の日はまだ来ないのだ。

Maxamillian John
英国　ロンドン

Ganbaro

I was sitting at my desk the afternoon of March 11th when my phone buzzed. That's all that happened.

I broke away from writing reports and picked up my phone to read an email from a friend. My friend said there had been an earthquake, and a tsunami was hitting the Japanese coast. I relayed the news to my wife and kids in the next room. My wife said, "Oh dear," but since earthquakes and tsunami are part of life in Japan, the news wasn't a shock. It was an early spring day in Kyoto. The plum blossoms were reaching full bloom, a good sign that winter is on its way out. I wanted to finish my reports so I could walk to the park with my kids. Taking a break, I went downstairs to make coffee and turned on the TV.

Nothing could have prepared me for what I saw unfolding before my eyes.

I couldn't make sense of the images at first. My eyes had to adjust as if getting used to the dark. What I saw was a wharf and dozens of cars on the Japanese coast being swept away like leaves in a gutter. So many cars. What I saw was almost too big to grasp. It was a movie that didn't seem real.

Of course, it was terrifyingly real. The people of Tohoku had been dealt an unimaginable blow that will require years to recover from. But they will. A word I keep hearing from people in the area is "ganbaro." They say it on the news every night, "ganbaro." I saw it spray painted on the side of a concrete wall in the midst of absolute ruin, "ganbaro." The word that has many nuances but in this case can best be translated as, "Stay strong, stand firm."

"Ganbaro" is a word that is sometimes overused. But not now, not in this place. At this time the people of Tohoku and Fukushima need to keep saying it and keep believing it, because the challenge they face is immense.

Lowlypoetic
Kyoto

がんばろう

3月11日の午後、書斎にいた私の携帯が鳴った。それがすべての始まりだった。

　書類を書く手を止め、友人からのメールを読むとこう書いてあった。 地震が起き、津波が日本の沿岸部に押し寄せている、と。隣の部屋にいた妻と子どもに伝えると、妻は一瞬驚いたが、地震や津波は日本では日常茶飯事であり、ショックを受けた様子はない。京都はちょうど早春の時期で、桜のつぼみは開花に近づき、冬の終わりを感じさせる陽気になっていた。私は子どもと散歩に出かけるため、書類を一気に終わらせようと思っていた。その前に、休憩がてらコーヒーをいれに階下に降り、テレビをつけた。

　そこには思いがけない光景が広がっていた。

　すぐには理解できなかった。まるで暗闇に目が慣れていくときのように、この光景を認識するまでには時間が必要だった。葉っぱのようにあっけなく流されていく一艘の船と多数の車が、私の目に飛び込んできた。とても多くの車。あまりにショックが大きく、その状況を把握することができなかった。 現実とは思えず、まるで映画を観ているようだった。

　もちろん、それは恐ろしい現実だった。東北は想像を絶する打撃を受け、復興まで何年もかかるだろう。しかし、必ず復興するだろう。「がんばろう」という言葉をよく耳にする。毎晩のニュースに映る東北の人々が言う「がんばろう」。廃墟の真ん中に大きくスプレーで描かれた「がんばろう」。さまざまな訳し方があるが、ここではこう捉えよう。「Stay strong, stand firm.（負けるな、踏ん張れ）」。

　「がんばろう」は乱用されがちな言葉である。しかし、今、ここに限っては、言いすぎということはない。東北の人々はこの言葉を口にし続け、信じる必要がある。彼らは今、とても大きな困難に立ち向かっているのだ。

Lowlypoetic
京都府

Gesture

I live south of Tokyo. I can't write about what it felt like to experience that disaster up north because I simply can't imagine it. But I will say this: The people here are to be admired. From the architects who design the skyscrapers in Tokyo, to first year elementary school children, everybody knows what they should do. People help each other out.

People get on with business as usual. The traffic lights in my town went out and a few of the locals took it upon themselves to go out and keep things safe by directing the traffic. A simple gesture. A small gesture. A gesture that wouldn't have crossed my mind.

N Cobayne
Shizuoka

しぐさ

私は東京の南に住んでいる。私には東北の震災を経験して、どう感じたかを書くことはできない。というのも、どうしても想像できないからだ。でも、これは言いたい。この国の人たちは賞賛されるべきだ、と。東京の高層ビルを設計した建築士から、小学1年生の子どもに至るまで、だれもが何をすべきかわかっている。互いに助け合い、自分がやるべきことをいつも通りやる。私の住む町の信号は消えてしまったが、地元の人が自ら外に出て、交通整理をすることで安全を確保している。それはとても簡単なしぐさだ。とても小さなしぐさだ。私には決して思い浮かばないだろうしぐさだ。

N Cobayne
東京都

Philipp Christoph Tautz

Goal

Watching the events unfold has shifted my focus in life. My vague goal of visiting Japan has grown stronger. It has become a resolution. I will go to Japan, I'll donate, I'll help in any way possible. If by doing so I can take in even some of the dignity, sense of duty and kindness that the Japanese people have in their core, it will be more than an even exchange.

Naomi
Canada

目標

いまだ収拾のつかない事態を目の当たりにして、人生の関心事が変わった。日本を訪れるという漠然とした私の目標は、確固たるものになった。決意に変わった。私は日本に行き、寄付をし、あらゆる方法で支援する。そうすることで、日本の人々の核をなす尊厳、責任感と親切心をいくらかでも身につけることができたら、私にとってこれ以上の収穫はない。

Naomi
カナダ

God

At first it didn't seem like that big of a deal. We are two hours south of Tokyo, and initial reports were all very conservative, with potential death tolls of under 500 people. We were actually kind of impressed, considering the death toll in Haiti not so very long ago.

But that has all turned out to be very, very wrong. Ten-thousand-plus people dead or missing. Certainly doesn't seem "low," especially when people you know are crying because of lost relatives and friends in the north. Everyone's trying go about life-as-usual, but it's not so easy to do. Today we had a graduation ceremony at my son's school. As soon as the speaker mentioned the disaster, half the place was in tears. The Japanese are very good at "gaman" (quietly enduring hardship), but as an over-expressive foreigner, I find that to be aggravating at times. Seems like a good national cry might be a better idea.

I find it hard to escape a certain sense of dread, like a dark voice in the back of my head that mocks my faith in light of meaningless destruction like this. You can't blame terrorists or human evil. Sometimes the earth just up and kills at random, and like Shusaku Endo repeated so many times in that haunting novel of his—God is silent.

I made up a fairy tale to make some sense of it. I'd like to believe that the only problem is that our communicators are broken. That once long ago, God had such an intimate relationship with his creation that we'd know long beforehand about any natural irregularities, and always be safely out of the way. Maybe we are just crippled by our inability to hear God, and we live out of step with his creation because of it.

I know some people will be offended by my telling of such children's stories at a time like this, so I'll stop there. Today the panic seems to be getting worse instead of better. No one is sure whether or not we'll be running from a radioactive cloud within the next few days. Frankly, I start to think that Twitter and Facebook are more interesting as a study in human psychology than they are useful sources of clear and true information. And CNN can be even worse with their "possible scenarios."

The question, "What is Truth?" is important on so many levels in a crisis like this.

John Janzen
Japan

神様

はじめはそれほどのこととは思えなかった。私たちは東京から南に2時間のところに住んでおり、当初の報道はどれも控え目で、予想される死者数も500人以下だった。先ごろのハイチでの犠牲者数に比べれば、ずいぶん少ないじゃないか、という思いでいた。

しかし、それは完全に間違っていた。死亡・行方不明者は1万人以上。家族や友人を亡くして涙を流している東北の知人を思うと、決して「少ない」人数には感じられない。だれもが何もなかったかのように生活しようとしているけれど、それは簡単なことではない。今日は息子の学校で卒業式が行われた。震災の話になったとたん、会場の半分が涙を流しはじめた。日本人は我慢をすることに長けているが、感情を表に出すことの多い外国人からすると、ときには非常にもどかしく感じる。国全体で一度思いっきり泣いたほうが良いのではないかと思う。

このような無意味な破壊を前にすると、ある種の恐ろしさ、頭の後ろのほうで私の信仰をあざける低い声のようなものから逃れられそうにないと感じている。テロリストや人間の悪意のせいにはできない。ときに大地は無差別に命を奪う。遠藤周作があの忘れられない小説で繰り返し言ったように……神は沈黙した。

この災害に何らかの理由付けをしたいと思って、おとぎ話を作った。できることなら、行き違いが生じただけなのだ、と信じたい。遠い昔、神とその創造物とは親密な関係を保っており、自然災害が起きる前に創造物はそれを感知し、安全な場所に避難していた。私たちは今、神の声を聞く力を失い、そのために創造物とうまく歩調を合わすことができないのだ、と。

こんなときにこのような子ども話をすると腹を立てる人もいると思うので、これくらいでやめておく。現在、パニックは収まるところどころか、ひどくなっているようだ。この2、3日で、放射性の雲から避難しなければならなくなるかどうかもわからない。正直に言うと、フェイスブックやツイターは、明確で正確な情報源としてよりも、人間心理を学ぶツールとして役立つように思い始めた。また、「想定されるシナリオ」を伝えるCNNはもっとひどい存在かもしれない。

このような災害においては、「真実とは何か」という問いは、さまざまなレベルで重要である。

John Janzen
日本

Graduation

We'd just come home from my elder daughter's farewell concert, when the unprecedented catastrophe occurred in Tohoku and Kanto. Our small daughter was in the toilet, but the kids' room door was shaking, banging. That's strange. Her sister is still at school. Is it a ghost? What a silly idea.

No! It's an earthquake! It's shaking like nothing ever before! It took me about one minute to realize this. And then, straight away, came the blackout. I rushed back to the school to pick up my older daughter. Someone was saying, according to forecasts a huge tsunami is coming, but at this point, I was thinking, "No way!" A neighboring granny said, "We're going to be all right here, dear. If something happens, we all escape together." The neighborhood agreed.

And then the lights came back. We saw the devastation, and wept. The huge black tsunami, swelling over the levee, swallowing homes and cars in its path. On the Chiba coast, an oil refinery was in flames, spewing bursts of fire.

I couldn't reach my mother. She wasn't answering her mail. Morning came, and finally, a friend living a couple of houses down from my parents told me mum was OK. Daddy got on a train when it finally started moving, came home in the morning, and fell asleep straight away. A friend sent me a message saying she walked all the way home. And then came the worries over the nuclear power plant, people scavenging batteries and non-perishables.

The university shut down as it was spring break anyway. A British colleague is taking refuge at our house. She has a granddad in New Zealand. She's pretty worn out what with one quake after another.

The rolling blackouts are indeed inconvenient, but they're nothing compared to the cold in the shelters. The cake shop didn't open on our little girl's birthday, so I did the baking. For the chocolate, I gathered all the Hershey's left from Valentine's and melted them. Finished baking exactly 10 minutes before the rolling blackout. Phew. We put emergency candles on the gateau chocolat, and together celebrated the little one's eighth birthday.

On the same day, navy-colored slip-on shoes arrived. I'd ordered them for the graduation ceremony. Our usual delivery man from Sagawa brought it. He never stopped his rounds, saying Sagawa will deliver no matter what. I thanked him from the bottom of my heart. "Thanks to you, I can wear new shoes for the graduation ceremony." The ceremony took place right in the middle of the blackout. But it was such a bright, sunny day, there was ample light inside the gymnasium. When the children paraded into the gym, backs straight, chests out, my eyes stung. There was no microphone or anything. Just the fifth-grade children playing instruments and singing songs for the departing sixth-graders. Everything seemed really solemn and holy. Everyone had their heads held high. Twelve-year-olds. How are they taking in this disaster?

The future of Japan will be theirs to rebuild. It will be up to their generation. We weren't sure whether there would be a graduation ceremony at all. I think of how fortunate I am to have been there at such a milestone event. Happy graduation. May you all have a good journey as you walk along your paths of life.

May Arai
Kamakura

卒業式

　未曾有の大災害が東北と関東で起こったのは、上の娘のお別れコンサートが終わって、家に戻ったときだった。下の娘がトイレに入っているとき、子ども部屋のドアがたがた揺れている。おかしいな、姉はまだ学校なのに。おばけ！？とばかなことを考えた。
　違う！　これは地震だ！　それも今まで起こったことのない揺れだ！　そう気がついたのは1分くらいたってからのことだ。それからすぐの停電。学校に引き返して姉を引き取る。大津波が来る、という予報があった、とだれかが言っていたけど、この時点では、まさか！と思っていた。ここは大丈夫よ、と近所のおばあちゃま。万一のときは一緒に逃げようと近隣一帯で声を掛け合う。
　そうして電気が戻ってきてみて、あまりの大惨事に涙が出た。堤防を超えて人家や車を呑み込み、黒く押し寄せてくる大津波。千葉の沿岸では石油コンビナートが火を吹いて燃えている。
　母とは連絡が取れない。メールに返事が来ない。一晩あけてやっと実家の何軒か先の友人から、母は無事だと連絡が来た。ダディは動き始めた電車に乗って、朝帰宅してそのまま寝てしまった。友人からは歩いて自宅まで帰った、とメールが入ってきた。そのあと続く原発への心配、乾電池や保存食品の買い占め。
　大学は春休みということもあって閉めてしまった。我が家にはイギリス人の同僚が避難してきた。彼女はニュージーランドにおじいさんがいる。地震につぐ地震でかなりまいっていた。
　計画停電は確かに不便だけど、避難所の寒さに比べたら何でもない。下の娘の誕生日にはケーキ屋さんは開かなかったので、自分で焼いた。チョコレートは、バレンタインのときのハーシーズを集めて溶かした。ちょうど計画停電の電気が止まる10分前に焼き上がった。ほっ。そのガトーショコラに非常用のロウソクを立てて、妹の8歳の誕生日をみんなで祝う。
　同じ日に、卒業式用に頼んでおいた紺のスリップオンの靴が届く。配達してくれたのは、地震の日も、サガワです、と配送をやめなかった担当の方だ。おかげで卒業式に新しい靴がはけます、と心の底からお礼を言った。卒業式もちょうど計画停電の最中だった。でも快晴だったので、体育館の中は十分に明るい。みなが胸を張って入場行進してきたときは、目頭が熱くなった。5年生の楽器の演奏や歌に送られた。マイクもなにも使われない式。とても厳粛で神聖な気がした。みんな堂々としていた。この大災害は12歳の胸に、どんな風に刻まれたのだろう。
　これから日本を立て直して行くのは彼らの世代になる。開かれるのかも危ぶまれた卒業式。ひとつの節目に立ち会えた幸せを思う。卒業おめでとう。それぞれの道をしっかり歩んでいってください。

荒井真弓
神奈川県　鎌倉市

Harmony

We were in Kofukuji, Nara, when it hit. It wasn't really much there, but we still felt the tremor. My parents were visiting us on holiday from England and at first the creaking temple was amusing, mum thinking it interesting that old temples creak in the wind. "But it isn't windy," I said. I was the first to realize it was an earthquake and told the others. Then the famously beautiful buddhist statues started rocking in harmony. We jumped out of the temple, only then realizing that standing under the eaves may be more dangerous than inside. But the swaying was gentle in Nara.

Tom Hope
Tokyo

調和

地震が起きたとき、私たちは奈良の興福寺にいた。大きくはなかったが、確かに揺れを感じた。英国から両親が遊びにきていた。お堂がきしみ始めた。母は、古い寺が風できしんでいるのだと思って、おもしろがった。「風は吹いていないよ」と私は言った。まず私が地震に気づき、両親にそれを伝えた。まもなく、有名な美しい仏像がそろって揺れ始めた。私たちはあわてて建物から飛び出したが、軒下にいるほうが中にいるより危ないかもしれないとすぐに気づいた。しかし、地震の揺れは奈良では穏やかだった。

Tom Hope
東京都

Andrew Woolner

Heart

Sitting around the dinner table earlier in half darkness, watching the latest press conference about exposed fuel rods at Fukushima No. 2 power station 247 km north of here, I asked the gathered Japanese housemates what they would do if the problems there worsened. One of them replied that her family lives in Fukushima, about 60 km from the troubled plant. I suggested that she would be safer here than returning home. She told me that if her family were exposed to the radiation she would return home to be with them, irrespective of the consequences for herself. "That's the heart of Japan, isn't it?" she said. This was met with a chorus of "Yes, that's right."

Yes, it is. To an extent, that's why I came here, why my life is here. It's why even now I don't want to leave. To leave is to abandon, yes? This is a critical time for Japan. Where do my loyalties lie? But I have been researching a route to Fukuoka, 1,100 km south of Tokyo. By the time things get worse, and by the time they actually tell anyone about it—in the absence of independent radiation monitoring by some impartial international agency, if one actually exists—it would probably be too late to make any difference. But I might pack a bag just in case. I've already had one half-packed for the past three days.

I was actually thinking about having a relaxing early night, perhaps finally getting around to that post-move shopping in Ikebukuro tomorrow if the trains were running. This is the surreal contradiction we're experiencing. Here in the house, they're talking now about which male idol has the most attractive face. In the background, experts from Tokyo University continue to discuss the melting-down reactors, and what to do if you're exposed to ionizing radiation. I know which conversation I'd rather be listening to.

Victoria
Tokyo

こころ

少し前に、薄暗い部屋のダイニングテーブルに座って、ここから247キロ離れた福島第一原発2号機の露出した燃料棒についての記者会見を見ながら、集まった日本人のハウスメイトたちに、もし事態がこれ以上悪化したらどうするかと聞いてみた。ひとりのハウスメイトは、家族が事故を起こした福島原発から60キロ離れたところに住んでいるという。それを聞いて彼女に、実家に帰るよりもここにいるほうが安全だねと言うと、彼女は、もし家族が放射線を浴びることになったら、自分がどうなろうとも家族のそばにいるために帰ると答えた。「それが日本人の心だと思わない？」と彼女は言う。その言葉に対して「そうだよね」という賛成の声がたくさん上がった。

彼女の言っていることは正しい。だからこそ私はこの国を訪れ、ここで生活しているとも言える。だからこそ、こうなった今でも日本を離れたくない。離れることは見捨てること、そうだよね？ 今、日本はたいへんなときだ。だが、私の忠誠心はどこにあるのだろう。実はいま、東京から南に1,100キロ離れた福岡へ行くルー

トを調べている。事態が悪化して、公平な国際機関による独立した放射線測定が行われていない現状でそれが公然とささやかれるころにはすでに手遅れで、脱出することは無意味かもしれない。しかし、万が一に備えて、私は荷物をまとめるかもしれない。現に、この3日間で、すでに半分荷物を詰め終えてしまった。

本当は、今夜は少しゆっくりしようと思っていた。明日もし電車が動いていたら、例の引っ越し後の買い物を池袋でするのもいいのかもしれないなどと考えながら。私たちは今、現実とは思いがたい矛盾に直面している。家の中で、どの男性アイドルがイケメンかなどと話している。その後ろでは、東大の専門家が、原子炉がメルトダウンしたらどうなるか、電離放射能を浴びたらどうすべきかという議論を続けている。そして私は、どちらの会話に耳を傾けるのがよいのかわかっている。

Victoria
東京都

Help

I feel really sad to know that the tsunami and the earthquakes took so many people's lives. When I watched the news on TV, I thought to myself, "Is it really happening in Japan?" I become very sad each time I see the destruction.

I've been considering what I can do to help. I decided not to waste electricity and water. I'll try to save the important things. I hope that Japan can find joy again soon.

Yui Nonaka (age 12)
Abiko, Chiba

I was with my 4-year-old daughter at home when the earthquakes hit. We were upstairs and I ran back downstairs holding my child since the shakes had gotten stronger and stronger.

I switched the TV on to find out what was happening. There were lots of aftershocks and a second big one. I was so scared and didn't know what to do.

I picked up my daughter and moved to our garden and hunched down in a ball. I certainly didn't expect to have two quakes in a row. I was really worried about my family. I rang and rang and tried to email, but it didn't work for some time.

At last I received an email from my husband confirming he was OK. I headed to the primary school where my two other daughters were.

We've never had this scary shaking before. Lots of people who worked in Tokyo could not come back on the day as all public transportation stopped. Nature is terrifyingly powerful. All the victims are now trying to revive their lives and towns.

I can't think of any particular things to help at the moment but I will find something one day and try the best I can.

Shizue Nonaka
Abiko, Chiba

いま私ができること

この地震で亡くなった人がたくさんいて、とても悲しいです。テレビのニュースで現場を見ると「ここって日本？」って思います。私はそれを見るとき、とってもつらいです。

なので、今、私ができることは何かを考えました。それは「電気の無駄使いをしない」と「水を必要な分だけ出し、無駄に使わない」です。これからもこれを実践していきたいです。そして、早く日本に笑顔が戻ったらいいなと思います。

野中唯（12歳）
千葉県　我孫子市

東日本に巨大地震が起きたとき、私は4歳の娘と2人でいた。地震だと思い、2階に行ったが下に降りなくてはと思い、子どもを抱きかかえ、あわてて下りた。その後どんどん揺れが強くなり、座って収まるのを待った。

すぐにテレビをつけてみると、東北地方で大きな地震があったと聞き、本当にびっくりした。その間にも余震が続き、私自身も怖くて足が震えながらもテレビを見ていたら、再び大きな地震がきた。どうしていいかわからなかった。

子どもを抱えたまま庭に出てしまい、そこで座り込み、また収まるのを待った。2回も大きな地震が来るなんて思いもしなかった。家族のことが心配になり、携帯電話にかけても繋がらず、何度かけても無駄だった。

でも、少したったころメールが入ってきた。「大丈夫だよ」と受け取り、本当に安心した。小学校では子どもたちも校庭に避難していた。

今回の地震は本当に怖かった。東北地方から関東にかけて広い地域が被災した。津波で家などが流れてしまったところ、都内では帰宅ができずたいへんだった人。福島の原子力発電所はいまでも予断を許さない。自然の力は本当に怖いと思った今回の地震。でも被災している人たちは、復興しようと少しずつ頑張っています。

私たちもなかなか何もしてあげられないかもしれないけど、必ずできることはあると思います。そのことをやっていきたいと思います。皆でがんばろうね。

野中志津江
千葉県　我孫子市

Home

Walking up the street to Yoyogi Station from my office, I passed a Starbucks and thought "Oh, double cappuccino? Mmm... No, I just gotta get home—so much to do today." Yoyogi crossing was crowded, when suddenly the concrete rolled and I got pitched forward. Instantly everything was a blur of seasickness, shaking buildings and traffic lights. The pole I grabbed to steady myself, everything nearby in fact, started shaking like crazy.

Traffic halted. A girl crouched down in the middle of the intersection. My sluggish brain told me I wasn't fainting or having a stroke and that this was a big, very big, earthquake. Earth....QUAKE!! I let go of the vibrating pole. Windows were about to blow out of the buildings because they were shaking so badly. I asked myself, "Should I run for it?"

Then it stopped. Japanese announcements came over the public loudspeakers telling people not to panic. I was frozen in front of a convenience store while texting my husband. "Big earthquake, really scary," I told him. "I'm OK—you?" The loudspeaker announcer said "6.0" and exclamations of "whoa" and "ahhh" rose out of the crowd. My text message to my husband failed. I tried to call but couldn't get through. The only thing working was the internet.

So, at 2:49 PM I posted on Facebook, "Big quake in Japan near Tokyo, it's pretty bad, but I am ok. No cell service, no trains. I'm at work." But at this point, as it was after the Towers went down in New York, I knew that things were going to get crazy. A determined energy collected in my gut. I said to myself, "I've just gotta get home." So I started walking, merging into a stream of hundreds of people, thousands. They were mostly dressed in suits, stepping on each other's heels.

In the crowd I walked a long time and saw some odd things. For example, Captain Jack Sparrow was on Meiji-dori for some reason holding a gift bag. At Shibuya Station I was pretty sure there was no way to get a cab. I kept telling myself, "Just keep going... gotta get home." Later, I ran into an actor friend of mine. We walked on together, chatting about showbiz until we got to Meguro Station. Here she kept walking and I waited another hour for a bus to Shinagawa Station. But it was utter chaos as a woman's voice announced: "We are now closing so please go home or someplace else. The trains are not running and we don't know about tomorrow." At this point I had hopes of finding a bus or even a cab, but the taxi line was two bodies deep and hundreds of people long.

So I kept walking. Alone, but surrounded by the hundreds of others, each one of us walking and thinking, "I just gotta get home."

Kimberly Tierney
Tokyo

うちへ

職場から代々木駅へ向かって歩きながら、スターバックスの前でこう思った。「お、ダブルカプチーノ？　うーん、いや、うちへ帰らなくちゃ。今日はやることがいっぱいある」代々木交差点は混雑していた。すると突然、コンクリートが波打って私はつんのめった。すぐに、なにもかも船酔いで頭がぼやけたときのようになり、ビルも信号機もすべて揺れていた。つかまって体を支えた柱も、近くにあるなにもかもが狂ったように揺れはじめた。

交通が止まっていた。女の子が交差点の真ん中でしゃがみこんでいた。頭はうまく働かなかったが、わかったのは、私が貧血とか発作を起こしたんじゃない、これは大きな、すごく大きな地震だ、ということだった。地面が震えてる！　揺れている柱から手を離した。ビルの窓ガラスがひどく震えて、はじけそうだった。「走って逃げるべきだろうか？」と考えた。

それから揺れは止まった。日本語のアナウンスがスピーカーから聞こえてきて、パニックにならないように呼びかけていた。コンビニの前で立ちすくんだまま、夫にメールを送った。「大地震、すごくこわい。私は大丈夫。あなたは？」。スピーカーのアナウンスが「6.0」と伝え、「うわっ」とか「ああ」というどよめきが起

こった。夫へのメールは送信エラーだった。電話をかけたが、つながらない。インターネットだけが機能していた。

だから、午後2時49分にフェイスブックに書き込んだ。「日本の東京の近くで大地震、かなりひどい、でも私は大丈夫。携帯電話は不通、電車もだめ。私は職場近くにいる」。このときには、ニューヨークでツインタワーが崩れ落ちた直後と同じように、収拾のつかない事態になるとわかっていた。自分のなかに、断固とした力が集まって気合いが入った。「うちに帰らなくちゃ」。それで歩き出した。何百人、何千人もの人の流れに加わって。ほとんどがスーツ姿で、ぞろぞろと連なっていた。

人混みに混ざって長い時間歩きながら、いくつかへんなものも見た。例えば、なぜか、明治通りにギフトバッグを持ったジャック・スパロウ船長がいた。渋谷駅では、タクシーはつかまえられないだろうと確信していた。自分に言い続けた。「とにかく行こう、うちに帰らなくちゃ」しばらくして、俳優をしている友人にばったり会った。映画や舞台についておしゃべりをしながら一緒に歩いて、目黒駅まで来た。友人は歩き続け、私はここで品川行きのバスを1時間ほど待った。混乱はきわまり、女性の声のアナウンスが言っていた。「駅構内を閉鎖しますので、帰宅なさるか、他の場所へ移動なさってください。電車は動いていません。明日についてもわかりません」この時点ではバスかタクシーを見つけられると希望を持っていたけれど、タクシーを待つ列は2列で数百人待ちの長さだった。

だから歩き続けた。ひとりきりで、でも何百人もの人たちに囲まれて。だれもが歩きながら考えていた。「うちへ帰らなくちゃ」

Kimberly Tierney
東京都

Illusion

I was at my job when I saw the news of the earthquake, followed by an announcement from city hall warning of a tsunami coming in around 4:30 p.m. We were told not to go near the ocean.

It was around 3:30 p.m. I wondered where my seven-year-old daughter was. I looked for her around our house. I also went to her friend's house, but it was empty. I went to city hall to look for them, but they weren't there. But when I went to the elementary school I found her playing there. I was only looking for 30 minutes, but it seemed longer and I was really relieved when I found her.

Gradually people started wandering up to the school. The next announcement told us that a small tsunami had arrived. Calculating that there would be enough time before another might hit, I decided to go home immediately. My husband was already there, along with my friend and her one-year-old son. They live near the beach so she was very nervous and decided to stay at my house. Although we live close to the ocean, our house is located on a cliff 30 meters above sea level, so we reckoned we should be safe.

We followed news of the earthquake, but things kept getting worse and worse. Continuous earthquakes meant a constant risk of tsunami for people like us who live near the ocean. When one tsunami is expected you can take the appropriate action and then carry on, but now we had to be on continuous alert and that was exhausting. Around 10:30 p.m., there was another announcement that the danger level was upgraded and we were warned of a big tsunami. We stayed up late into the night, listening to the multitude of announcements on the public address system. In the end a 1.5-meter tsunami hit, which luckily caused no real problems for the town.

After what seemed like a very long weekend, I went back to work and asked my students where they had stayed after the big tsunami warning. To my surprise, most answered they had stayed at home. One kid said, "All of my family was watching TV as usual. I live right next to the ocean. I am brave, aren't I?"

Local people have become used to natural disasters and warnings, and most of the time experience tells them the worst case won't happen. Therefore, their minds don't switch to real emergency mode. The friend who stayed at my house said old people laughed at her when she said she was moving to higher ground. What is this laid-back attitude?

I was particularly shocked to find quite a lot of families didn't evacuate even though they had small children. I cannot imagine what's going on in those people's heads. They think they will be OK because "experienced" older people say it should be OK? For me, it seems like something bordering on superstitious belief. I want the older people to be more sensible, not to be optimistic to the extent of stupidity! Most of the inhabitants of my town are old and the power of old people is still strong.

I overheard some high school kids chatting. They were boasting of how little they or their family had been bothered by the tsunami alert. I was so frustrated and told them, "You don't need to panic and run around in circles, but you should run up the hill!" Every individual needs to take responsibility for their own life.

Why don't parents teach this to their kids?

Japanese people are good at not thinking about the worst-case scenario. They stop thinking. To stop thinking is easy. To stop thinking is safe, because it is the same as everyone else! I think that's an illusion! It is not safe!

Hiromi Sakai
Kochi

幻想

東北地震のニュースをテレビで知ったとき、私は仕事場（自営の英語教室）にいた。すぐに市の放送があり、「4時半ごろ、津波が到達するとみられます。海のそばには近づかないように」と伝えていた。

すぐに7歳の娘のことが気にかかった。娘はどこだ？ 時計は3時半。家の周りを探し、友人の家も訪ね、市役所にも行ってみたがどこも空っぽ。最後に小学校に行ってみると、そこで友人と遊んでいた。その間、ほんの30分ほどだったが、もっと長いように感じ、娘を見つけたときには心底ほっとした。

次第に避難組の人々が小学校に集まってきた。しばらくしてまた放送があり、小さい津波が到達したとのこと。次の津波が来るまでに帰宅する時間はありそうなので、急いで家路につくことにした。家に到着すると、主人はもう帰宅していた。友人と彼女の1歳の息子も家にいた。彼女たち親子は、海のすぐ近くに住んでいて心配なので、今晩はうちに泊まることに。うちも海に近いことは近いが、家は海抜30メートルの高台にあるので大丈夫だろうと判断した。

地震のニュースを追っていると、状況はどんどん悪化しているようだった……。まだ次々と余震もある。と

いうことは、私たちのように海の近くに住んでいる住民にとっては、常に津波を警戒し続けなければならないということ。津波の到達予想時刻はわからず、ほとんど24時間、警戒体勢でいなくてはならないのには、神経を消耗した。10時半頃また放送があり、危険レベルが引き上げられ、大津波警報へと切り替わった。深夜まで起きて、次々に入る市内放送を聞き続けたが、幸い1.5メートルの津波が来ただけで、町に大きな被害は出ずにすんだ。

この途方もなく長く感じた週末を終え、仕事に戻り、生徒たちに質問してみた。「大津波警報の後、どこで過ごしてた？」驚いたことに、ほとんどの生徒の答えが「家にいた」「家族みんなで普通にテレビを見てた」だった。「海のすぐ近くに住んでるけど、逃げなかったよ。勇気あるでしょ！」などと答える小学生の生徒も。

地元の人たちは自然災害や警報に慣れすぎてしまっていて、そしてほとんどの場合、最悪の事態には到らずにすんでいるので、緊急モードに切り替えられないのだろうか。うちで過ごした友人は、「高台に避難していたと周りの人たちに言うと、笑われた」と話していた。この危機感のなさはなんなんだ。

小さな子どもがいる多くの家でも、避難しなかったという話にはショックを受けた。どうして避難せずにいられるのだろう……。私には想像がつかない。「経験のある」年寄りたちが大丈夫だと言えば、自分も大丈夫だとでも思っているのだろうか。迷信すれすれの思い込みにすがっているのではないだろうか。年輩の方たちからは、楽観視しすぎず、良識のある意見が欲しい。わたしが住んでいる高齢化が進んだ町は、多数派の年輩の意見がまかり通るようなところが今もある。

女子高生たちが、津波警報時、自分や自分の家族がどれだけそれを気に留めなかったかという自慢話をしているのも耳に入ってきた。ものすごく違和感を感じ、思わず彼女たちに「パニックになって逃げ惑う必要はないけど、せめて危機感は持って高台に移るくらいはしなくちゃ」と口をはさまずにはいられなかった。自分の人生に責任を持ち、命を守るのは自分にしかできない。なぜ親はこのことを、自分の子どもにすら伝えないのだろう？

日本人は「最悪のシナリオ」を想定することに慣れていない。そのことは、ただの「思考停止」にもつながる。考えることをやめるのは簡単だ。考えることをやめるのは安全だ、なぜなら周りの他のみんなもそうだから……！　いいや、そんなの幻想にすぎない！　安全なんかではない！

堺　洋美
高知県

Leaving

A Twitter exchange I saw a few days after the earthquake:
"Anything a returning gaijin can bring back that would be helpful?"
"People who run away don't need to bother bringing back anything—including themselves."

Rice and milk may be in short supply, but there has been no lack of accusations and vitriol in the foreign community following the quake. Those who stay are brave loyalists; those who leave are turncoat cowards. There are as many reasons to stay or go as there are suitcases. Tokyo is my home now, and I wanted to be there to do what I could. I'm not scared of radiation or inconvenience. I walked toward the burning World Trade Center on 9/11. Running away isn't normally what I do. I have a close friend who works at Tepco Systems in Tokyo—she didn't leave. Abandoning friends isn't normally what

I do either.

Yet here I am, on a borrowed couch in L.A. I didn't have an answer compelling enough to stand up to frightened family who demanded my "solid reasons" to stay. It's hard to stand up to 1 a.m. phone calls asking, "Leaving is easy, so WHY are you making us all worry like this?" Circumstances did make it easy for us to leave. Since I can work from anywhere, it came down to balancing a remote but tangible threat against abstract ideals.

So I left a key behind hoping that someone who truly needs our apartment will use it. I comfort myself knowing that we are one less household drawing power and two fewer stomachs taking food and water that is desperately needed up north. I don't think my reasons for leaving are any more valid than someone who just felt nervous. Everyone has to do what's best for them. When we were talking about it the night before we decided, I considered that the worry suffered by my family would take more years off their lives than radiation could from mine. All I had to fall back on, finally, was the belief that leaving would damage my idea of who I am. Jim agreed, but asked if that was worth possibly putting my life at risk.

Part of me is glad to be where the only radiation threat is from the constant sunshine. My family is certainly relieved I left Japan. And if that's not worth it, what is?

Sandra Barron
Los Angeles

離れてみて

地震の数日後、ツイッターで見かけたやり取り。
　「日本にこれから戻る外人だけど、何を持って帰れば役立つ？」
　「逃げていったやつなんか何も持ってこなくていいよ。自分の身を含めてね」
　あの地震のあと、米や牛乳は不足しているかもしれないが、日本在住の外国人の間でとびかう非難や辛辣な言葉は、あり余るほどだ。留まる者は勇敢で忠実、去っていく者は裏切り者で臆病。留まる理由も、去る理由も、スーツケースの数だけある。東京は私の第二の故郷であり、そこにいてできることをしたかった。放射線は怖くないし、生活の不便もどうでもいい。9/11の日だって、私は燃え上がる世界貿易センタービルに向かって歩いていったのだ。いつもなら逃げるなんて考えられない。東京にあるテプコシステムズという会社に勤めている親友がいるが、彼女は去らなかった。私だって、いつもなら友人を置き去りになどしない。

　だけど今、私は、ロサンゼルスで人から借りたソファに座っている。怖がる家族が東京に留まる「確固たる理由」を求めてきたとき、彼らを説得できる答えは浮かばなかった。「離れるのは簡単。なのにどうしてあなたは私たちをこんなに心配させるの？」夜中の1時の電話で問われて、言い返すのは難しい。確かに、簡単に離れられる状況ではあった。私の仕事はどこにいてもできるので、漠然とした理想と、遠いように見えてすぐそこにある脅威とを天秤にかけて考えることとなった。

　そこで私は、本当に必要としている人がいれば使ってくれることを願い、部屋の合鍵を置いてきた。私たちがいなくなったことで、東北でいますぐ必要な電力を使う世帯がひとつ減り、食料や水を消費する胃袋がふたつ減った、と自分を慰めている。ただの不安から日本を離れた人より、私が去った理由が正当だ

とは思わない。みんな自分のために最善のことをしなくてはいけない。私たちが東京を離れると決めた前夜、この件について話していて、私はこう考えた。放射線が私の寿命を縮める可能性よりも、家族が心配によって寿命を縮める可能性のほうが大きいだろう、と。結局私は、去ってしまったら、私という人物像に傷がつくと思い込んでいたのだ。ジムはわかってくれたが、命を危険にさらすほど価値のあることだろうかと言った。

放射線の脅威といえば、いつも降り注ぐ太陽光線ぐらい、という場所にいる私は、心のどこかでホッとしている。家族ももちろん、私が日本を離れたことで安心している。これに価値がないとしたら、何にあるというのだろう。

Sandra Barron
米国　カリフォルニア州　ロサンゼルス

Lingering

It's been a week since the Great Earthquake hit us at 2:46 p.m. on March 11. Our region of Soso has now been designated as an area of radioactive contamination, meaning that we have to head outside the 30-kilometer exclusion zone from the nuclear plant to pick up relief supplies.

Many people from Fukushima Prefecture have had to evacuate, but many still remain. Many haven't relocated because they are too old to move to emergency shelters.

Many linger because of their deep attachment to the land handed down from their forefathers.

Medical workers, working in devastated facilities with extreme shortages of medicine, also remain to help the many people who need them. Local government officials stick around to fulfill their duty to protect residents until the government orders them to evacuate.

We pray deeply for all the victims, and as remaining residents, we vow to protect our beloved cities.

　Stay strong, Soso.
　Stay strong, Fukushima.
　Stay strong, Tohoku.

Soso Bureau staff,
Soma and Futaba cities

いつまでも

3月11日（金）2時46分頃に発生した今回の大震災から、ちょうど1週間がたちました。今、相双は、南のいわき市と同様に、「放射能汚染地域」とされ、国の定めた屋内退避30キロメートルの外まで自分たちで物資を引き取りにこいと投げ出されました。

多くの方々が生まれ育った土地を泣く泣く離れ、県外避難が始まっています。しかし、留まる方々も数多

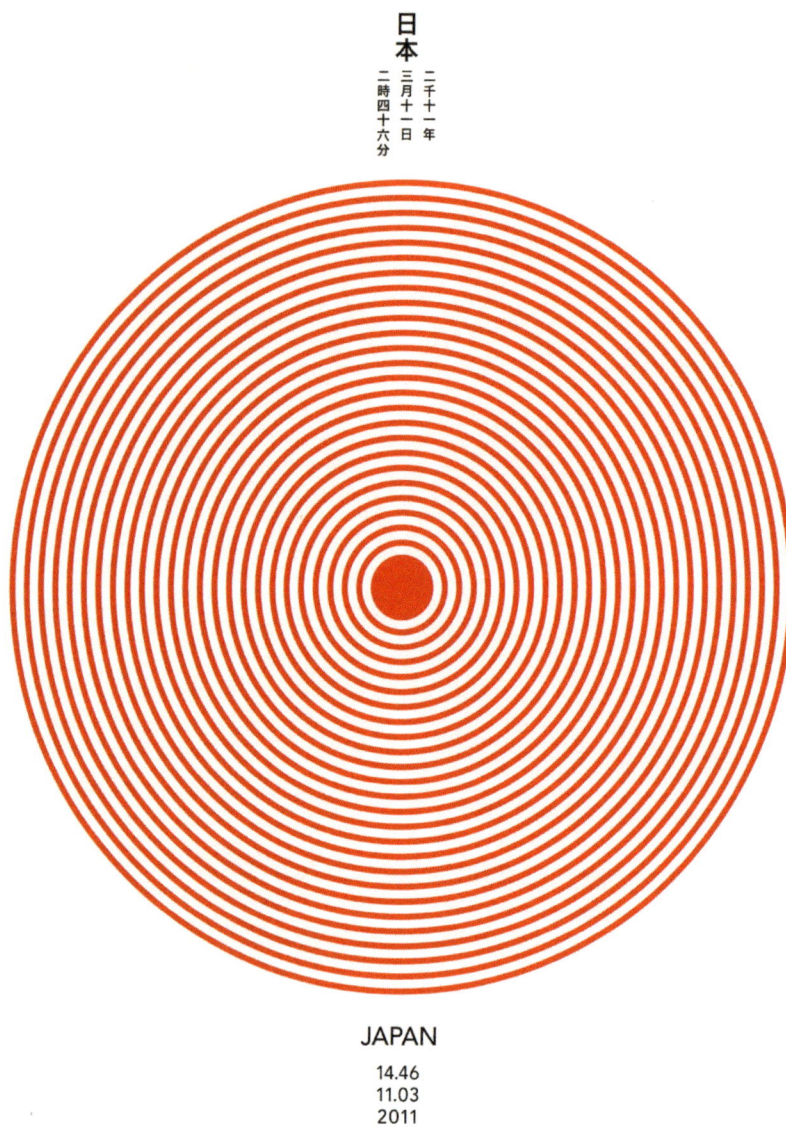

くいらっしゃいます。高齢のために避難所に移ることかできないという理由で留まっているのです。
先祖代々受け継いできた土地に深い愛着を感じるからこそ留まっているのです。
医療従事者は、極端な医療品不足のなかを被災した施設で働き、彼らを必要とする多くの方々のために留まっています。地元公務員は、政府による避難命令が出るまでは、住民を守る義務を果たすために留まります。
犠牲になられた皆さんに深く黙祷を捧げ、皆さんが愛した町は、残った全員で守っていくことを誓いたいと思います。

　がんばろう。相双。
　がんばろう。福島。
　がんばろう。東北。

相双ビューロースタッフ（ゆっ太郎・どっさりん子・Cross）
福島県 相双地域（相馬、双葉）

Lost

I am not the person you are looking for or, indeed, the story...
　This exchange is not between rescue-worker and missing person, parent and child, embassy and expat, but journalist searching for a tale of woe here in Tokyo, of all places, and me.
　I could give them an angle, yes, and an account of what was happening or had happened to me, no problem, but the "grim reality" was that here, life pretty much carried on.
　My thoughts are with those in the north and east of the country, and those around the country (and world) who have lost family members and friends.

Matthew Holmes
Shimokitazawa

僕じゃない

あなたのお目当ては僕じゃない。僕の話もきっとそう……。
　レスキュー隊員と行方不明だった人のやり取りとか、親と子どもの会話、大使館と日本在住の自国民の連絡とかじゃない。悲惨な話をなぜか東京で探すジャーナリストと私との間に交わされたやり取りなんだ。
　ネタになるような話をできるかって？ここで何が起き、僕自身に何が起こったかを説明できるかって？もちろん。でも、「厳しい現実」といっても、実際、東京の生活は、だいたいいつも通りだったんだよ。
　むしろ僕は、東北や全国（あるいは世界中）の、家族や友人を失った人々へ心からお見舞い申し上げたいと思う。

Matthew Holmes
東京都　世田谷区　下北沢

Loving

Though I have lived nearly nine years in Japan, I have experienced many earthquakes that have not frightened me. March 11th was my first time to be frightened.

As I took leave from work to go to the doctor's, things didn't go as well as I had planned. I'd only gotten ready to go at around 2:30 p.m. As my son came home after school, I waited a little longer until he settled down with his homework.

Then suddenly the earthquake struck.

As everyone probably thought, I thought it would end soon, but it didn't. It became more furious the more time passed. I saw things shaking vigorously around and falling. Even the building was shaking (as we are on the fifth floor) and it made me frightened. I told my son to put on a jacket and we ran outside for safety.

We were safe outside. We returned home after about two hours. Thank God that everyone was safe. At home, on the news, the real truth of the disaster unfolded. The tragedies that have happened to innocent people are too much to bear. The earthquake, the tsunami and then the nuclear power plant radiation.

Since we're safe, it taught me a good lesson about life. The importance of loving and taking care of your loved ones when they are alive. It can be family, neighbors, friends, or relations. As natural disasters can happen anywhere at any time, we should all be loving, friendly and happy while we are alive.

Shehan Raban
Kohoku, Chiba

愛をもって接すること

日本に住み始めて9年ほどになりますが、数多くの地震を経験しました。一度も怖いと感じたことはありませんでしたが、3月11日の地震ははじめて怖いと感じました。

その日私は仕事を休んで病院に行く予定でしたが、予定通りに物事が進まず、病院に行く準備ができたときには、もう2時半でした。息子が学校から帰ってきたので、宿題にとりかかるまで、しばらく待っていました。

そのときに、地震が起きたのです。

だれもがそう考えたように、私も地震はすぐに終わると思っていました。でも、そうはなりませんでした。それどころか、時の経過とともに激しさを増していったのです。身の回りの物が激しく揺れ、落ちてきました。建物さえも揺れて（私たちは5階に住んでいます）、怖くなりました。息子にジャケットを着るように言い、安全のため外に出ました。

戸外は安全でした。2時間ほどして帰宅すると、幸いみんな無事でした。家でニュースを見ると、震災の真の姿が映し出されました。罪もない人々をあまりの悲劇が襲ったのです。地震、津波、そして、原発の放射線漏れ。

被災を免れた私は、この震災から人生について学びました。愛する人たちが生きている間にこそ愛し、慈しむことが大切なのです。愛する人とは、家族、隣人、友人、あるいは親族かもしれません。天災はい

つ、どこで起きるかわかりません。私たちは、生きているからこそ、愛情を持ち、親しみを持って、楽しく過ごしていくべきでしょう。

Shehan Raban
千葉県　我孫子市　湖北

Lucky

I was in Shinagawa, Tokyo, in a meeting on the 19th floor. I wondered if this would be the end of me. The sounds were unnerving—not just rattling and banging, but loud creaking and groaning. We had a panoramic view across the city and over Tokyo Bay. Across the street we could see other skyscrapers swaying like palm trees in the breeze. Fires sprung up in various places and huge plumes of black smoke rose from Odaiba.

Had the quake stopped? The building kept moving for ages. Worried about my girlfriend, I peered anxiously down the coast towards the towers of Yokohama Thermal Power Station, looking for smoke. None. But across the bay in Chiba, vast, terrifying explosions could be seen on the horizon.

We decided to stay where we were because we were in a relatively safe building, at least if a tsunami hit Tokyo Bay. Our meeting continued for the next three hours, interrupted by several big aftershocks. I can't remember anything that was discussed. I had motion sickness from the constant swaying.

Eventually, my girlfriend rang from home. She had walked. I took that as my cue. I descended the many flights of stairs and joined an orderly pedestrian exodus along the old Tokaido Highway. After a while, I passed people gathered around a TV that an old lady had set up outside her shop. Only then, seeing the aftermath of the tsunami, did I realize how serious this really was and how lucky we were to be in Tokyo.

Stephen Lyth
Tokyo

幸運

私は東京の品川にいて、19階で会議中だった。これが人生の終わりなのかと思った。音に度肝を抜かれた—激しくたたきつけるだけでなく、大きくきしんでうめくような音だった。東京の街と東京湾を一望する眺めがそこにはあった。通りの反対側では、他の高層ビル群が、そよ風を受けたヤシの木のように揺れている。いくつもの場所で炎が上がり、黒い巨大な噴煙がお台場から立ち昇った。

地震は収まったのだろうか。建物は長い間揺れ続けた。恋人のことを心配する私は、横浜火力発電所の塔へと向かう湾岸を不安な思いで見下ろした。煙を探したが見当たらない。だが、対岸の千葉では、恐ろしく大きな爆発が水平線上に見えた。

私たちはこのまま留まることにした。少なくとも津波が東京湾を襲っても、比較的安全な建物だったから

だ。会議は、いくつかの大きな余震に中断されながら、さらに3時間続いた。何を議論したかまったく思い出せない。揺れ続けた私は乗物酔いの状態だった。

　ようやく、恋人が家から電話をかけてきた。彼女は歩いて帰ったのだ。これを合図に、私は何段もの階段を下り、旧東海道沿いを整然と歩いていく帰宅者の集団に加わった。しばらくして、高齢の女性が店先に設置したテレビに群がる人たちを追い越した。このときになってようやく津波の被害を目にした私は、この地震がどれだけ深刻な被害をもたらし、また、東京にいたことがどれだけ幸運だったかを知った。

Stephen Lyth
東京都

Morals

It's been one week since the evacuation. Yesterday we found 260,000 yen in cash under the rubble. Our shelter has 150 people in it. Looks like we'll be here for a while yet. We all discussed what to do with the money. Everybody agreed to take it all to the police station. I'm proud to say that we decided that lowering our moral standards would be too terrible, even during such a great emergency. We survivors are left to consider what makes us who we are, and what needs to be protected at all costs.

P.S. Thank you very much for leaving lots of comments. I'm relieved to know we're still connected to the rest of the world. I'll try to gather more information from Miyagi.

Yuichiro Ito
Kesennuma, Miyagi

モラル

避難生活が1週間になろうとしています。昨日……がれきの中から、現金26万円が出てきました。この避難場所には150人ほどの人たちがいますが、まだまだ、ここでの生活が続くでしょう。もし、このお金が使えるならば……と考えましたが、みんなの意見で、警察署に届けることになりました。緊急時ですが、本当に怖いのはモラルの低下だと判断した仲間たちを誇りに思います。僕らが僕らであるために、守っていかなければならないことを、改めて考えました。

P.S.たくさんの書き込みをありがとうございます。世界と繋がっていると思うと少し安心します。少しでも情報を集めますので、待っていてください。

伊藤雄一郎
宮城県　気仙沼市

Brian Lynn

Mountain

I remember the moment I first looked at the Zushi City tsunami hazard map. It was after we'd moved here. I enlarged the map on my computer screen, traced the road to our house and found that it was partly covered by a rude green splotch indicating up to 50 cm of flooding. The map-makers had postulated a maximum tsunami of five meters. I guessed that in a worst case scenario we'd end up with the ocean gently lapping at our doorstep, kind of like when a large wave races up the beach and soaks just a corner of your towel.

This memory flashed before my eyes at exactly 3:36pm on Friday, March 11. I know the time precisely because it was also at this time that I sent an email to my wife: "Climb the mountain," I wrote. "Escape!" By then, about 45 minutes had passed since the earthquake, and I hadn't once got through to her mobile or our landline. In those 45 minutes the tsunami warnings for the Miura Peninsula, where Zushi is located, had grown more urgent by the minute. Monitoring the television in my office in Tokyo I had first seen predictions of a 50 cm wave, then one meter. Next, they said three meters. Zushi was shifted from the orange category to red: "tsunami" to "major tsunami."

"This was it," I thought. "The real thing."

I tried again and again to call my wife, but it was hopeless. With the tone of a dead line still thumping in my ear, I stood in front of the television at work. NHK was broadcasting images from up north. What I saw wasn't a gentle lapping, nothing like it. A massive wave was rolling over houses and buildings like they were sandcastles. Large fishing boats were being thrown through barns several hundred meters from the sea.

Then, as if they knew I was watching, NHK cut to their revised list of tsunami warnings. Miura Peninsula, it said, "Six meters."

I was shaking as I bashed out another email. "Climb the mountain. Take the emergency radio. Listen to it. Climb the mountain," I wrote. Like the first email, this one received no response. The only real precaution I'd taken in choosing where in our seaside idyll we'd rent a house was to make sure we'd be near high ground. Our house is about 20 meters from the foot of the high-wooded ridge that divides Zushi from neighboring Hayama. Hop a fence, cross the neighbor's garden and you're at a path leading up the "mountain," as we call it. I was praying my wife had already gone.

With the Zushi City Government website down, I turned to Twitter for local updates. There I learned that the city had been in a blackout since the quake. No one could make calls in or out. Someone had tweeted, however, that the sea was receding rapidly at Enoshima. "I've never seen it this low," they wrote. Enoshima is about 10 kilometers west of our house. I remembered that the mobile phone carrier my wife and I used operated a disaster message board. I registered myself and checked if my wife had done the same. She hadn't. Back on Twitter I realized that I wasn't alone in seeking information about Zushi. There were dozens of tweets echoing my own desire for information. "Anyone who knows what's happening at Sakurayama, Zushi, please tweet," said one. I hit retweet. Sakurayama is where we live.

Scrolling through the tweets, I noticed that most were from men. Most seemed to be in Tokyo. Most were at work. I wondered if they, too, had been the ones in their families to suggest living by the sea. I wondered if they'd done so because they wanted to surf, sail, fish or just walk along the beach every now and again. I wondered if they, too, now felt responsible for endangering the people they loved most.

The authorities had only made plans for a five-meter tsunami. I hadn't even done that. NHK's tsunami warning for Zushi still stood at six meters. I kept following Twitter looking for information on whether it had hit. I found nothing.

I did a Google transit search and plugged in the Tokyo district where my office is located, and Zushi. On its default "train journey" setting it came back with a travel time of 80 minutes. All the trains had stopped, so I switched to "walking journey" mode. Ten hours, it said. Like many of my colleagues, I was about to spend a night in the office. I tried to think about work, about how we should respond to this, how this was going to affect what we had planned. But I couldn't. I couldn't concentrate. I couldn't stop thinking about what might be happening at home, to my wife. I couldn't, that is, until 6:40 p.m.

I know the time because there's an email in my "sent" box with that time stamp. It's addressed to my father, and it explains that I had just managed to get in contact with my wife. "She climbed the mountain," it says. "Now she's moved to the public library with our neighbors and she'll stay there tonight. No major tsunami has hit Zushi, yet."

Edan Corkill
Zushi, Kanagawa

山

　逗子市の『津波浸水予測図』をはじめて目にしたときのことをよく覚えている。この場所に引っ越してきた後のことだ。コンピューターの画面で地図を拡大して、自宅に続く道を確かめたところ、最大で50センチの洪水が起こることを示すいやなグリーンに色分けされた地区に、部分的にかかっていた。地図の制作者は、最大津波を5メートルと仮定していた。しかし、私は、最悪のシナリオが訪れたとしても、玄関前の階段にさざ波が打ち寄せるように海水が上がってくる程度、それはだいたい、海辺で大波が打ち寄せたときにタオルの端が少し濡れるようなものだと思っていた。

　この記憶が、3月11日金曜日午後3時36分、私の目前によみがえった。その時刻を正確に覚えている。なぜなら妻にメールを送信したのが、まさにその時刻だったからだ。「山に登れ！」と書いた。「逃げろ！」地震発生からすでに約45分が経過していた。妻の携帯にも、自宅の固定電話にもまだつながらない。その45分間のうちにも、逗子が位置する三浦半島の津波警報は刻々と緊急性を増していた。東京都内のオフィスでテレビを確認していたのだが、当初50センチの予測だった波の高さが1メートルに変わった。次には3メートルだと言う。逗子は、オレンジ色の区分けから赤色に変わった。「津波」が「大津波」に変わった。

　「このことだったんだ」と私は思った。「本物が来てしまった」

　妻に電話をしようと何度も繰り返し試みたが、どうにもならなかった。電話の不通音がいつまでも耳元で鳴っているのを聞きながら、私は職場のテレビの前に立っていた。NHKは東北からの画像を中継していた。私の目に映ったのは、さざ波ではなかった。巨大な波が家々やビルの上に襲いかかり、まるで砂の城のように次々と押しつぶしていく。海から数百メートルも離れた倉庫から大型漁船が放り出される。この後、NHKの画面は、私が見ていることを知っているかのように、津波警報の最新リストに切り替わった。

　三浦半島は、なんと「6メートル」とある。

　私は身を震わせ、急いで再度メールを送ろうとした。「山に登れ。緊急ラジオを持って、それを聴いて。山に登るんだ」と書いた。最初のメールと同じく、このメールにも返信はなかった。のどかな海辺で家を借りる場所を選ぶときに私が注意したことといえば、高台の近くであることを確認するぐらいだった。私たちの自宅は、逗子と、隣接する葉山とを分ける山の稜線から20メートルほど離れたところにある。フェンスを越えて隣家の庭を通り抜ければ、私たちが「山」と呼んでいるところに出る。妻がもうそこに行っているようにと、私は祈った。

　逗子市役所のウェブサイトが落ちていたので、最新の地域情報を求めてツイッターに移った。そこで私は、地震発生以来、市内は停電していることを知った。だれも電話をかけたり受けたりできなかった。だが、ツイッターには、江ノ島では海が急速に引いていると書いている人が何人かいた。「こんなに浅いのは見たことがない」と書いてある。江ノ島は、自宅から10キロ西方にある。私と妻の使っている携帯電話会社には、災害伝言板があることを思い出した。自分の名前を登録して、妻のメッセージがあるか調べてみた。まだなかった。ツイッターに戻ると、逗子の情報を探しているのは私だけでないことに気づいた。情報を求める私と同じような声が数多くツイッター上でこだましていた。「逗子桜山がどうなっているか、ご存じの方はツイートをお願いします」というツイート。すぐさま私はリツイートした。桜山に私たちの自宅はある。

　ツイートをスクロールしながら見ていくと、ほとんどが男性からの発信であることに気づいた。ほとんどが東京にいるようだ。また、ほとんどが職場にいる。この男性たちも私と同じように、海の近くに住もうとそれぞれの家族に勧めたのではないだろうか。自分たちがサーフィンやヨット、釣りや海辺の散歩をしたいためにそうしたのではないだろうか。だから、愛する家族を危険な目に遭わせていることに責任を感じているのではないだろうか、と思った。

　当局は、最大5メートルの津波にしか対応計画を用意していなかった。私はといえば、そんな計画すらしていない。NHKの津波警報では、逗子はまだ6メートル。津波が来たかどうかの情報を求めてツイッターを確認し続けた。何も見つからなかった。

私は、グーグル乗り換え案内で、会社のある東京地区と逗子を入れて検索した。初期設定の「列車の旅」で調べると、移動時間80分という結果が返ってきた。列車はすべて運転中止だったので、「徒歩の旅」に変更した。10時間だった。同僚の多くと同様に、私も会社で一夜を過ごすことになりそうだった。仕事のことを考えようとした。この事態にどう対処したものか、我々の計画してきたことにどう影響するのか。だが、できなかった。私は集中することができなかった。家で何が起きているのか、妻の身に何が起きているのか、考えずにはいられなかった。無理だった、午後6時40分までは。

　その時刻がわかっているのは、送信ボックスにある1通のメールにその時刻が記録されているからだ。父に宛てたメールで、妻とやっと連絡が取れたことを説明した。「彼女は山に登っていました」と書いた。「今は近所の人と一緒に公立図書館に移動しました。今夜はそこで泊まるそうです。逗子には大きな津波はまだ来ていません」

Edan Corkill
神奈川県　逗子市

Muenbotoke

On March 11th, 2011, an earthquake of almost unprecedented magnitude...

Last year I had my palm read, for a lark. It was part of an event at a boutique hotel—wine, cheese, and a palm reader. The woman doing it seemed pleasant enough, maybe early forties, long black curly hair, wearing a long red skirt, leather jacket over a purple blouse, an Egyptian ankh necklace with a thin black silk rope holding it around her neck instead of a chain.

　She cheerfully took my palm in her hand as I sat down, and as we made small talk she honed in on my palm, slightly pushing the palm with her tiny, thin finger and said something a little odd. "You have a square in the mount of Mercury. You will lead and have lead an exciting life shadowed by fatality wherever you have been and will go."

　"Couldn't I get a slightly cheerier reading?" I quipped and she laughed and I pretended to have to meet someone, that I was late, and I left.

　I don't need someone to tell me that life involves fatality. We all know that amusing little Buddhist proverb on why we are mortal: "The cause of death is birth."

　True. Death is part of my business. That's the extreme end of being a crime reporter or an investigative reporter.

　For many the coming of spring is symbolic of birth, rebirth, vitality. For me, it used be a reminder that a lot of people are going to start dying and I'll be busy. People are a little less active in the fall and winter—the cold slows them down, cools down tempers, bodies don't rot quickly, the odor doesn't give away their secrets. But by the early spring or late summer, what's killed rots quickly and what's been laying dormant begins to stink. The heat makes temperature and tempers rise, anger flares in sync with the solar spots on the sun. Hot tempers lead to fatal mistakes, impulsive murders, rape, arson, lethal assaults. Hasty attempts to cover up crimes don't go so well. The missing are uncovered and/or their deaths known much faster.

Please don't think as a reporter that I dreaded the summer. Death is always a good story. It's always tragic.

....devastated Japan. Thousands died and thousands are missing. It was a natural disaster compounded by a partially man-made disaster, the collapse of a nuclear power plant in Fukushima Prefecture.

However, as a reporter in Japan, it's not just enough to find a tragic event to write about—it has to be a good tragic event. There are plenty to choose from. Sometimes, however, a tragedy is just a plain tragedy.

In 1999, covering the 4th District of the TMPD was an interesting assignment. There was enough crime and sleaze in Kabukicho alone to keep me busy, but I had to cover a wide area and a lot of police stations.

On a weekend in July, the body of a sixty-two year old man and his fifty-nine year old wife, Mr. and Mrs. Akutagawa, were found dead in their apartment. It looked like a double suicide or in Japanese what they call "*murishinju.*" *Shinju* in medieval times meant a suicide pact between a man and his lover, or even a family. *Muri* means unreasonable in Japanese and together the term refers to a suicide/murder in which one persons kills a loved one(s) and then him or herself. I was asked to go talk to the police and see if I could get a human interest story out of it.

I went to the home of Mr. and Mrs. Akutagawa before going to the police station. The door was slightly open, so you could see into the place. The apartment was filthy, totally covered in trash. Newspapers, magazines, clothes, randomly strewn about and a TV on the floor. The neighbors had stuck close to ten notices on the door asking them to clear the hallway and the area in front of their apartment.

Empty plastic bowls of ramen were stacked outside the door. The postbox was filled with bills.

I went to the police station but they didn't have much to tell me. One cop did break protocol and showed me photos of the couple.

In the photo of the crime scene, a towel was placed over Mrs. Akutagawa's face, and there were no signs that she put up a fight at the time of her death. As background information on the incident, the detective working the case told me the couple not only had outstanding loans on their condominium apartment, but likely held a significantly large sum of consumer debt as well. Probably borrowed money from loan sharks.

They'd drunk poison. The husband had boiled a pack of cigarettes, Peace or Hope brand, in some alcohol and water. There was enough nicotine in a pack of cigarettes that if you distilled it and drank it down, it could kill you very quickly. She'd died first and he died shortly afterwards. I gathered that death had been quick. Painless or not, I didn't know.

The assistant chief told me, "He was a faithful salary man that had just been laid off, and had just started at a new job, then that didn't work out. It happens like that. A guy gets put in a situation where even when living a relatively simple way of life, a man can't save enough to repay loans and this eventually leads to suicide becoming an apparent solution to the problem. It's evident that the guy was not skilled in money matters and didn't know how to handle his finances. Gambling was most likely involved."

Many of the staff at the nuclear power plant stayed on the job long after radiation levels had risen past even the laxest of safety standards, to prevent a full melt-down. Why?

"You can call it double suicide, but if he killed his wife without her consent, it's murder. He should be prosecuted for it accordingly with all facts investigated and necessary paperwork submitted."

The cops do this in Japan a lot; they file papers on dead perpetrators. Just because you're dead doesn't mean the wheels of justice stop turning.

I tried to flesh out a story by talking to people who knew the man, but no one did. I had gotten a photo of the guy from the police. I thought that would be helpful. It wasn't. He was practically invisible. Akutagawa was temporarily employed at a construction company located in the Shinagawa Ward of Tokyo. If he had any friends or acquaintances in the area, no such individual having a close relationship with Mr. Akutagawa could be identified.

The female managing the apartment complex stated, "I didn't have a personal relationship with the man, though he has seemed a bit strange recently. I didn't notice any indications of ruckus related to debt collection." When she was told that the man may have had a heavy loan burden, she commented, "It could be true. It does seem that he enjoyed pinball and gambling, but I just really can't say for sure. We're not supposed to speak about that in public or to the media, even if it was true."

It's because they are willing to give their lives to save the lives of thousands of other people, people they know, people they don't know, and people they will never meet.

Another resident of the complex, a middle-aged woman working part-time said, "We were living in the same apartment building, but I never got to know him. I may have met him before, but I can't place his face. Since I've moved into this complex, I haven't gotten acquainted much with those living around me. Yesterday, I was told that the wife of the person living in Room 201 died, and thought that it must've been a double suicide. It wasn't. She just killed herself. It probably would've been helpful if she had someone to confide in, but it seems that she had no one she could talk to."

Questioning the owner of a Japanese pub next door resulted in, "I'm not familiar with the man. If he was a customer, I'd mostly likely recognize his name."

On the first floor of the complex was a beauty salon, but questioning was not possible due to Tuesday being the salon's off day. An attempt to gain further clues from speaking with someone in the salon was set for the following day, as was a visit with the elderly woman working at the nearby ramen shop which I hoped would give me something to go on. I came back the next day. No luck.

It's amazing to me that people can live in an apartment complex right next to each other for years and not know each other at all, not even in passing. This was the case with the Akutagawa family. They had no friends, no social life or interaction with the neighbors. Mr. Akutagawa lost his job, they ran out of money, and they made a suicide pact. A lot of Japanese people hate to ask others for help—even from close friends.

That was the whole story. All they could tell me at Mr. Akutagawa's former company was that he worked hard and didn't talk much. Work was slow, they had to let people go and Mr. Akutagawa wasn't young or fast or particularly good at building. So they laid him off. He'd only been working there a few weeks.

Those who are still working there may survive a few weeks, a few months, but the unseen radiation they were exposed to has probably already killed them. They are living yet already amongst the deceased.

I went back to the police and asked them if they had found anything else about the husband and wife or the circumstances leading up to the suicide. The detective showed me the note he had left behind. It was addressed to no one—they didn't have any children.

The note said simply: "Don't worry about us. We've been dead for a long time. Sorry we didn't clean up before we left. We didn't have the energy."

Very Japanese, very apologetic.

The police had found some very nasty letters from a consumer loan company, Yamaguchi-gumi backed, in the mailbox of Akutagawa. Debt collectors had also shown up at his workplace. He was apparently being threatened and harassed at regular intervals. Still, the suicide couldn't really be blamed on the loan sharks. Not in a criminal justice sense, the detective told me.

I asked when the funeral was going to be held and where but they didn't have anyone claiming the body. They were *muenbotoke*, literally, Buddhas without connections. There was no one to mourn for them. There was no one who would miss them, pine for them. At least not in Tokyo. There would be an ad put in the paper, and if no one came forward, the cremated ashes would be transferred to a temple on the outskirts of the megalopolis.

The detective asked me if I could write something in the paper but I didn't have much for a story. I told him as much. He nodded.

I asked him where the temple was. I checked back with him two weeks later. The ashes had been moved there. I took a cab to the temple the same day, and the priest showed me where they housed the ashes. I'm not sure I remember it correctly but there were about three stories of urns in the pagoda dedicated to the *muenbotoke*. On one floor, there were the ashes of children and infants—people who had had loved ones. Someone had stuck a photo of one child onto his urn. A cute kid, little round face with big lips, fuzzy eyebrows (for a Japanese kid). He had on a navy blue Hanshin Tigers baseball cap in the picture.

The priest took me to where Mr. and Mrs. Akutagawa had been put to rest. I lit a stick of incense, put my hands together, mumbled the only Buddhist prayer I could remember and left.

By now, the ashes of the Akutagawas have probably been evicted or displaced by the ashes of other *muenbotoke*. This happens. When family members don't pay the upkeep fees on gravestones and burial plots in Japan, the remains are moved and new tenants are sought. Even the dead can only rent in Tokyo.

I think I'll still visit the temple this summer anyway and pay my respects to the Akutagawas before even the memory of their memory is gone. It seems like the least I could do. Everybody needs someone to mourn them. I hope that when my time comes, there's someone who will do the same for me. I couldn't tell you why that's even important to me but it is.

May their memories last longer than the accident that took their lives. Because remembering them is all we can do for them now and for all those who lost their lives. And in that act of remembering, hopefully we will lead better lives and remember to care for all living things. We owe the dead that much.

Jake Adelstein
Tokyo

Originally published in Shambhala Sun, rewritten for #quakebook.

無縁仏

2011年3月11日　空前のマグニチュードの地震……。

昨年、おもしろ半分に手相を見てもらったことがある。おしゃれで気のきいたホテルのイベントで、ワインとチーズが振る舞われ、手相占いをしてくれるというものだった。手相を見てくれる女性はなかなか感じが良くて、たぶん40代前半。長い黒髪はカールしていて、赤いロングスカートを履き、紫色のブラウスの上に革のジャケットをはおり、胸元には、チェーンの代わりに細めの黒いシルクのひもをつけたエジプトのアンク（十字架）の首飾りを下げていた。

腰をかけると、彼女はにこやかに私の掌を自分の手の中におさめ、少し言葉を交して、私の掌を磨くように自分の小さな細い指で軽く押した。そして、少し奇妙なことを言った。「水星丘が四角ですね。今までもそうだったようですが、今後もあなたは、刺激的で死の影をおびた人生を送るでしょう。いままでどこにいたとしても、これからどこへ行くにしても」

「もう少し明るいことは言ってもらえないかな？」と私が軽口をたたくと、彼女は笑った。人と会う約束に遅れそうだからという振りをして、私は席を立った。

人生には死がつきものだということはわかっている。なぜ死ぬのかという問いに対しては、「死は生を受けたが故に訪れる」というちょっとおもしろい仏教のことわざをみんな知っているだろう。

死は私の仕事の一部である。事件記者あるいは調査報道記者にとって、死は終着点である。

多くの人々にとって、春の到来は誕生、再生、活力を象徴するだろう。しかし、かつての私にとっては、死者が増えて忙しくなるという思いをもたらすものだった。人は、秋と冬はあまり活動的でない。寒いと動きが遅くなり、感情にも冷静になるし、肉体が急速に腐敗することもなく、秘密を漏らすような臭気もない。しかし、早春から夏の終わりまでは、殺されたものはすぐに腐敗し、眠っていたものからは臭気がたち始める。熱のせいで気温は上がり、感情は熱しやすくなり、怒りは太陽系の太陽黒点の動きに伴って燃え上が

る。感情的になると死に至る間違いが起こる。衝動殺人、レイプ、放火、暴行致死。犯罪を急いでもみ消そうとしてもうまくはいかない。行方不明だったものは見つけ出され、死はすぐにわかる。

記者だから夏を怖れていたと思わないでもらいたい。死は常に物語として楽しめる。そこには常に悲劇がある。

日本は被災した。死者数千人、行方不明者数千人。自然災害に始まり、人災が重なり、福島県原子力発電所が壊滅した。

しかし、日本在住の記者にとっては、記事になりそうな悲劇的な出来事を見つけるだけでは十分でない。悲劇的で、しかもおもしろい出来事でなくてはならない。そうした出来事には事欠かない。しかし、ときとして悲劇は、どこまで行っても悲劇でしかない。

1999年、警視庁の第4地区を担当したが、興味深い任務であった。歌舞伎町ひとつとっても犯罪やスキャンダルが多くていつも忙しかったが、私の担当は広域にわたっていて、警察署がたくさんあった。

とある7月の週末、男性（62歳）とその妻（57歳）、芥川夫婦が自宅のアパートで死体で発見された。心中らしかった。日本語では「無理心中」という。「心中」は、中世には、男性とその愛人との間、ときには家族間で交わされる自殺の約束を意味した。「無理」は日本語で理にかなわない状態を意味し、両方の語を合わせて「自殺／殺害」を言う。人が愛する人を殺害して、その後自殺することを言う。警察に行き、この事件で何か人間模様となる話が聞けないか取材してくるよう言われた。

警察に行く前に、芥川夫婦の自宅に行った。ドアが少し開いていて、中が見えた。アパートは汚れていて、部屋中ゴミだらけ。新聞、雑誌、衣料品が散乱し、テレビが床にあった。ドアには隣人のメモが10枚近く貼られていて、廊下や玄関前を片付けるようにと書かれている。

玄関ドアの外には空になったプラスチックのラーメン用丼が重ねてあって、郵便受けには請求書があふれていた。

警察署に行ってみたものの、たいした話は聞けなかった。警察官の一人が規則を破って夫婦の写真を見せてくれた。

犯行現場の写真では、芥川夫人の顔にはタオルがかかっていたが、死に際に抵抗したような形跡はなかった。この事件の背景情報として担当刑事が教えてくれたのだが、夫婦には分譲マンションの未払いローンがあり、おまけにかなり多額の消費者負債も抱えていたらしい。恐らくサラ金から借りた金だろう。

二人は毒を飲んだ。夫がピースだかホープだかのタバコ1箱を、アルコール入りの水に入れて沸騰させた。タバコ1箱にはかなりの量のニコチンが含まれており、蒸留して飲めばほぼ即死する。妻が先に死んで、しばらくして夫が死んだ。死ぬのに時間はかからなかっただろう。痛みがなかったかどうかは、私にはわからない。

警察の副本部長が私に語ったことには、「彼は誠実なサラリーマンだったが、解雇され、新しい仕事を始めた。だが、それもうまくいかなかった。よくあることだね。比較的質素な暮らしでもローン返済に十分な貯金ができない状況に置かれて、結局そこからこの問題を解決するには自殺しかないと思い詰めたんだろうな。男は明らかに金のやり繰りが苦手で、自分の資産管理をどうしたらよいかわからなかったんだろう。ギャンブルが関係していたことは確からしい」

原子力発電所職員の多くが、放射能レベルが最も緩い安全基準を超えて上昇した後も長く現場で作業を続けた。完全なメルトダウンを避けるために。なぜ？

「心中と呼ぶこともできるが、妻の同意なく夫がその命を絶ったのであれば殺人になる。捜査で解明された全事実と必要書類を提出したうえで、夫はしかるべく起訴される」

日本ではよくあることで、警察は、死亡した犯罪者についても訴追手続きを進める。死をもって司法手続きが終わるわけではないのだ。

私は、この話に肉付けしようと、夫を知っている人々と話そうと試みた。だが、彼のことを知る者はいなかった。男の写真は警察から入手していた。役立つかと思ったが、だめだった。実際のところ、彼はだれの目にも見えない存在だったのだ。芥川は、東京都品川区にある建設会社で一時雇用されていた。その地域に友人か知人がいたとしても、芥川氏と親しい関係にある人物を特定することはできないだろう。
　マンションの管理人の女性は、「個人的関係はなかったけど、最近少し様子がおかしかったみたい。借金の取り立てのような騒ぎには特に気づかなかったけど」と話した。だが、彼が多額の借金で苦しんでいたようだと聞くと、彼女は、「そうかもしれません。パチンコやギャンブルが好きだったようだし。でも、確かなことは言えません。その件については、公にもマスコミにも話さないことになってますから。たとえ真実だとしても」と答えた。

　なぜなら、何千人もの人々の命を救うために自分たちの命をすすんで捧げようとしている人々だからだ。
　自分たちの知っている人たちも、知らない人たちも、決して会うことのないような人たちのために。

　マンションの別の住人で、パート勤務の中年の女性はこう言った。「マンションの同じ建物に住んでいるけど、彼のことはあまりよく知りませんでした。以前会ったことがあるかもしれないけど、顔は思い出せません。このマンションに引っ越してきて以来、近所の人たちとあまり知り合う機会がありません。昨日、201号室の奥さんが亡くなったと聞いて、心中に違いないと思ったんですけど、違っていました。奥さんは自殺したんです。だれか信用して話せる人がいればよかったのに。だれも話せる人がいなかったみたいです」
　隣の部屋の住人で居酒屋経営者に尋ねると、「その男性のことは知らないねえ。お客さんだったら、だいたいは名前でわかるはずなんだけど」という答えだった。
　マンションの1階は美容室だが、火曜日だったので店は休業日で取材できなかった。美容室の人に取材して何かヒントを得ようという試みは翌日にまわした。同様に、近くのラーメン店で働く年配の女性を訪ねれば何が起きていたのか手がかりがつかめるかと期待していたのだが、これも翌日にした。次の日改めて訪ねてみたが、だめだった。
　マンションで長年隣同士で住んでいるのに互いのことをまったく知らない、すれ違っているかさえわからないというのは、私には驚くべきことだ。しかし、それが芥川家の生活だった。友人もなく、社交的な暮らしや隣人との付き合いはまったくない。芥川氏は失業して、金がなくなり、夫婦は心中の約束をした。日本人の多くは、他の人に助けを求めたがらない。親しい友人に対してでさえ。
　話の全容はそんなところだ。芥川氏の以前の会社で聞けたのは、彼が仕事熱心で口数の少ない人だったということぐらいだ。仕事があまりなく、解雇せざるを得なかった。芥川氏は若くなかったし、仕事が速かったわけでも建設作業が得意だったわけでもない。だから解雇された。2週間ほど働いただけだ。

　原子力発電所でまだ働いている人々は、あと2週間、あるいはあと2か月は生き残るかもしれない。しかし目に見えぬ放射線が、恐らくすでに彼らの体を蝕んでいるだろう。生きてはいるが、すでに死者の仲間入りをしているのかもしれない。

　警察署に戻り、夫婦のこと、あるいは彼らを自殺に追い込むような状況について何かわかったか尋ねた。刑事は男が残したメモを見せてくれた。それはだれに宛てたものでもない。彼らには子どももいなかった。
　そこには、「私たちのことは心配しないでください。とうの昔に私たちは死んでいたのです。片付けもしないでこの世を去ることになってしまい、申し訳ありません。そうするだけの力が残っていません」とだけ書かれていた。
　たいへん日本的で、謝罪の気持ちがあふれている。
　警察は、芥川の自宅の郵便受けに、消費者金融会社からのいやがらせの手紙を発見した。山口組が背後にいる会社だ。借金の取り立て人が職場にも来ていた。男は定期的に脅迫されたり、いやがらせを受けていたようだ。しかし、だからといって自殺をサラ金会社のせいにはできない。少なくとも刑法上は、と刑事

が教えてくれた。

葬儀はいつ、どこで開かれるのか尋ねたが、遺体の引き取り手がいないという。無縁仏である。文字通りの意味では縁のつながりのない仏。彼らを悼む人はいない。寂しがる人もいなければ、恋しがる人もいない。少なくとも東京にはいない。新聞広告が載るかもしれないが、だれも現れなければ、火葬された遺灰は首都の郊外にある寺に移送される。

刑事に、何か記事を書けそうかと聞かれたが、記事が書けるほどの情報がない。私は彼にできる限りのことを話した。彼は頷いた。

彼に寺がどこにあるのか尋ねた。2週間後にまた連絡してみた。遺骨はすでにそこに移されていた。その日のうちにタクシーで寺へ行った。僧侶が、二人の遺骨の納められているところへ案内してくれた。正確に覚えているか自信はないが、寺の塔には、無縁仏の骨壺を置くための場所が3段あった。ひとつの段には、子どもや乳児の遺骨が安置されていた。愛する者がかつていた人々。子どもの写真が骨壺の上に置かれていた。かわいい子だ。小さな丸い顔に大きな唇、（日本人の子どもにしては）濃い睫毛。紺色（原文のまま）の阪神タイガースの野球帽を被っている。

僧侶が、芥川夫婦が安置されているところに案内してくれた。お香に火をつけ、両手を合わせて、唯一覚えていたお経をつぶやいて、席を立った。

今ごろはもう、芥川夫婦の遺骨はたぶん移動されているか、他の無縁仏の遺骨と入れ替えられているだろう。そういったことが起きる。家族が墓石や墓地の維持費を払わなければ、動かして新たな借り手を捜すことになる。死者でさえ東京では賃貸するしかない。

私は、今年の夏も寺を訪れ、芥川夫婦に敬意を払おうと思う。二人についての記憶がなくなってしまう前に。私にできるせめてものことだから。どんな人も死を悼んでくれる人が必要だ。私に死が訪れたときには、私のために同じようにしてくれる人がいてほしい。そうであることがなぜ私にとって重要なのかはわからないが、でもそうなのだ。

彼らについての記憶が、彼らの命を奪った事故についての記憶以上に長く続きますように。なぜなら、彼らのことを覚えていることが、私たちが彼らのために、そして命を失ったすべての人々のために今できる唯一のことなのですから。願わくば、思い出すという行為において、私たちはより良い人生を送り、生きとし生けるすべてのものを気づかうことを忘れないでいられるように。私たちがあるのは、死者のおかげなのだから。

Jake Adelstein
東京都
(Shambhala Sun に掲載された原文を本書のために書き直しました)

Neighbors

We lost all of our lifelines immediately after the earthquake. We had no idea what had happened as we were unable to use our cell phones or watch TV. We were so scared that we just could not stay inside of our home that night. We chose to stay in our car. There were aftershocks, one after another throughout the night, preventing us from getting any sleep.

It was not until two days later that the electricity in our house finally came back on. The gas came on soon after. I can't describe how happy and lucky we felt to eat warm food under the bright light. We had not been able to drink much liquid for the past two days, so the coffee we were having that day was especially tasty.

It's now ten days after the earthquake, and we still do not have running water in our house. However, I think about how lucky we are to still have that house. Especially since there are a lot of people here in Ibaraki whose hometowns are in Fukushima Prefecture and who still have not been able to contact their families.

We managed to carry on with our lives without running water. Our neighbors provided us with water from a well in their garden. They also gave us some drinking water, instant noodles and some dishes to use for meals. I honestly think we could not have done anything without their help. I told them that words could not express how much we appreciated their help. They told me, "You'd do the same thing if we were in trouble." I'm so grateful for the kindness we received, from neighbors who provided well water to strangers, who shared their water to fill out our bathtub.

My neighbors' kindness reminded me that it is very important to stay connected with our neighbors, and to help each other. I would like to urge everybody to be more actively involved in their local community in their everyday life. Because nobody can survive without the support from others.

Yumiko Takemoto
Hitachinaka, Ibaraki

ご近所さん

今回の地震ではすべてのライフラインが途絶え、その日の夜は余震の恐怖から家の中では寝られずに車の中で夜を明かしました。携帯もつながらず、もちろんテレビも見られないわけですから、いったい何がどうなっているやらと不安な夜でした。たびたび来る余震と寒さでほとんど寝られませんでした。

2日後、ようやく電気が、そしてその後ガスが復旧したとき、明るい電気の下で温かいものを食べられる幸せは言葉にはできません。そして地震後はじめて飲んだコーヒーのなんておいしかったこと！　水分をあまりとっていなかったので、とくにそう感じたのかもしれません。

地震発生から10日、まだ水は出ていませんが「まだ私たちは家があるだけ幸せ」とつくづく思います。ここ茨城は実家が福島という人もけっこういて、実家のお父さんの消息がわからないという人もいます。

まだ水は出ませんが、近所の井戸水が出るお宅からお水を汲ませてもらってなんとか生活できています。また、ご近所さんから飲料水やカップラーメンなどをいただいたり、夕飯のおかずからおすそ分けをもらったりと、改めて近所付き合いの大切さを感じています。自分たちだけでは何もできなかったと思います。いくら感謝してもしきれません。「困ったときはお互いさま」と見ず知らずの人たちにも井戸水を解放してくれている近所の友人。ホースをつないで自宅から浴槽に水を入れてくれた裏のご主人。ほんとうに、ほんとうに、ありがとうございます。

近所付き合いが希薄になってきていると言われていますが（特に都市部では！）、ここで声を大にして言いたいです。日々の生活の中で、積極的に地域に入っていって近所付き合いをしましょう、と。今回の地震で強く感じたことです。

武本由美子
茨城県　ひたちなか市

Normal

In the space of one week I've been through fear, sadness, paranoia, anger, tiredness and euphoria—each day bringing with it more or less a different feeling. Until today, when I stepped out to have a cigarette and coffee and for the first time in a week felt as if everything was normal. No wind, sun shining, warm air, people going about their business in Koenji as usual.

Laurent Fintoni
Koenji, Tokyo

いつも通り

この1週間の間に私は恐怖、悲しみ、疑念、怒り、疲労、絶頂感などの思いを味わってきた。毎日どこかしら異なる感情がこみあげてくる。しかし今日、コーヒーを飲み、タバコを一服しようと外へ足を踏み出して、1週間ぶりにすべてがいつも通りに戻ったように感じた。特に風もなく、好天で暖かな外気の中で、人々が普段通りに暮らす高円寺の姿があった。

Laurent Fintoni
東京都　杉並区　高円寺

OK

More than 6,000 people have passed away, and many more are not found yet. Many survivors lost their homes and are living in the gym as shelter. There is not enough food, water or heating oil.

One of the nuclear plants has been damaged. It is very serious. It's very close to meltdown. And the weather is still cold.

I'm OK, but it's a pity for the children. Sometimes the electric power is cut off. Gas stations are closed and trains do not come as usual. But we are OK. We are living. Please do not worry about me, please worry about people in the north.

It's cold, but I'm OK. Keep in touch.

Naotoshi Nabekawa
Abiko, Chiba

返信

　6千人以上の人が亡くなっており、それ以上の人たちが行方不明になっている。多くの生存者は家を失い、体育館などを避難所として生活している。食料、水、暖房用灯油が不足している。
　原子力発電所のひとつが被災した。かなり深刻な状態だ。メルトダウンに近いようだ。そして、依然として寒さが続いている。
　私は大丈夫、でも子どもたちはかわいそうだ。ときどき停電がある。ガソリンスタンドは閉店し、列車もいつものようには動かない。しかし、私たちは大丈夫、生きているよ。私のことより、北方の人たちのことを心配してほしい。
　とても寒いが、私は大丈夫。また連絡する。

鍋川尚孝
千葉県　我孫子市

Options

The most surprising thing for me was that my life never flashed before my eyes. Other than the twenty or so minutes during which I couldn't get hold of my wife to check if she and my daughter were safe, I like to think I didn't really panic or feel much fear. My co-workers might like to differ, but this is my story and I'm going to make myself seem brave.

　I was at work in Tama Centre, Tokyo, preparing for a day of lessons. I teach English at an eikaiwa where most of the students are kids, along with a few near-mute adolescents and assorted adults thrown in for good measure. All five of the school's teachers were together when the quake struck.

　We fled the building and decamped to a nearby car park right under the Tama Monorail, which at that point was swaying like it was made of rubber, and screeching. One co-worker advised us to pray. The rest of us tried to get signals on our phones so we could call loved ones. We had all figured out pretty quickly that the quake was big, and that somewhere people were suffering.

　I spent the next few days glued to the computer, while my wife's family was glued to the TV. Slowly but surely, news about the tsunami was overtaken by panicked reporting on the nuclear reactor problems in Fukushima. And that's when the e-mails started from home.

　"Please come home", "We will pay" and "You have options" were common themes, but never once did I want to leave. This is my home. It is a country I love. It is where my daughter was born and where I met my wife. It is the only place I have enjoyed working, and I couldn't pack it in just because the chips were down.

Jason Morgan
Kawasaki

選択肢

　驚いたことに、自分の人生を走馬灯のように思い浮かべたことなどなかった。妻と娘の無事を確認しように も、妻と連絡が取れなかった20分かそこらの時間を除けば、自分がパニックになったり恐怖を感じたりした ことはなかったと考えたい。同僚の見方は違うかもしれないが、これは僕のストーリーだし、自分が強く、肝 が据わっているかのように書こう。

　地震のとき、僕は東京の多摩センターでその日の授業の準備をしていた。僕が英語を教えている英会話 学校の生徒は子どもたちが多いが、無口な年頃の若者から大人も交えてうまく人数を調整している。地震 が起きたとき、教師5人は全員一緒にいた。

　僕らはビルから脱出し、すぐ近くの多摩モノレールの下にある駐車場に避難した。その時点でモノレール はゴムでできているかのようにブラブラ揺れ、荒く甲高い音をたてていた。同僚のひとりから祈るように言 われたが、僕たちは家族や恋人と連絡が取れるよう、携帯が通じるのを待っていた。この地震がかなり大 きなもので、多くの被災者が出ると察するまでに時間はかからなかった。

　地震から数日間、僕はコンピューターに、妻の家族はテレビに釘付け状態だった。少しずつ、でも確実に、 津波のニュースに代わって、福島の原発事故についての狂乱報道が多くを占めるようになっていった。母 国の家族からメールが次々と届き始めたのはそういうときだった。

　「お願いだから帰ってきて」「旅費は私たちが払うから」、そして「選択肢があるよ」が主なテーマだった が、僕は一度も日本を離れようとは思わなかった。ここが僕の家だ。ここが僕の愛する国だ。ここは妻と出 会い、娘が生まれた場所だ。働くのが楽しいと思った唯一の場所でもある。不運に見舞われたからといっ て、見捨てるわけにはいかない。

Jason Morgan
神奈川県　川崎市

Overwhelmed

Am I supremely lucky or cursedly unlucky? Neither I nor my immediate family have been in harm's way for even one second. Friends and extended family—even while at risk—have come through mostly fine. But I have experienced from afar the destruction of the two places in the world that I call home.

　I've never been a good one for specific times and dates. However 12:51 p.m., February 22, and 2:46 p.m., March 11 will always stick in mind. Christchurch and Tohoku. Earthquakes are nothing unusual to either country. Neither is it unusual to have a friend or two overreact to such events on Facebook. The TV went on. But placid, boring old Christchurch looked like a war zone—the sort of place that is anywhere but Christchurch.

　At 6:46 p.m. New Zealand time on March 11, I was getting ready to head home for dinner. I was about to close Twitter and the same flood of concern from Japan was overwhelming. My wife is from Fukushima City and my son was born there. Fukushima City was my Japanese home, and Sendai, as my frequent weekend host, was my second Japanese home. My sister-in-law lives there with her husband and young son. I called my wife. She said, "If you are calling about an earthquake it must be quite serious." At that moment NHK started showing that dreadful, dark and irrepressible wave heading towards the outskirts of Sendai. "Yes, I think it's quite serious. I'm pretty sure I am watching a tsunami hit Sendai. Maybe Fukushima City is fine, but make sure your sister is not dithering around in some shopping mall!" The wave kept going and going. I had always had this idea of a tsunami being akin to Hokusai's Wave of Kanagawa—a massive thing that rises out of the water, has a huge impact as it hits land but quickly recedes after its short-term but destructive energy is spent. Not so.

As I write this there is a massive torrential downpour outside. Suddenly the water dripping from the roof, soaking the carpet of our central Auckland home doesn't seem to be such a big deal.

Corey Wallace
Auckland, New Zealand

圧倒

このうえなく幸運だったのか、それともひどくついていなかったのか。私自身も家族も、1秒たりとも危険にさらされることはなかった。危険の中にいた友人や親戚も、大事なく無事でいる。故郷と呼ぶふたつの地域からはるか離れての、僕の体験だった。

日時を覚えるのは得意じゃないが、2月22日午後12時51分、そして3月11日午後2時46分、この2つは今後もずっと頭から離れることはないだろう。クライストチャーチ、そして東北地方。どちらにとっても地震はめずらしいものではないし、地震が起きたからといって、フェイスブックで大騒ぎするような友人もいないだろう。テレビをつけて目に入ったものは、いつもの静かで古くさいクライストチャーチではなく、まるで戦争でも起こったかのような、まさかそれがクライストチャーチだとは思いもよらない映像だった。

ニュージーランド時間、3月11日午後6時46分。僕は夕食のために帰宅する用意をしていた。ツイッターを閉じようとしていたところで、日本から届く、またも不安な知らせで圧倒され始めた。妻は福島県福島市出身、息子もそこで生まれた。福島市は僕の日本の故郷で、週末によく行った仙台市は日本での第二の故郷だ。義理の姉も結婚して、夫と小さな息子とそこで暮らしている。僕は妻に電話をした。「あなたが地震のことで電話してくるなんて、きっとすごくたいへんなことなのね」と妻は言う。

ちょうどそのときNHKが、真っ黒で制御不可能な、ものすごい勢いの波が仙台市郊外に向かっている映像を流し始めた。「ああ、すごいことになってる。津波が仙台を襲っている。福島市は無事かもしれないが、念のためお姉さんがショッピングモールとかで取り残されてないか確認するんだ!」波はグングンと突進していく。津波とは、葛飾北斎の描いた『神奈川沖浪裏』のような巨大で水面に伸びた波が、破壊的な強さで陸地に衝撃を与えるものの、すぐに引いていく、そういうものだと思っていた。しかし、本物はそうではなかった。

オークランドの自宅でこれを書く今、外は急な豪雨だ。僕たちのオークランドの住まいの絨毯を濡らし始めた屋根からの雨漏など、たいしたこととは思えなくなった。

Corey Wallace
ニュージーランド　オークランド

Pajamas

Keiko, my wife, was alone in her ninth floor office at Waseda University in the center of Tokyo when the earthquake hit at 2:46 p.m. on March 11th. After several minutes, she was able to come out from under her desk and run down the nine flights of stairs to the outside.

She first ran to our apartment building and up six flights of stairs to our apartment, where our six-year-old son was with a babysitter and Keiko's mom. Our son Danny was quite scared and was comforted throughout the entire earthquake by the babysitter. Things had fallen in the apartment but there was no structural damage.

They all walked downstairs to wait in the lobby while Keiko ran to the kindergarten/day-care center where our five-year-old twins were. She had to ring the buzzer a long time before the teachers heard it over the commotion and let her in. Kids were in pajamas and bare feet, having been awakened from their naps. The teachers were getting their shoes on and getting ready to evacuate everyone to a nearby open space.

Keiko took our twins and walked home with them. We suspect that the teachers and many of the children ended up sleeping at the school that night because, with trains shut down in Tokyo, parents may have been unable to arrive from work. My whole family—Keiko, the three kids, grandma, and the babysitter—walked back upstairs to our apartment. Surprisingly, power, water and local phone service were all working. Long-distance phone service, however, was not available.

Since she lives far away, our babysitter was stranded. She spent six nights at our apartment, the first night alone in the front bedroom and the other five nights huddled in the back bedroom with the rest of the family. With aftershocks hitting every few minutes—some the size of good-sized earthquakes themselves—it was difficult for everyone to sleep.

It is Saturday morning in Tokyo now, and my family is still in the apartment. Fortunately, we have enough food to last for a while. Elevators are still not working. We are trying to decide whether to remain hunkered down all day in the apartment or venture out to the park and playground a few blocks away. The kids are doing well today, though, in the living room in their pajamas. They're disappointed that their favorite Saturday morning cartoons have been usurped by 24-hour news broadcasts.

Mark Warschauer
Tokyo

パジャマ

妻のケイコが、都内にある早稲田大学の9階にあるオフィスにひとりでいるとき、地震は起きた。3月11日午後2時46分。数分して、ようやく机の下から出られるようになり、階段を駆け下りて外に飛び出した。

彼女が最初に向かったのはマンションの自宅。6階まで階段を駆け上がり、6歳になる息子、ベビーシッ

ター、そしてケイコの母が待つ自宅にたどり着く。息子のダニーはひどく怯えていて、ベビーシッターは地震の間ずっとダニーを励まし続けてくれた。家の中は物が落ちた程度で、建物自体は無事だった。

全員階段を下りてロビーに避難する。ケイコは5歳になる双子を迎えに幼稚園兼託児所に向かった。園内は呼び鈴が聞こえないほど混乱をきたしていて、先生が音に気づくまで長いこと呼び鈴を押し続けた。子どもたちは、全員パジャマ姿に裸足、昼寝の途中で起こされたのだ。近所の空き地に避難するため、先生たちは彼らに靴をはかせているところだった。

ケイコは双子を連れ、歩いて家に帰った。その晩、おそらく先生たちは大勢の子どもたちと一緒に園内に泊まったに違いない。都内の交通機関が麻痺し、親たちが職場から子どもを迎えにくることは難しい。ケイコ、3人の子ども、おばあちゃんとベビーシッターといううちの家族は階段を上がって自宅に戻った。驚いたことに、電気と水、電話回線は使えた。でも、長距離電話は不通だった。

うちに来てくれるベビーシッターは、家が遠いので帰れなかった。6泊のうち初日は手前の寝室にひとりで寝て、残る5泊は奥の部屋で私たち家族と一緒に寝た。数分おきにやって来て、中には地震並みの大きさもある余震のために、だれも眠れなかった。

今は東京の土曜日の朝で、私たちはまだ自宅にいる。幸い、食料の備えはしばらくは大丈夫だ。エレベーターは停まったままだ。自宅にこもるか、近所の公園や広場に出かけようか迷っている。子どもたちはずいぶん元気になったが、パジャマ姿のままリビングで過ごしている。毎朝楽しみにしていたアニメが24時間放送のニュースで中止になってしまい、がっかりしている。

Mark Warschauer
東京都

Photographs

I've never been to Japan. My Japanese mother didn't tell me much of her family when she was alive. I have many photographs of her family—brothers, sisters-in-law, nieces, nephews, great-nieces and great-nephews. My mother died in 2000, and I have all of her letters and photographs. The letters I cannot read, and I know only two of the faces in the photos for sure—my aunt and uncle. My son is very curious about his Japanese heritage and wants us to visit. I have been slow in thinking about how to go about that. How to communicate.

The morning of March 11, 2011, I awoke at 5 a.m. and switched on the radio to listen and stretch before arising. I heard the news of an earthquake and tsunami in Miyagi prefecture and my heart jumped as I leapt out of bed and turned on my computer. I knew the name of that place, because of the return addresses on those letters. The addresses were the only parts written in text that I could read.

For a week now, I obsessively read Twitter messages, read stories, look for pictures and video online—all in a hopeless effort to know that the people in my mother's photographs are OK. I may never know. I worry and fret. I donate money. I want to wrap up in safety those people who loved my mother in another country. I'm hiring a translator to help me find them. I could have done that a year ago.

I'm ashamed that it took this disaster to motivate me to try and make contact with my Japanese cousins. I regret letting so many years pass by with no effort made. My mother had a favorite niece she spoke about when I was still a girl. I hope it's not too late to meet her. My son is studying Japanese. I hope it's not too late.

I love Japan. Something about it feels like home.

Mari Aquarian
Concord, New Hampshire, USA

写真

私は日本を訪れたことがありません。日本人の母は生前に日本の家族について話すことはありませんでした。2000年に母が亡くなり、残されたのは読めない何通かの手紙と母の兄弟、義理の姉妹、姪たち、甥たち、姪と甥の子どもたちが写っているたくさんの写真だけ。手紙は読めないし、写真に写っている人物で見覚えがあるのは、叔父と叔母の2人だけ。私の息子は日本とのつながりに興味津々で、私と一緒に日本に行きたがっています。私はどうしたものか考えるのをためらっていました。会話もできないのだから。

2011年3月11日は、早朝5時に目が覚め、ラジオを聞きながらストレッチをしていました。宮城県での地震と津波のニュースを聞いた途端、心臓が破裂しそうになり、ベッドから飛び起きてコンピューターの電源を入れました。母の残した手紙の差出人住所から、宮城という地名だけは知っていました。差出人の住所だけは読めたからです。

あれから1週間が経ち、私はとりつかれたようにツイッターのメッセージ、ストーリーを読みながら、オンラインで写真やビデオを探しました。無理だとはわかっていても、母の写真に写っている人たちが無事であることを確かめたかったのです。一生知ることはできないかもしれません。心配でイライラするばかりです。募金はしたけれど、日本で母を愛してくれた人たちを抱きしめ、守ってあげたかった。とりあえず通訳を雇って日本の家族を探すことにします。1年前にもできたと思うと、いたたまれない気持ちです。

この大災害があるまで、日本のいとこに連絡を取ろうと思わなかったことを恥ずかしく思います。何の努力もせず、こうして何年もの月日が経ってしまったことが悔やまれます。子どものころ、母はよくお気に入りの姪っ子の話をしてくれました。いまからでも彼女に会えるのでしょうか。今、息子は日本語を勉強しています。今からでも遅くないことを願っています。

故郷のように感じる日本。その日本を愛しています。

Mari Aquarian
米国　ニューハンプシャー州　コンコード

Positive

March 18 2011. I switched the TV on yesterday morning before going to school for class and I wished I hadn't.

I can't get the image out of my head:
The TV crew just happened to be there at that moment.
A boy (maybe 10 years old) was looking through the wreckage of a tsunami-ravaged

town with his aunt and grandfather.

The grandfather came running out from a wrecked building—he'd found the missing mother's car.

The boy looked so excited.

Like somehow everything was going to be OK.

Like some miracle was about to happen.

The aunt screamed and ran into the building followed by the boy and TV cameraman. She looked again at the car's numberplate and called out her sister's name. The car had been forced up towards the ceiling of what might have been a car park. The woman climbed up and put her palms on the window of the car.

She could see her sister strapped into the car that had been swept into a building by the tsunami and called her name again.

Still the boy's expression was filled with hope, he didn't understand.

His mother was found…everything was going to be all right, phone the police, phone for an ambulance, everything was going to be OK…

He didn't realize…

Face filled with hope.

I couldn't watch anymore. In half an hour I would be in class at elementary school and I would need to be positive: Teaching 10-year-old kids, showing them what an exciting and fun world was waiting for them.

Arthur Davis
Kochi

ポジティブ

2011年3月18日。昨日の朝、学校の授業に行く前にテレビのスイッチをつけた。つけるんじゃなかった。

そこで見た映像が頭から離れない：

テレビの取材陣が、ちょうどその瞬間、現場にいた。

祖父、叔母と一緒に、少年（たぶん10歳くらい）が、町を襲った津波のがれきの中、懸命に何かを探していた。

祖父が崩れかけたビルの中から駆け出してきた。行方不明になっていた少年の母親の車を見つけたのだ。

少年はかなり興奮してるようだった。

まるで、これでなんとか、すべてがうまくいくかのように。

まるで、今まさに奇跡が起こるかのように。

叔母は叫びながら、男の子とテレビのカメラマンと共にビルの中へと走っていった。再び車のナンバープレートを確認し、妹の名を大声で呼んだ。車は天井付近まで打ち上げられていて、駐車場で何が起こったのかを物語っていた。叔母はよじ登り、車の窓に自分の手のひらを押し付けた。

津波によってビルの中へと押し流された車の中に、妹がはさまっているのを見て、妹の名を再び呼んだ。

少年の表情は、まだ希望に満ちあふれていた。彼には理解できていなかった。

お母さんが見つかった……よし、これですべてうまくいく、警察に電話だ。救急車を呼ぼう、だいじょうぶ、これですべてがうまく……。
彼は気づいていなかった。
希望でいっぱいの顔。

もうこれ以上見続けることができなかった。30分後、僕は小学校の教室にいる。ポジティブでいなければ。10歳の子たちを待ち受けているこの世界は、刺激に満ちて、楽しいところだということを教えにいくために。

Arthur Davis
高知県

Precious

It was 10 minutes before our daughter was due to arrive back from her kindergarten by school bus. The earthquake started and got stronger and stronger. Suddenly the TV died and all the furniture started shaking. Lots of things fell from the bookshelves and the fridge door opened. I was at home by myself and told myself, "I'm scared. I'm scared."

I could not calm down after the big earthquake and headed to the bus stop to pick up my daughter. The school bus didn't arrive on time and I couldn't get hold of my husband at work nor my daughter's kindergarten. Much, much later, the red bus carrying my daughter came. I was so relieved I couldn't stop crying when I found she and her friends were all safe. We were too scared to go back into our house and so were our neighbors. We decided to stay outside together for a while.

I managed to get hold of my husband at that time. I still remember clearly how grateful I was that we were all alive. Later that night we finally contacted our parents in Tochigi and heard that everybody was fine. I learned from the news that lots of people lost their families and houses in the tsunami.

It's not just somebody's story, as a mother, to know that many people lost their precious children and many children lost their parents in such a short time. If there is anything I can do to help, I am happy to contribute. I only hope that all the survivors can stay strong and feel happier about life soon.

Keiko Fujii
Abiko, Chiba

Andrew Woolner

愛しきもの

あと10分ほどで娘が幼稚園バスで帰ってくる時間だった。急に長い揺れが……徐々に揺れは大きくなり、テレビが消えた。大きな音とともに家具がすごい勢いで横揺れとなり、書棚のものが一斉に落ちた。冷蔵庫が開き、揺れは収まった。ひとりで家にいたこともあり、思わず「怖い、怖い……」と口から言葉が出た。

　初めての大地震に落ち着く間もなくバス停へ。いつもの時間にバスは来ない。幼稚園はもちろん、仕事中の夫とも電話が繋がらない。他のママたちと大きな余震の中、お互い抱き合って不安を抱えてバスを待った。バス走行中に地震にあっていたら……と不安が募る。かなり遅れて赤いバスが……、無事、娘が帰宅。娘もお友達も皆無事だと知って安堵し、涙が出た。家に入るのが怖くて、しばらく娘とご近所さんと外にいた。

　夫の無事もわかり、無邪気に遊ぶ娘を見て「生きてて良かった」とご近所さんと話したのを思い出す。栃木に住む夫、私の両親と連絡がついたのは夜になってから。全員無事だった。それだけで幸せだと感じた。そんななか、東北、関東沿岸は津波の被害があり、壊滅的な町もあった。家族を失ったり離れ離れになったり……、ライフラインも失っているとニュースで知り、心が痛くなった。

　娘と同じような幼子をなくしたご家族の気持ち、親をなくした子どもの気持ちを思うと他人事とは思えない。私にできることがあれば，なんなりとお役に立ちたい。被災された方々、そのご家族など、関係される皆さまが早く元気に、少しでも幸せな気持ちになれますよう、お祈り申し上げます。

藤井桂子
千葉県　我孫子市

Prepared

At 2:46 p.m. on March 11, 2011, I was at home in Tokyo's Shinjuku ward, writing an abstract to a research paper I'd just completed. Our apartment started to shake. I thought, "Oh come on, not now, I'm trying to concentrate. Abstracts are tough."

You get used to earthquakes in Tokyo. The city rumbles every now and then but the shaking rarely lasts more than a minute. This time, it kept going. It got stronger. I shut my laptop and went to stand in the doorway. The shaking got even stronger. I started to think that standing in front of a glass door wasn't the best thing to do, so I stood under the steel frame of our front door and watched the skyscrapers in our neighborhood wobble.

I know I wasn't the only one thinking, by then, that this was the big one. I know I'm not the only one who followed that thought with the silent protest, "But I'm not prepared!"

There was an emergency earthquake kit under our bed. A list of emergency landline numbers by our phone. A childhood's worth of earthquake drills in my memory. I had prepared, yes, but I wasn't prepared.

Annamarie Sasagawa
Shinjuku, Tokyo

準備

2011年3月11日午後2時46分、私は東京の新宿区にある自宅で、完成させたばかりの研究論文のための要約を書いていた。アパートが揺れはじめた。「ああ、こんなときに来ないでよ。集中しようとしてるの。要約を書くのは難しいんだから」と思った。

東京に住んでいると地震に慣れる。この街が揺れることはしょっちゅうあるが、揺れが1分以上続くことはほとんどない。今回は続いた。激しくなった。私はノートパソコンを閉じると戸口へ向かい、そこに立った。揺れはさらに強くなった。ガラスの扉の前に立つのは最善の策ではないと考えはじめて、玄関のドアの鉄骨フレームの下に立ち、近所の高層ビルがグラグラと揺れるのを眺めた。

この時点で、これは大地震だと考えていた人間は自分だけではないってことを私は知っている。その考えに続いて「でも、私は準備ができてない！」という静かな抗議をしたのが自分だけではないことも、私は知っている。

私たちのベッドの下には緊急用の地震対策セットがあった。電話のそばには、緊急用の固定電話番号リスト。私の記憶の中には子ども時代に行った防災訓練。そう、昔の私は準備をしていたのに、今の私は準備ができていなかったのだ。

Annamarie Sasagawa
東京都　新宿区

Radioactive

I'm in a small club in Koenji, drinking beer with a group of 20 or so young Tokyoites. A man in a hard hat and face mask is conducting a mini orchestra of vintage 1980s synthesizers.

Beneath the cheer and good humor, however, they are only too aware of the new uncertainty that Japan is facing. The man's getup is just one of the eerie reminders of the tragedy that had struck northeastern Japan less than a week ago. His father was from Fukushima, close to the nuclear power plant, and the band's drummer also hails from the same area. There are smiles and laughs around the room when Kraftwerk's 1975 song "Radioactivity" comes on in the background, but it's a dark, ironic sort of humour on display, rarely seen in Japan.

A small TV in the corner remains tuned to NHK, Japan's national broadcaster, and all eyes turn to the screen. An aftershock has been recorded near Tokyo. Here in our Koenji basement, no one felt a thing, but as numbers recording the strength of the tremor start to appear on the onscreen map, a cheer goes up among some of the people present; the Koenji area scored 4, putting it in the level of most extreme shaking. There's a sense of victory: we took the worst of that tremor and didn't even feel it.

The party goes on. For now.

Ian Martin
Tokyo

「放射能」

高円寺の小さなクラブで、東京の若い人たち20人くらいとビールを飲んでいる。ヘルメットを被ってマスクをした男が、1980年代ビンテージのシンセサイザーでミニオーケストラを指揮している。

歓声とユーモアの裏で、彼らは日本が直面している新たな不確実性に十分すぎるほど気づいている。あの男の扮装は、まだ1週間も経っていない東北地方を襲った悲劇を思い起こさせる、気味の悪いものだ。彼の父親は原子力発電所に近い福島の出身で、バンドのドラマーも同じあたりの出身だ。BGMでクラフトワークの1975年の曲「Radio-Activity」（放射能）がかかると笑みや笑い声が上がった、でも、それは陰気で皮肉な種類のユーモアで、日本ではあまり見られないものだ。

片隅の小さなテレビではNHKがつけっぱなしになっていて、全員の目が画面へ注がれる。東京の近くで余震が記録されている。この高円寺の地下室ではだれも何も感じなかったけれど、震度が画面の地図上に現れると、ここにいる何人かが歓声を上げた。高円寺あたりは震度4、最も激しい揺れのレベルだった。ちょっとした勝利の感覚：我々は最悪の揺れを経験しながら、気づきもしなかったんだ。

パーティーは続く。まだしばらくの間。

Ian Martin
東京都

Really?

Pour cereal. Check email. Check the online news. WHAT! Is this for real? What the hell is going on? Can't find any in-depth info on the Canadian news websites. The American news articles are frightening. I settle on reading tweets from a live blog on an Australian news website. At least those tweeters are actually there.

I feel helpless. Why don't I feel safe even though I'm miles away? I'm worried about my relatives. I'm worried about the evacuees. I'm worried about the nuclear plant workers.

I go to Facebook to see everyone else's reactions.

Baby pictures. Ski trips. Weddings.

Really?

Chikae Singleton
Calgary, Alberta, Canada

うそでしょ？

シリアルをボウルに入れる。メールをチェックする。オンラインでニュースを読む。えっ！うそでしょ？いったい何が起こってるの？カナダのニュースサイトでは詳しい情報は見つからない。米国の記事を読むと恐ろしいことになっている。とりあえずオーストラリアのニュースサイトにあるブログでツイートを読むことにした。少なくとも、この人たちはちゃんと日本からツイートしてるみたい。

自分が無力に感じる。なぜ、こんなにも距離は離れているのに不安に駆られるんだろう？　親戚のことが心配。避難している人たちのことも心配。原発の作業員たちのことも心配。

みんなの反応を見ようと、フェイスブックを開いた。

子どもの写真。スキー旅行。結婚式。

うそでしょ？

Chikae Singleton
カナダ　アルバータ州　カルガリー

Rebuilding

Exactly one week after the disaster and it's a sunny day, albeit a bit chilly. Spring is supposed to return in force soon and get the Tokyo temperatures up to almost 20 degrees. As gasoline is still hard to get, my family and I head out on foot today to get some groceries at the local supermarket. Things almost seem back to normal. All the small shops close to our house are open for business. To our great joy the fantastic-but-expensive local bakery is open, which allows us to get hold of some good bread for the first time in a week. The supermarket is reasonably well stocked and we manage to get some diapers and the other stuff we need, even though toilet paper, tissue paper and rice are still sold out.

The situation in the Fukushima plant is still worrisome, but the worst doomsday advocates seem to have calmed down a little bit. Perhaps this is because the reality is bad enough, and the foreign media has switched its reporting to the situation in Libya and other, more dramatic news stories.

Minor aftershocks keep on coming, but the frequency and intensity are growing less. They hardly grab my attention as long as I know my wife and baby are safe with me. Rolling blackouts still affect the greater Tokyo area, but power hasn't been interrupted where I live. Maybe they have forgotten our secluded little valley, or it is sitting on some big, secret thing we don't know about that needs constant power. You never know.

But as I write this, there is also the sense of a return to "normalcy." I'm drinking a beer and finally relaxing after a week of constantly trying to learn more about the situation, about earthquakes, about tsunami, about radiation and about the extent of death in this tragedy. I know that strong aftershocks will follow, but I am okay with that.

It doesn't mean this whole thing will repeat itself. For now, I can relax a bit for the first time in what feels like an eternity. I think next I'll enjoy a large whiskey.

Perhaps we're seeing the end of the disaster and the start of the rebuilding.

Mr Salaryman
Tokyo

再建

地震からちょうど1週間が過ぎた。少し肌寒いけれど、太陽が出ている。春が再び力を取り戻し、やがて東京の気温を20℃にまで押し上げるころだ。ガソリンはまだ調達困難なので、家族と一緒に近所のスーパーへ歩いて買い物に出かけた。事態はほぼ平常に戻りつつある。近所の個人商店はすべて営業を再開した。うれしいことに、味はすばらしいが値の張る地元のパン屋も営業を再開し、1週間ぶりにおいしいパンにありつくことができた。スーパーはそれなりに品物がそろっており、オムツや必要なものを手に入れることができた。しかし、トイレットペーパーやティッシュペーパー、米は売り切れの状態が続いている。

福島原発の状態はまだまだ気懸かりだけれど、最悪の事態を訴えていた終末論者たちも少しおとなしくなったようだ。たぶん現実がこれ以上悪くなりようがなく、海外メディアがリビア情勢や、他のもっと話題性のある時事ネタに切り替えているからだろう。

小さな余震は続いているが、その頻度や強さは減少傾向だ。妻と赤ん坊と安全に一緒にいられる限り、

余震は気にならない。計画停電は依然として首都圏に影響を与えているが、なぜか私が住むところではまだ電力供給は途切れていない。私たちが住む、この小さな人目につかない谷間の地は忘れられているのか、それとも、常時電力を必要とするような、私たちの知らない何か大きな秘密がここに存在するのか。理由はだれもわからない。

しかし、こうして書いている間にも、「正常」へ戻りつつある気がしている。ビールを飲みながら、ようやく緊張が緩んできた。現状、地震、津波、放射線、そして、この悲劇による死者数について知ろうと努める1週間だった。まだ強い余震が続くだろうが、それはそれでかまわない。

余震が続くからと言って、この大震災がそっくりそのまま繰り返されるわけではないからだ。永遠に続くように思われた時の流れの中で、初めて少し気持ちが安らいでいる。次の一杯は多めのウィスキーにしようと思う。

きっと今が悲劇の終わりであり、再建のはじまりなのだ。

Mr Salaryman
東京都

Recovery

I have seen images of the disaster area that was affected by the tsunami caused by the eastern Japan great earthquake. I have no words to describe the dreadful scenes.

I'm experiencing for the first time empty shelves at supermarkets and gasoline stations with no gasoline, all because of the two big earthquakes and aftershocks. The radiation from the nuclear power plant makes me nervous because you can't see it. There is a lack of electricity. I can only hope that when I save electricity it helps others.

I pray for a quick recovery as soon as possible, and that we never have a disaster as great as this again.

Yoko Kobayashi
Abiko, Chiba

復旧

今回の東日本大地震の津波で被害を受けた被災地の映像をテレビで見て、あまりのすごさに言葉を失ってしまう。

私の住んでいる千葉県我孫子市でも、2度の大きな地震と何回も続く余震に震え、買いだめと出荷未定によるスーパーの品不足、ガソリン不足をはじめて体験した。地震に伴う原発事故を受け、放射線も問題になっている。目に見えないので不安だ。地震による影響で各地が電力不足に陥っている。少しでも協力できればと思い節電を心がけている。

早く被災地が復旧し、もうこのような大きな災害がないことを祈る。

小林陽子
千葉県　我孫子市

Relief

"What a ridiculous time to be awake," I groaned to myself. I had only gone to bed three hours earlier, but a dull ache in my left knee left me restless.

Looking at my Twitter stream I failed to see any significance in a tweet which arrived from my friend in Japan. Indeed, I'm sure neither of us realized what a massive understatement the phrase "That was a big aftershock" was at the time.

Shortly afterwards, other tweets started to appear from news organizations reporting the quake, but nothing seemed extraordinary. I didn't give much thought to what seemed to be a standard post-earthquake tsunami warning.

It was much later at work when people started to contact me to see if I'd heard from my friend in Japan. I took a quick glance at the BBC and I saw an image of the devastation for the first time. I instantly returned to Twitter to check that my friend was OK. Thankfully, he'd been one of the lucky ones, with family nearby. They were reunited quickly, with none of the uncertainty which plagued so many others.

Relieved, I went back to the BBC. Dark sludge made its way across farmland. This wasn't the bright blue sea I remembered from videos of the 2004 tsunami. This one looked far more sinister. It didn't stop. I kept waiting for it to retreat, as a wave is supposed to do. But this wasn't a tidal wave, this was a TSUNAMI and it swallowed everything in its path.

Now I am left with a pang of guilt. As I watched footage of the dark water swallowing up entire communities my overwhelming emotion was that of relief. Relief that my friend and his family were safe.

Don Myles
Falkirk, Scotland

安堵

「なんて時間に目が覚めるんだよ」と、うなった。3時間も前にベッドに入ったばかりなのに、左ひざの痛みでよく眠れない。

ツイッターの画面を眺めていると、日本にいる友人からのツイートが入った。その重大さに気づかなかった。「大きな余震だった」というそのメッセージが、ものすごく控えめな表現だということに、そのとき私も友人も気づいていなかったと思う。

まもなく、地震について伝える報道機関からのツイートも入りはじめたけれど、大災害には見えなかった。地震の後の津波警報も、おきまりのものだと思って、あまり気にとめなかった。

ずっとたってから、日本にいる友人から連絡があったかという問い合わせを仕事中にいくつも受けた。すぐにBBCを見ると、甚大な被害の映像が初めて目に飛び込んできた。すぐにツイッターに戻り、友人の無事を確認した。ありがたいことに彼は難を逃れた。近くにいる家族もだ。友人と家族はすぐに合流できたので、ほかの多くの人たちのように確認のとれない苦しみを知らずにすんだのだ。

安心した。BBCの画面に戻ると、黒い泥が畑を越えて進んでいく。記憶にある2004年の津波の映像の

ような明るい青い海ではない。もっとずっと邪悪な感じだった。泥は止まらない。波なら自然に引くはずだ。泥流が引くのを私は待ち続けた。だが、これは並みの津波ではなく、超の字が付く津波だった。行く手にあるものすべてを呑み込んだ。

今は罪悪感にさいなまれている。濁流が一帯をすべて呑み込む映像を見ている私の心を占めていたのは、安堵の気持ちだった。友人一家は無事だったことに安堵したのだ。

Don Myles
スコットランド　フォルカーク

Remoteness

I won't forget the first video I saw of the tsunami. This black mass rolled over the landscape, gulping, chewing and spitting out everything in its path. I waited for the ebb to come, but it didn't. The black water just kept going and going. I reversed the video and hit pause, staring at the scene frozen on my computer screen. I was frozen, too.

Even with video, it is hard to comprehend the speed of the event and the noise that huge volume of water surging past must have made. The people in front of it must have felt hunted, terrified that they couldn't escape. In seven minutes of video the whole landscape disappeared. They started tallying the death toll. One dead, then thirty-seven, then... Hundreds, thousands. Here in the UK, it struck me that these people were dying without ever knowing if their loved ones survived.

There was more video, of course, of the aftermath. It showed boats where cars should be, cars where people should be and very few people at all. I saw some tearful survivor reunions, which caused me to cry. I know, I have no right to these emotions in my geographic remoteness, but I do feel for them, too.

Sybil Murray
United Kingdom

遠くで

あの津波の最初の映像を忘れることはないだろう。黒い塊が風景に覆いかぶさって進み、行く手にあるすべてを呑み込み、嚙み砕き、吐き出す。その潮が引くのを待ったが、そうはならなかった。黒い海はただただ前進を続けた。その映像を巻き戻して一時停止し、パソコン画面上でその静止画面を見ていた。私も動けなかった。

映像でも、津波の進む速さや、膨らみながら通り過ぎる巨大な水の塊が発したに違いない轟音の大きさは理解しがたい。津波を目の前にした人々は、追い詰められ、逃げられないという恐怖におののいただろう。7分間の映像が終わるころには、その一帯は姿を消していた。死亡者数の確認が始まった。ひとり…37人…数百人…数千人。英国にいる私は、これらの人々は愛する人が助かったかどうかも知るすべなく死んでいったということにがく然とした。

もちろん、直後の映像もあった。車があるべき場所に船があり、人がいるべきところに車があり、そして人はほとんどいなくなってしまった。生存者が涙を流しながら再会する場面もあった。それを見る私もまた涙した。地理的な隔たりの中で、被災者と同じ感情を抱くのはおこがましい。それでも、彼らの心情に共感してしまうのだ。

Sybil Murray
英国

Same

I was walking toward Kikuna station in Yokohama. As soon as I entered the station I saw two cops running towards me, and they were looking up instead of at me. I followed their eyes and saw that the power lines and poles were swinging. In fact, everything was swinging and shaking! That's when my legs got wobbly, like I had a sudden charley horse. But I stayed cool. Eight years in Japan and I was used to the terrestrial hiccups that occur here almost daily. And these tremors are usually pretty short. You can forget they even happened in a matter of moments.

But, as I looked around trying to keep my balance, I realized this was not a tremor. In addition to the power lines and poles, the train station and surrounding buildings were shaking! I heard loud noises, rattling, clanging, banging metal and glass like a thousand chandeliers shaking. Sounds I'd never heard before were coming from all over.

It was like the street was screaming.

I staggered out of the station to the sidewalk. Traffic was still moving since some motorists seemed unaware of what was happening. I groped for a building wall to lean on, and as I looked above my head I saw a sign swinging on flimsy hinges. All around me were things that could kill me if they fell. Structures had become lethal. The dry cleaner's nearby, for example, was literally a shaking, swaying two-storey ton of bricks. I spotted what I thought was a safe place to run, but I changed my mind when a window there exploded into a shower of glass.

But through all this, there were no screams. There probably would be anywhere else, but there were none in Yokohama.

For a moment, I looked around into the silent faces of nearby Japanese people. Normally, they were strangers to me, people I usually hold in contempt. But despite my uneasy relationship with them, in that moment I felt no spite, no disgust, no animosity and no contempt for them nor from them. For the first time in years we were one and the same! They looked at me and saw a person, a very scared person, not some foreigner to be feared.

It was an amazing moment. The people around me and I had shared something I would not immediately discard. Finally, after eight years in Japan, that short time made the Japanese my kin. And I realized how sweet and fragile and the same we all are. The temblors stopped and I went into a coffee shop next to Kikuna station. I sat down and

watched the unflappable old-timers sip coffee and read their newspapers.
I smiled, and sat there resting and feeling very Asian.

Baye McNeil
Yokohama, Kanagawa

同じ存在

　私は横浜の菊名駅へ向かって歩いていた。駅に入るやいなや、ふたりの警官が私の方に向かって走ってくるのに気づいた。彼らは私でなく空を見上げていた。彼らの視線を追うと、その先では電線や電柱がぐらぐらと揺れている。いやむしろ、ありとあらゆるものが震動し、揺れていた！　と同時に、突然脚がつったときのように、私の脚も立っていられなくなった。しかし、それでも私は冷静だった。日本に暮らして8年、ほぼ毎日のように起こる、こんな地球のしゃっくりには慣れていた。それに、揺れてもいつもすぐに収まる。地震があったことを次の瞬間には忘れてしまえるくらいに。
　しかし、体勢を保とうとしながら周りを見渡すと、これは小さな地震ではないということがわかった。電柱や電線だけでなく、駅も周辺のビルも揺れていた！　千個のシャンデリアが揺れているかのように、金属やガラスがガタガタ揺れ、カーンと鳴り響き、ドーンと大きな音をたてるのが聞こえた。聞いたこともないような音ばかりが、あちこちから聞こえた。
　まるで街の通り全体が泣き叫んでいるようだった。
　私はなんとか駅構内から歩道に出た。車はまだ走っていて、運転手は何が起こっているのか、気づいていない様子だった。建物の壁につかまろうとした。上を見ると、簡単に固定されただけの看板が私の頭上で揺れていた。もし落ちてくれば、命を奪われるかもしれないものが周りにはたくさんあった。建物が崩れてきたら死者が出ていたかもしれない。近くで激しく横揺れする2階建てのクリーニング屋がもし崩れてきたら、文字通りレンガの山になる。私は安全と思える建物を見極め、そこに走っていこうとした。しかし、その建物の窓ガラスが破裂した瞬間、考え直した。
　このようなひどい状態にもかかわらず、人の叫び声はなかった。ほかの土地ではあったのかもしれないが、横浜ではなかった。
　少しの間、あたりを見回して、近くにいた日本人数人のもの言わぬ顔をのぞき込んだ。いつもなら彼らは私にとって完全な他人であり、私が「軽蔑」する存在だ。彼らとの関係は居心地の良いものではなかったが、そのとき私は、何の悪意も、嫌悪感も、敵意も、侮蔑心も一切自分の中に感じなかったし、彼らからも感じなかった。日本に何年も住んではじめて、私は彼らとひとつになり、同じ存在となった！　彼らが私を見て目にしたのは、恐れおののくひとりの人間であって、恐れるべき外国人ではなかった。
　それは驚くべき瞬間だった。私の近くにいた人々と私は、すぐには手放したくない何かを共有した。日本で8年を過ごして、ついに日本人が私の家族のように思えた。私たちのだれもが思いやりにあふれ、もろいながらも、同じ人間であることを私は悟った。地震が収まり、私は菊名駅の横にあるコーヒーショップに入った。私は席に座り、何事にも動じない老人たちがコーヒーをすすり、新聞を読むのを眺めた。
　私は頬を緩め、自分の中にあるアジア的なものを強く感じながら、ゆったりとそこに座っていた。

Baye McNeil
神奈川県　横浜市

Scenarios

I'm sure everyone is reading scary reports about the radiation situation in Japan in the foreign press, and yes, it is most definitely a serious situation in the vicinity of the plant. I'm following the information extremely closely. Still, according to US, UK and Japanese governments and science officials, there is no risk in the Tokyo area currently.

If this situation changes, we will of course take appropriate action immediately, but at this time, we are safe here, 200 km away. Sadly, a side effect of the wonderful immediacy that Twitter and Facebook bring us is that as much misinformation seems to propagate as real info, and in these circumstances, it's so easy to panic.

The foreign media in the US, UK and France are also not helping. I wish they'd put as much effort into raising awareness, support and donations for those currently affected by the tsunami who are without food and shelter as they are now putting into producing Hollywood-esque nightmare scenarios or segments about how iPad 2 sales are impacted by this. Please.

This situation is being defined by the heroism of those working on-site at the power stations and those providing critical support in the areas devastated by the tsunami. Please direct all your concerns and warmest wishes in their direction.

Miles Woodroffe
Tokyo

シナリオ

皆、外国のメディアを通じて、日本の放射線状況に関する恐ろしい記事を読んでいることだろう。そう、確かに、発電所付近では深刻な状況だ。私は情報をきわめて注意深く追っている。それでも、米国、英国、そして日本の政府や科学当局の職員によると、今のところ首都圏に危険はない。

もしこの状況が変化したら、もちろんすぐに適切な行動を取るつもりだが、現時点では、200キロ離れたこの場所は安全だ。悲しいことに、ツイッターやフェイスブックがもたらすすばらしい即時性の副作用は、間違った情報も本当の情報であるかのように広まることであり、このような状況下では、すぐにパニックを引き起こす。

米国、英国、そしてフランスなどの海外メディアも役に立たない。これらのメディアが、食べ物も避難場所もない津波被災者たちへの寄付や支援に力を注いでくれたら、と思う。これらのメディアがいま力を注いでいることといえば、ハリウッド映画式の悪夢のシナリオや、この震災によってiPad 2の売上にどれだけ影響が出るかという記事を書くことでしかない。

現在の状況は、発電所の現場で作業している人たち、そして津波によって壊滅的な被害を被った地域で重要な支援を提供する人たちの勇敢な行動にかかっている。あなた方の関心のすべてを、心からの祈りのすべてを、この人たちへと向けてください。

Miles Woodroffe
東京都

Shaken

It was the most terrifying day of my life. The country came to a standstill. My wife walked home for nearly eight hours in her new shoes, about 20 kilometers, arriving home just before midnight with a fellow refugee in tow. Being home was comforting, but it was not the end.

That first night was infinitely more terrifying than the initial earthquake. Aftershocks hit time after time, little shakes and big bumps, each time forcing us to question whether it was time to flee the building.

We started the night with just a single emergency rucksack on standby at the entrance, but by early morning we'd assembled two further bags with clothes and blankets—the basic essentials that might make a disaster a little bit more comfortable.

Every creak, every muscle spasm, every electronic beep from the television set us into flight mode. While there were few major aftershocks in the daytime, as night descended that thick tension set in once more, confirmed by a large aftershock, as occurred every night that week.

James Simpson
Kawasaki

動揺

それは人生で最も恐ろしい日だった。この国は機能を停止した。妻は新しい靴で約20キロの距離を8時間近くかけて歩いて夜中前に帰宅し、帰宅難民になった仲間を連れてきた。家にいれば心は安らぐが、それで話は終わらない。

地震後最初の夜は、最初の地震以上に恐ろしかった。余震が次々に襲う。小さい揺れや、ドーンという大きい揺れ。そのたびに建物から逃げ出すべきかどうか考えることになる。

その晩、私たちは玄関に緊急避難用のリュックをひとつ用意しておいた。朝方までには、衣服、毛布を詰め込んだバッグをさらに2つ用意した。災害を多少は快適に乗り越えるための必需品だろう。

きしむ音、揺れ、テレビからの緊急地震速報を伝える信号音。そのたびに部屋から飛び出そうと身構えた。日中のはっきりとした揺れは少なくなったが、その週は毎晩のように大きな余震があり、夜がふけるにつれて緊張感が高まった。

James Simpson
神奈川県　川崎市

Signs

Three days before the earthquake, my dog—who has slept upstairs in my son's room ever since he was a puppy—refused to go up. If we took him per usual, he'd whine and scratch at the door all night and no amount of taking him outside for one final pee or presenting him with a tasty rawhide treat to gnaw on changed his mind.

A little before noon on March 11, while sitting at my kitchen table drinking coffee with friends, several crows dropped from the sky and began making a huge ruckus in my front yard. It was a weird moment. So striking that one of my friends exclaimed it was like a scene from a horror movie.

It's silly, I know, but I've always been on the look-out for signs. I live in Shizuoka Prefecture—over 400 km southwest of the Tohoku Pacific Earthquake—and we are long overdue for our own magnitude 8-or-above temblor. Last year my city even gave out emergency radios that automatically switch on and give early (by mere seconds) warning if a large quake is coming. Earthquakes are, and always have been, on people's minds here.

However, despite years of watching cloud formations, keeping an eye out for earthworms fleeing to the surface and observing the newts I keep in my foyer, I completely missed the fighting crows and the dog's reluctance to go upstairs. (Yeah, I know, whether those two things are related to the earthquake up north at all is anyone's guess.) It's just something I did: looked for signs of impending doom.

When the Tohoku Pacific Earthquake actually hit, the dog was sleeping on the sofa and the birds outside were quiet. Lamps swayed, pictures rattled against the walls and the house creaked and moaned. It wasn't until I turned on the TV that I learned the epicenter was up north and the devastation was incomprehensible, even at that early stage. It was a true horror show.

On March 16th we had a magnitude 6.4 earthquake in Shizuoka Prefecture. I began sleeping in my coat with a flashlight in the pocket and suspecting every wind-blown creak of the house was our Big One. I'm as prepared as I can be, but I realize I cannot keep focusing on the negative. It's so easy to get overwhelmed with the devastation—the earthquake, the tsunami, and the nuclear plant in Fukushima.

I've decided to change strategies. I've started looking for more encouraging signs, anything that inspires hope. It's been a little over a week since the Tohoku Pacific Earthquake. The birds are back to normal, but the dog still refuses to go upstairs. He prefers to spend the night downstairs with the cats, sometimes in the litter box. It's a very small thing and I'm sure it will take awhile, but I am looking forward to the day when he makes his way back upstairs to sleep at the foot of my son's bed.

Terrie Matsuura
Shizuoka

前兆

地震の3日前。子犬のときからずっと2階の息子の部屋で寝ていた飼い犬が、上の階に行きたがらなかった。いつものように連れていけば、一晩中クンクン鳴いてドアをひっかきそうだったし、寝る前のオシッコに外に連れ出しても、おいしい骨ガムをあげても、気が変わりそうにはなかった。

3月11日正午少し前。自宅で友人数人と食卓でコーヒーを飲んでいると、カラスが数羽、突然空から舞い降りて前庭で大騒ぎを始めた。奇妙な感じだった。驚いた友人のひとりは大声で、ホラー映画の一場面みたい、と言った。

ばかな話とはわかっている。でも、私はいつも前兆は警戒してきた。私が暮らすのは静岡県で、東北地方太平洋沖地震が発生したところから南西400キロ以上のところだが、マグニチュード8以上の地震がいつ起きてもおかしくない、と以前から言われてきた。昨年は市から非常用ラジオまで配布された。大地震の発生が近づくと自動的に電源が入り、わずか数秒で早期警報を流す。地震はずっと人々の頭から離れたことがない。

しかし、何年も雲のでき方を観察したり、ミミズが地表に逃げ出してきていないかと目を凝らしてみたり、玄関で飼っているイモリを観察してきたにもかかわらず、カラスのケンカや犬が2階に行きたがらないことについては見落としていた。(この2つの出来事だって、北で起きた地震とはたして関係あるのかどうか、だれにもわからない、ということもわかっている)単なる私の習慣だった。危険が迫っていることを示す前兆を探す、ということは。

実際に東北地方太平洋沖地震が襲ったとき、犬はソファで寝ていて、外の鳥たちは静かだった。電灯は大きく揺れ、壁の絵はカタカタと音をたて、家屋はギィギィきしみ、うなった。テレビをつけてはじめて震源地は北方にあり、地震発生から間もない時点ですでに壊滅的な惨状であることを知った。まさにホラーだった。

3月16日、静岡県でもマグニチュード6.4の地震が起きた。私はコートを着て、ポケットに懐中電灯を入れて寝るようになり、風で家がきしむたびに、今度はこちらの大地震ではないかと思うようになった。可能なかぎりの備えはできているが、このまま否定的なことばかり考え続けるわけにはいかないと気づいた。簡単に地震、津波、福島原発の惨状にまいってしまうから。

私は、対処の方法を変えることにして、もっと前向きになれる予兆、何か希望を抱かせるものを探し始めた。東北地方太平洋沖地震から1週間あまり。鳥たちは平常に戻ったが、犬はまだ2階に行こうとしない。夜は猫たちと一緒に階下で過ごしたいようだ。ときには猫用トイレに入ってしまう。ささいなことだし、しばらく時間がかかりそうだが、いつかまた2階に戻って、息子のベッドの足元で寝られるようになることを願っている。

Terrie Matsuura
静岡県

Strength

Each time I see the devastation on TV, my heart aches and I can't stop crying. I saw an old woman on TV one day say, "The crying stage has already past. From today, we don't have any time to cry. There are so many people who suffer much more than I do."

Even while trying to accept that she has to face this terrifying situation and move forward, she still remembers to care for others. That is the true strength of people. I only hope that all the victims can spend some peaceful time with their precious loved ones as soon as possible, and that their smiles will soon be back.

Ai Hinton
Kashiwa, Chiba

前に進む

テレビで被災地の様子を見るたび、胸が痛み、涙が出てしまう。地震から数日後、テレビで見たあるおばあさんは言った。「泣くのは昨日まで。今日からは泣いている暇なんてないんだから。私よりもたいへんな人はいっぱいいるんだから」

どんなにたいへんな状況にあっても、他人を思いやる気持ち、つらくても、現実を受け入れ、前に進もうとする姿に、人間の本当の強さを見た気がする。一日も早く、大切な人たちと心休まる時間を過ごせる日が来ますように。心から笑える日が来ますように。

ヒントン愛
千葉県 柏市

Strong

Here in South Korea, talking about Japan can be tricky.

During colonial times, a group of Korean women were taken from their homes to provide sexual services for Japanese soldiers. They were called "comfort women," the nicest possible way to say "sex slave." Every Wednesday, the survivors, very old now, still stage demonstrations in downtown Seoul, demanding the Japanese government recognize their plight, and pay reparations. They have lived hard lives: many were unable to have normal lives afterwards because of the stain on their pasts.

Of all people, these "comfort women" wouldn't be blamed for drawing some satisfaction from Japan's misfortune, yet they set aside their old hurts, and held up signs of comfort and consolation to Japan: "Be strong."

Robert Ouwehand
Seoul, South Korea

強靭

ここ韓国では、日本が話題にのぼるときには注意が必要だ。

植民地時代に、日本軍によって故郷から連れ去られ性的な奉仕をさせられた韓国人女性たちがいた。「性の奴隷」をこのうえなく穏やかに言い換えて「従軍慰安婦」と呼ばれる。今でも毎週水曜日のソウルの繁華街では、すっかり年老いたかつての慰安婦たちによって、日本政府に謝罪と賠償を求めるデモが行われている。彼女たちの人生は壮絶なものだった。過去の汚点のために、その後も彼女たちの多くは普通の人生を送ることができなかった。

こうした「慰安婦」たちが日本にふりかかった災難に喜びの声を上げたとしても、だれも責めはしなかっただろう。しかし、彼女たちは長年の痛みを脇に置いて、日本に向けて慰めと励ましのプラカードを掲げた。「くじけないで」と。

Robert Ouwehand
韓国 ソウル

Television

It passed through my head that I may be mistaken. Perhaps my neighbor was indulging in some afternoon lovemaking. While the ground in earthquakes often sways from side to side, it seemed to be going up and down.

And then it got serious. I grabbed the flat screen television to prevent it from hitting the ground as a wine glass fell. Luckily, I'm messy—it landed on a jumper strewn across the floor.

And then it got violent again. I dove under the table, unsure whether what I was doing was correct. My backside was sticking out from under the table. If the ceiling came through, would I be paralyzed by falling rubble? I started to shake as the tremors failed to subside. I live within earshot of the Yamanote Line that circles Tokyo, and I could hear a cacophony of announcements competing with the city council. This was the sound of an earthquake.

Finally, the intensity subsided. I got out from under the table and left the house. All the stairways and elevators were inaccessible. Leaving via the fire escape, when I got outside I saw everybody was dazed yet relieved. Our neighborhood had not been turned to rubble.

I asked a neighbor what to do, again embarrassed by my lack of preparation for an earthquake in the world's center for such disasters. He told me, "Go home and watch the television."

I headed to meet my wife and friends; we had decided to stick together in case there were further quakes through the night. Walking to the main roads, Tokyo was like I had never seen it. Train stations were empty. We found an open restaurant displaying news.

"You feel different watching news coverage of a disaster if you've been a part of it," my wife said as we walked home a couple of hours later.

Richard Smart
Tokyo

テレビジョン

　これは自分の勘違いかもしれない、という考えが頭をよぎった。たぶん隣人が昼下がりのセックスに夢中になっているんだと思っていた。地震によって地面は左右に揺れることが多いのに、今回は上下に揺れているかのようだった。
　揺れが激しくなった。ワイングラスが落ち、僕は薄型テレビが倒れないよう必死につかんだ。幸い僕は家を散らかす人間なので、ワイングラスは床の上に広がったジャンパーの上に落ちていった。
　そして、また暴力的な揺れが来た。自分の行動が正しいかどうかわからないまま、とりあえずテーブルの下へもぐった。お尻はテーブルからはみ出していたが。もし天井が落ちてきたら、下敷きとなって身動きがとれなくなるのではないか？　揺れが収まらないなか、自分の身も恐怖で震えだした。僕は東京を循環する山手線の近くに住んでいる。駅の構内放送と防災無線放送が不協和音を奏でながら同時に聞こえてきた。これが僕にとっての地震の音だった。
　やっと揺れが弱くなり、テーブルの下から這い出て家の外へ出た。階段とエレベーターはどれも使用できなくなっていた。避難口を使って脱出すると、近所の人たちはみんな茫然としながらも、ホッとした様子を見せていた。近隣に被害はなかったようだ。
　地震大国に住みながら震災への備えが不十分だったことを恥ずかしく思いつつ、近所の人に何をすべきか尋ねた。彼は「家に帰って、テレビを見なさい」と答えた。
　ひとまず、妻と友人に合流しようと出かけた。夜通し地震が続く場合に備えて、一緒にいることにしたのだ。幹線道路を歩いていると、今まで見たことのない東京の姿があった。駅には人の気配がなかった。僕らはニュースを放送しているレストランを見つけた。
　「実際に災害を体験すると、それについての報道の見方が違ってくるのよね」と、数時間後に自宅に向かって歩く途中、妻が言った。

Richard Smart
東京都

Together

I wasn't there.

　I wasn't in the shit. I wasn't grasping my wife's hand in a final expression of love as the Earth violently convulsed. I wasn't watching in horror as the sea reached out, groping, tearing families apart. I wasn't close to the reactors as radiation fears spurred evacuation orders and an exodus of my countrymen from their adopted homeland.

　No. I was far away, reading, watching, downloading news of the events 180 miles north. But the quake and all that followed shook me from my expatriate perch. It has cost me nothing more than a single day of work; more a reward than a punishment.

　Yet there I was, on the verge of bursting into tears.

　Working at a newspaper, seeing the images and reading the accounts of the devastated regions should have been something I was inoculated against. But as the crises deepened, I became increasingly tense. Nuclear plants near the quake's epicenter threatened an uninformed Japanese capital. Aftershocks drove me under tables. I soon couldn't tell if it was me shaking or actual residual tremblors.

As the threat of a nuclear disaster loomed, friends and acquaintances packed up—some leaving Tokyo without an utterance, others professing their guilty consciences to the Internet ether. It was fine. Really, I thought. But the sense of dread it instilled in me was more dangerous to my psyche than any radioactive agent my imagination could conjure up.

Their departures forced me to consider my own. I weighed my options. As a friend said, you'd be a fool not to leave. But I couldn't come up with a solid reason to. I was staying.

Thinking about it now, I can't help but feel guilty. With hundreds of thousands suffering and tens of thousands more dead or missing, what right did I have to feel this way? None, I thought.

But I was wrong. We are all in this together.

Jesse Johnson
Abiko, Chiba

Yukiko Kurokawa

ともに

私はその場にいなかった。

私はその渦中にはいなかった。地球が暴力的なほど身悶えしていたときに、最後の愛情の表現として妻の手をしかと握っていたわけではない。ジワジワとにじり寄ってきた海が家族を離散させるのを恐怖のなかで眺めていたわけでもない。放射線の恐怖が避難勧告や、同胞らの第二の祖国からの脱出に拍車をかけたときに、原子炉の近くにいたわけでもない。

そう、私は北から290キロほど離れた場所で、これらのニュースを読んだり、見たり、ダウンロードしたりしていた。しかし、地震とその後に起こったすべての出来事は、国外居住者という私の立場を揺るがすことになった。災害のために私が失ったのは一日分の仕事だけだった。罰を受けたというよりは、報われた思いだ。

それでも、私は涙があふれるぎりぎりの状態だった。

新聞社に勤務する身として、直撃を受けた被災地の画像や記述を目にすることには免疫ができているつもりだった。しかし、危機が深刻化するにつれて、自分自身の緊張は高まっていったのだ。地震の震源地に近い福島第一原発は、情報が乏しい日本の首都を脅かしていった。余震のたびに私は机の下にもぐることになった。そのうち自分自身が揺れているのか、それとも余震の揺れなのかすらわからなくなっていった。

原子力災害の恐怖が影を落としはじめると、友人や知人は荷造りを始めた。一言の知らせもなく東京を去った者もいれば、良心の呵責をネット上で表明しながら東京を離れた者もいる。でも、それもしかたがない。本当にそう思っていた。その人たちが去ったことで私の中で増していった不安感のほうが、想像力の力を借りて思いつくどんな放射性物質よりも私の精神状態を脅かした。

彼らが去っていったことで、私自身のことを考えざるを得なかった。自分の選択肢を天秤にかけてみた。友人は「この地を離れないなんてバカだ」と言った。しかし、私は離れるための確固とした理由を見つけられなかった。私は残ることにした。

いま改めて考えてみると、罪悪感を感じずにはいられない。何十万人もの人々が苦しみ、数万人が犠牲になり、行方不明でいる一方で、あのように自分の感情に浸っている権利が私にはあったのか？　ない、と私は思った。

でも、それは違った。我々は、だれもがこの困難な状況に直面しているのだ。

Jesse Johnson
千葉県　我孫子市

Tremors

I left work and got on the train at around 14:40, heading to Shibuya for another train home. Between stations, the train ground to a sudden halt and slammed me into the back of a seat. Initially I thought an accident had occurred, but the driver announced, "Tokyo is experiencing a huge earthquake, please brace yourself." Seconds later, the train shook violently, like a ship on rough seas. It shook from side to side, front to back. Nobody showed signs of panic or distress, except that most people's faces turned very pale.

After this first shock, the train crawled to the next station, Omotesando. I got off, and hesitated as I wondered what I'd find when I got above ground. People seemed calm enough, but many were trying to exit the station since train services had been stopped. When I got up to the street it was swarming with people. A few were crying, but most were waiting in lines to use the public phones, which are free in emergencies. Cell phone coverage had been knocked out.

I realized that I was going to have to walk home, so I headed off in the right direction for the long journey. I had only walked a couple of yards when I heard a group of guys ahead of me shouting, "MOVE! DANGER!!" I looked up and the buildings were moving and swaying. An aftershock hit and I felt the pavement drop and ripple under my feet. People moved quickly to the center of the street. Some people abandoned their cars. The sky turned an ominous black color. I thought this was the "main event."

Luckily, the tremor soon ended and I was able to continue. In Shibuya glass had fallen from high windows on to pedestrians, and there was mass disorder. Two and a half hours later I was home. My house was relatively unscathed, but when I switched on the TV I realized the extent of what had just happened.

Since then, a lot of people have left Tokyo fearing what may come. However, my life is here, and that has almost returned to normal. The situation in Japan is serious, undoubtedly, but people northeast of here have it far worse than I. And I would rather stay and help the people in a country that has embraced of me for a long time.

Iain Hair
Tokyo

余震

その日、私は職場を出て午後2時20分ごろに地下鉄に乗った。渋谷で別の電車に乗り換えて、自宅に帰ろうとしていたところだった。駅と駅の間で、突然、私の乗った電車は急停車し、その反動で私は座席の背もたれに叩きつけられた。はじめは何か事故でも起こったのだろうと思った。だが、運転士から「大地震が発生しています。揺れに備えてください」というアナウンスがあった。その数秒後、電車は荒れ狂う海に揉まれる船のように猛烈に揺れた。前後左右にも揺れ続けた。パニックを起こしたり、苦痛の色を見せた人はいなかったが、大多数の人は青ざめていた。

この最初の地震の後、列車はノロノロと徐行運転を始め、次の表参道駅に着いた。電車を降りたものの、地上に出て目にするであろう光景を想像すると気が進まなかった。ほかの人たちは落ち着いているように見えたが、地下鉄が運行を停止したので、多くの人は駅から外に出ようとしていた。地下鉄の駅を外に出ると、道は人間であふれ返っていた。何人かは泣いていたが、多くの人は公衆電話に列をなして並んでいた。携帯電話の電波環境は完全にダウンしていた。

歩いて自宅まで帰らなければと察した私は、長い帰路となる方角へ歩き始めた。しかし、2メートル歩いたかどうかのところですぐに、前を歩いていた数人の男性が「危ない！　そこをどいて！」と叫んだ。見上げると、周辺の建物が揺れに揺れている。大きな余震が起こり、足元で歩道が陥没して波打っているように感じた。人びとは道路の真ん中へ急いで避難していく。運転をあきらめ、車をそこに乗り捨てる人もいた。空は真っ黒な不吉な色を呈していた。今日がこの世の終わりだと思った。

幸運にもその余震はすぐに収まり、歩き続けることができた。渋谷では、高層ビルの窓ガラスが歩行者の頭上に降り注ぎ、現場は大混乱していた。2時間半歩き続けて、自宅に着いた。部屋はそれほど乱れてはいなかった。だが、テレビをつけて、今回起こった地震の規模がどれほどのものであったかを知った。

以来、さらなる事態を恐れて多くの人が東京を離れた。しかし、私の生活はここにあり、日常はほぼ正常な状態に戻っている。日本の状況が深刻であることは確かだが、東北の人々は私よりずっと悲惨な状況にある。だからこそ、あえて私はここに残り、私を長い間受け入れてくれたこの国の人々を助けたいと思っている。

Iain Hair
東京都

Trousers

Three days after the earthquake I found myself accompanying a journalist to the north. After six hours spent locating a can for spare fuel (sold out citywide), and then another couple of hours looking for fuel, we set out on Route 4, destination: Koriyama evacuee center, 70 km south-west of the Fukushima nuclear plant.

As we crawled north on local roads, we saw convoys of Japan Self-Defense Forces vehicles on the motorway beside us. The further north we got, the more quake damage we saw. Houses that had lost their walls. Great fissures across the road. A four-story office block reduced to two.

Arriving at Koriyama we headed to the Radiation Detection Unit, a series of tents set up in a parking lot staffed by men dressed in full-body radiation-proof suits, armed with geiger counters. We had walked onto the set of *E.T.*

A father, mother, two children and their dog had just arrived, and one-by-one were checked over. There was a commotion—the father had radioactive trousers. The family rushed back to the car to find a spare pair as he was stripped down and washed. That day, 144 of 4,295 people that had been scanned had tested positive.

We interviewed a few teenagers living with their families in the baseball stadium converted into a rescue center. One said, "I used to hate going to school, but now all I want is to go back, study hard, see my friends. I want my normal life back."

Joseph Tame
Tokyo

ズボン

あの地震の3日後、私はあるジャーナリストに同行して北へ行くことになった。6時間かけて予備燃料の缶を探し（都内では売り切れだった）、それからさらに数時間燃料を探し回ったあげく、我々は福島第一原発から南西におよそ70キロのところにある郡山の避難所を目指して国道4号線を出発した。

北に向かってノロノロと一般道を走っていると、自衛隊の車隊が横の高速道路を行くのが見えた。さらに北上するにしたがって、地震の被害が大きくなっていく様子を目の当たりにすることになる。壁がなくなった住居、道路を横断する大きな亀裂、4階建てのオフィスビルは2階建てになっていた。

郡山に到着すると、我々は体に付着した放射線を計るチェックポイントへ向かった。一連のテントが設置された駐車場には、放射線防護服に身を包み、ガイガーカウンターを持った男たちが配置されていた。我々は『E.T.』の撮影現場に迷い込んだようだった。

そこにふたりの子どもとその両親が飼い犬を連れてやってきた。そして、ひとりずつチェックを受けていたとき、騒ぎは起こった。父親のズボンから放射性物質が検出されたのだ。父親がズボンを脱がされ体を洗われている間に、家族は急いで車に戻り、代わりのズボンを探した。その日、放射線検査を受けた4,295人のうち144人が陽性と判定された。

我々は、避難所となった野球場に家族とともに暮らす何人かの十代の若者にインタビューを行った。そのなかのひとりはこう話した。「以前は学校に行くのがきらいだった。でも今は学校に戻りたい。勉強も頑

張るし、友達にも会いたい。普通の生活に戻りたい」

Joseph Tame
東京都

Underground

Central Tokyo, Friday, March 11, 2:46 p.m., I was three levels underground waiting for a train and privately hoping for my last business meeting of that day to be short, so I could get home for an early weekend.

It was not to be.

"To all passengers. Please stay calm. The station and platforms have been designed to withstand earthquakes, and you are safe where you are." The stationmaster's panicked voice over the intercom was hardly reassuring. But with the ground under me vehemently trying to sweep me off my legs, it was not as if I had much of a choice anyway. I held on to a signboard and tried to call my wife, waiting for the wave of aftershocks to subdue. When it finally did, I walked the stairs up to the first level. By now, water had started to leak from a crack in the station's ceiling, and suddenly the "You're safe" announcements changed 180 degrees into "Evacuate, now!"

Elevators not working, a mother in front of me was struggling with a baby in a big stroller. I told her to take my bag and hurriedly carried the stroller with its precious content to the daylight.

Outside, the usually quiet park adjacent to our office was literally packed with thousands of people taking refuge, the better-prepared ones wearing hardhats. In the distance the sound of ambulances, and at a particularly large aftershock the sound of breaking glass. Like me, many people were frantically typing on their mobile phones, and I finally managed to get a text message through the overloaded network to my wife, and then to my parents back in Europe.

It was only when, after what seemed the longest of times, I finally received an answer back from my wife, saying she and our children were fine, that I could breathe normally again.

Bigger in Japan
Kamakura

アンダーグラウンド

東京の中心部、3月11日金曜日午後2時46分、私は地下3階で電車を待っていた。週末を自宅で早く迎えたい一心で、今日最後の会議が短く終わればいいのにと、内心願っていた。

しかしその通りにはならなかった。

「乗客の皆さま、冷静に願います。駅とホームは耐震設計になっております、ここは安全です」スピーカー越しに聞こえる駅長の動揺した声は、とても私たちを安心させてくれるようなものではない。しかし、激しい揺れで足下がおぼつかなくなり、この場に留まるほか私に選択肢はなかった。余震が静まるまで看板にしがみつき、妻へ電話をかけ続けた。余震がおさまって、やっと私は地上階まで階段を上った。その頃にはすでに駅の天井の亀裂から水が漏れ出し、「安全です」のアナウンスから急展開を見せ「今すぐ避難！」に変わっていた。

エレベーターは作動しておらず、私の目の前にいた母親らしき人は、ベビーカーを運ぶのに苦戦している。私のかばんを持ってくれるよう彼女に言い、私は尊い命を積んだベビーカーを陽の光に向かって急いで運んだ。

外に出ると、会社の隣にあるいつも閑散な公園は、避難してきた数千もの人でひしめき合っていた。そのなかにはヘルメットをしっかりかぶっている準備のよい者たちも見受けられる。遠くでは救急車のサイレンが聞こえ、ひときわ大きい余震の後にはガラスの割れる音も聞こえた。私と同様、周りの人たちはみな必死にメールを打ち、私もやっとパンク寸前の回線を通じて妻と、ヨーロッパに住む両親にメールを送ることができた。

永遠とも思える時間が過ぎた後、妻から彼女自身と子どもたちの安全を知らせる返信があり、私は一息つくことができた。

Bigger in Japan
神奈川県　鎌倉市

Underneath

Morning, 19 March 2011. Woke up thinking, "Oh my, I slept through a whole night." Then I immediately felt guilty in my bed with enough bedding to keep me warm even without the heat on. Knowing full well this is called survivor's guilt.

What else am I feeling? A constant, nagging dread. Am I afraid? Of course I am. I'm terrified. Am I panicking? Uhh, I don't think so. But compared to my normal state, I suppose I'm rather quietly frantic. I'm a Japanese woman, 45, born in Tokyo. I grew up here and in New York, and eventually went to university in Oxford. In the 1990s I was a reporter for the Asahi Shimbun, a Japanese national daily, and I covered the Hanshin earthquake on the ground in Kobe from day one. Until March 11th, 2011, that had been the most traumatic experience of my life.

On the morning of January 17th 1995, I was about 80 kilometers (50 miles) away from the epicenter of the Hanshin quake. What I felt then was a gigantic bang beneath me, followed by deadly silence. That was the effect of a magnitude 7.3 quake. The data show that the initial tremors lasted for 15 seconds. On the afternoon of March 11th 2011, I was about 350 kilometers (220 miles) from Sendai, the largest city near the epicenter. This time the earth groaned and shrieked, even as far away as that. And it went on and on and on, for what seemed like an eternal five minutes.

I think I thought about death. I don't really remember. That was the force of a magnitude 9.0 quake. I'm not a scientist, but I understand that means that it was 1,000 times more powerful than the Hanshin quake, which killed nearly 6,500 people. I don't ever remember being so constantly afraid. "Then why do Japanese people look so calm?" you may ask. Why so orderly? Why do we insist on queueing? Paying at the cash register? I can't speak for all of us, but those around me, the family, friends, colleagues and university students I know, have all said: "Because that's what we do."

Of course, violent crime and petty theft are commonplace in Japan, as in any other country. I used to cover the police as a reporter, so I know this well. But the majority of us, the people you see going about their daily business despite a sick, sinking feeling in the stomach, don't loot. Neither would you, right?

A few nights ago, I received an SOS e-mail from a high-school friend I hadn't seen in nearly 30 years. She and her husband are doctors in Fukushima. Her husband's family runs a mid-sized hospital and elderly care home outside the evacuation zone. The SOS said the hospital/home was running out of fuel and diapers. I did my best to dig out old government contacts from my days as a reporter, and eventually had someone from the Tokyo government call the besieged hospital to assess their situation.

I understand from my friend that the doctor on call told the government official, "Well, we're all right, I think." My friend was furious and proud at the same time; his answer was so typical of a modest, proud Tohoku man. So to see someone from that region, an elderly gentleman, break down in front of the TV cameras even for a fleeting moment is ...well... I have no words to explain.

The depth of one's emotions is not necessarily proportional to the level of emotion being expressed. I live in Tokyo. As of the morning of March 19th, the incessant aftershocks have abated somewhat, and the fear now is of course the still-burning power plants. In the past week, we have all scrambled to become nuclear radiation experts. Initially after March 11th, I had thought I could more or less project the future chain of events, because we've experienced major quakes and tsunamis before. But I have no clue whatsoever about what may, can or will happen with Fukushima No. 1. I have never felt so helpless about something that might have such a profound effect on the well-being of my family, friends, my compatriots and myself.

Of course I'm terrified.

But we in Tokyo, the people I know, the people I see bustling about in the streets, sitting next to me on the trains, are all going about our lives. Some call us naïve, deluded and fool-hardy. Perhaps. But many of us have no other choice. Many people have fled because they could and they wanted to.

For those of us with pets, or with ailing or elderly family members, or with any other circumstance that makes a quick evacuation impossible, the situation would have to become much, much worse before we would make that big push. But that doesn't mean we aren't thinking about it. People here seem to have a constant sick, sinking feeling. I constantly feel dizzy, as if I'm rocking and swaying all the time in a boat on the Cherwell. And this doesn't help at all.

From the outside, we may act calm and cheerful to the point of seeming creepy. But do understand: We are crying inside, we are gritting our teeth, often literally. I seem to have developed a constant crease in my forehead.

I asked a friend the other day, "I wonder if this is a bit like living in a war zone?" She said, "Darling, this IS a war zone. We're just lucky we have no enemy to hate." Right. So I'm now in a war zone. So the streets turn dark at night. Right. We put on extra jumpers and socks to keep ourselves warm. Yes. Well, I can just remember the 1960s, before Japan became a super-rich country. Back then, nights were dark and winters were cold. I feel sorry for the younger people who have only known bright nights, warm winters, and very little material want. They don't know how to react.

But we can teach them, as we wait for the cherry blossoms to come out. And I think I will daydream of the daffodils in Christ Church Meadow. With, of course, a very stiff upper lip.

Yuko Kato
Tokyo

下にあるもの

朝だ。2011年3月19日の朝。目が覚めるなり、「ああ、一晩通して寝られたんだ」と思う。思うなりたちまち、ベッドの中で罪悪感に襲われる。暖房をつけてなくても十分に暖かいほど、たっぷりの布団や毛布にくるまれて。この罪悪感は「サバイバーズ・ギルト」、生き残った人間に特有の感覚だとわかっていても。

ほかに何を感じてる？　絶え間ない、しつこい、重たい気持ち。怖いのかって？　もちろん怖いよ。ものすごく怖くてたまらないよ。パニクってるかって？　えーと、それはないと思う。でもふだんの自分と比べれば、たぶん静かにあわてふためいてる気がする。私は45歳の日本人女性。東京出身。ここ東京とニューヨークで育って、やがてオックスフォードの大学に行った。1990年代には朝日新聞の記者として、阪神大震災は初日から現場で取材した。あの震災取材が今までの自分にとって、一番大きい衝撃的な体験だった。2011年3月11日までは。

1995年1月17日の未明、私は阪神大震災の震源地から80キロくらいの場所にいた。あのとき感じたのは、体の下からつきあげる巨大なバン！という音。そして続いた、恐ろしいほどの沈黙。それがあのときのマグニチュード7.3の衝撃だった。データをみると、当初の震動は15秒ほど続いたという。そして2011年3月11日の午後、私は仙台から350キロくらい離れたところにいた。それほど離れていても、地面は唸り、雄叫びをあげて、揺れた。揺れて揺れて、揺れ続けた。永遠に続くのかと思われた5分間。

死について考えたかもしれない。あまりよく覚えてない。マグニチュード9.0の衝撃というのは、それほどのものだった。私は科学者ではないけど、つまり阪神大震災より1,000倍のエネルギーだったという意味らしい。阪神大震災では6,500人近くが亡くなったのに。常に何かに怯えてる、こんな状態、経験したことがない。「だったらなんで日本人はそんなに落ち着いて見えるんだ？」日本人じゃない人は、不思議に思うのかもしれない。なんでそんなに整然と行動できるのかって。きちんと行列して。レジで代金を払って。日本人全員の

代弁はできないけど、自分の周りの人たち、家族とか友人とか同僚とか、知り合いの大学生とかはみんな口をそろえてこう言う。「だって、そういうものだから」

もちろん日本だってほかの国と同じで、凶悪犯罪もあるし、つまらない窃盗事件だって日常的にある。私は記者だったころ警察も担当していたから、その辺はよく知ってる。けれども大半の人は、毎日すれ違う人たちは、腹の底にまとわりつくような重たい不快な気持ちを抱えながらも、それでも毎日やるべきことをやるために動き回っている人たちは、略奪なんかしない。あなたもそうでしょう？

数日前の夜、30年近く音信不通だった高校時代の友人からSOSのメールが舞い込んだ。彼女とその夫は福島で医者をしている。彼女の夫の家族は、退避圏外の街で中規模の病院と老人ホームを経営している。この病院とホームで、燃料と老人用おむつがなくなりつつある。それがSOSメールの内容だった。私は記者時代に知っていた政府関係者の連絡先をなんとか掘り出した。そしてめぐりめぐって結局、政府の人が、危機的状況にあるその病院に、状況把握の電話を直接かけたのだという。

しかし友人によると、当直の医師は政府関係者からの問い合わせに対して、「えーと、大丈夫だと思います」と答えてしまったのだとか。友人は怒り狂い、それでも誇らしそうだった。なんていかにも典型的な、謙虚で慎ましく、そして誇り高い、東北の男だろう。東北人気質というのは、そういうものだと。だからこそ、なおさらなのだ。東北の人が、東北のお年寄りの男性が、よりによってテレビカメラの前で、一瞬でも涙ぐみ声を詰まらせるというのが、どれほどのことなのか。どれほどの悲しみか。語る言葉が見つからない。

想いの深さは、表に出る感情の量とは必ずしも一致しない。私は東京で暮らしている。3月19日の朝現在で言うと、絶え間なく続いていた余震はこのところやや落ち着いている。今の恐怖の対象はもちろん、発熱の止まらない原発だ。ここ1週間、私たちはだれもが、原子力や放射能のにわか専門家になろうとバタバタ慌てふためいていた。3月11日の地震直後の私は、これからどうなるのかだいたいの展開は予測できると思っていた。大地震や津波は、初めてじゃないので。けれども福島第一原発がこれからどうなるのか、どうなり得るのか、私にはまったく想像がつかない。自分の家族や友人や、この国の人たちや自分自身の安全にこれほど巨大な影響を与えかねないものについて、これほどの無力感を覚えるのは、まったく初めての経験だ。

むちゃくちゃ怖いに決まってるでしょう。

だけど東京にいる私たちは、私の知り合いたちは、街中で忙しそうにしている人たちは、電車で隣に座ってる人たちは、みんなそれぞれに毎日をこなしている。そういう私たちをおめでたい能天気だと、だまされてると、愚かだと言う人たちもいる。そうかもしれない。でもほかにどうしようもない人だっている。すでに東京を出た多くの人は、出たいと思うだけでなく、出られるから出たのだ。

その一方で、動物と暮らしていたり、親が高齢だったり病気だったり、そのほかこの街を速やかに脱出できない何らかの理由がある人にとっては、状況がもっともっと悪化しない限り、東京脱出の大決断はおいそれとできるものじゃない。だからといって、東京を離れようかと考えてないわけじゃないのだ。不穏で不快で重たい、この身が沈み込んでいくような感覚を常に抱えながら。そして私はと言えば、常にぐらぐら揺れている感覚が消えない。まるでオックスフォードのチャーウェル川で、舟に揺られているみたいに、ぐらぐら揺れている。まったく困ったものだ。

端から見れば私たちは気持ちが悪いほど、冷静で明るくふるまっているように見えるかもしれない。だけどわかって。私たちは内側で泣いているんです。内側で歯を食いしばっているんです。あるいは実際に歯を食いしばってることもあるかもしれない。自分のことをいえば、眉間の皺が消えてくれない。

先日、友人にこう尋ねてみた。「戦時下に暮らすって、こういう感じなのかな」友人の返事はこう。「いや、間違いなく今は戦時下でしょう。憎む敵がいないだけ幸せなんだよ」そうか。私は今、戦時下にある。だから夜になると道が暗くなるんだ。なるほど。セーターや靴下を重ね着して暖をとるわけだ。そうか。まあ、私はぎりぎり1960年代を覚えているので、日本がものすごい金持ち大国になる前の。当時の日本では、夜は暗かったし冬は寒かったのだから。逆に、明るい夜と暖かい冬を経験したことがない若い人たち、物がな

い状態を知らない若い人たちは、気の毒だと思う。今の事態にどう反応していいかわからないみたいだ。けれどもそれは私たちが教えていけばいい。桜の花が咲くのを待ちながら。私の場合はそれに加えて、クライストチャーチ コレッジ裏の野原に咲き乱れる水仙を思いながら。ギュッと口を引き締めて。

加藤祐子
東京都

Understanding

My apartment is 5,629 miles from Sendai. At 10:46 PM on Thursday March 10, local time, I was getting ready to go to bed when posts started flooding my Twitter client. My first reply was, "Hey Japan, are you ok? #EarthQuake #GetToHighGround."

 I was horrified by the nightmare visions on NHK World's online broadcast: A sea of burning debris pouring across Sendai farmlands, racing up embankments and sweeping houses aside like matchsticks. I started posting to Twitter and Facebook and stayed glued to the live feeds. Days passed.

 I can't pretend to have even an ounce of understanding of what the survivors are going through right now, searching debris for missing loved ones, finding parents and children crushed in the rubble of what used to be their homes. Right now there are so many survivors who might die because of inaction. I'm afraid and tired, and I'm worried for my two friends who haven't made contact. But I set aside my own feelings and translate and repost messages by the thousands, hoping that maybe one message will make a difference to one person. Just one.

 Useless? Naïve? Stupid? Maybe. But I keep doing it, because the only alternative I have is to stop, and fall apart at the horror of it all.

 がんばります (I'll do all I can.)

Mari Kurisato
Denver, Colorado, USA

理解

私は仙台から9千キロあまり離れたアパートに住んでいます。こちらの時間で3月10日木曜日午後10時46分、ちょうどベッドに入ろうとしたときに、ツイッター画面に洪水のような投稿が始まりました。すぐさま「ねぇ日本、大丈夫？ #EarthQuake (ハッシュタグ：地震) #GetToHighGround (ハッシュタグ：高台へ)」と返信しました。

 NHKワールドのオンライン放送から流れる悪夢のような映像に恐ろしくなりました。燃え上がるがれきを巻き込んだ海が仙台の耕作地に押し寄せ、堤防を乗り越えて、マッチ棒でもさらうかのように家屋を押し流す。私はツイッターとフェイスブックに書き込みながら、ライブ映像に釘付けになりました。そして数日が経ちました。

今、被災者が体験していることのほんのわずかでも理解しているように振る舞うことは、私にはできません。愛する人々を求めてがれきを探し回る人。自分たちの家だったがれきに押しつぶされた親や子どもを見つける人。今、この瞬間にも多くの生存者が、救いの手が届かなかったために命を落としているかもしれません。私は恐れ、そして疲れました。まだ連絡の取れない友人2人のことも心配です。でも、自分の感情には押し流されず、何千もの人からのメッセージを翻訳して再投稿し続けました。たったひとつのメッセージでも、それがたったひとりの人でもいいから助けになることを願って。たったひとつでも、たったひとりのためになるなら……。

何の役にも立ちませんか？　考えが甘い？　愚か？　そうかもしれません。でも、私は続けます。さもなければ、何もしない私はあまりの恐怖に崩れ落ちてしまいます。

がんばります（I'll do all I can.）

Mari Kurisato
米国　コロラド州　デンバー

Values

I've been thinking about lots of things since I married a Sri Lankan. The great earthquake made me realize clearly that in seeking convenience and riches, Japan has been losing sight of the most valuable things. Now is the time to bring back the lost values—bonds, family, love and nature.

Whether Japan can really revive or not depends on that.

Kaoru Raban
Kohoku, Chiba

大切なもの

スリランカ人と結婚したことで常々感じていたことを、今回の大地震で再認識させられた。利便性や豊かさを追求し、大切なものを失った日本。それを取り戻すのは、今。「絆・家族・愛・資源……」

本当の意味で、日本が「復興」できるかは、そこにある。

ラバン薫
千葉県　我孫子市　湖北

Vertical

I certainly don't believe any of that "divine retribution" crap, which happens to unify the philosophies of right wing American broadcaster Glenn Beck and right wing Tokyo governor Shintaro Ishihara. But I can appreciate a cosmic joke.

The massive earthquake that hit northeast Japan on March 11th came right in the middle of moving season. The Japanese fiscal year and the school year begins April 1 or thereabouts, and traditionally many people move house during the month of March, because of job transfers, university admission, or because they just like to do what everybody else is doing. Consequently, there were a few trucks outside our 38-story building in the Shitamachi district of Tokyo the weekend after the quake, carrying furniture for folks who were moving in. Fortunately, the freight elevator was operational again by the morning of the 12th, but what did those new arrivals think standing in their new apartment while it swayed back and forth during one of the many aftershocks?

Maybe they had lived in a high-rise before, but in any case the quake helped test a theory, at least partially: Would all these earthquake-proofed structures actually withstand a massive quake? Of course, the epicenter of the one we experienced was a hundred kilometers off the coast of Iwate Prefecture, but according to reports, no buildings collapsed in Sendai, the nearest large city to the quake and one with its own share of skyscrapers. So the technology seems to work, and while it certainly saves lives and property, it doesn't solve a more intractable problem: Once you've been in a large earthquake in a high rise, you don't want to be in another one.

I was writing an email when the quake struck at 2:46. I've lived here on the 24th floor for more than 10 years and been through a good share of quakes. Usually, they start with a disconcerting jolt and then the whole apartment sways gently if sickeningly. From what I understand there are two types of technologies for high rises in Japan. One is designed so that the building is flexible: the entire structure absorbs the energy and disperses it evenly throughout the frame. That means the higher you live, the wider and longer the sway. The other type, which is more expensive, involves spongy shocks in the foundation that absorb much of the energy. We live in the former type. This time, I didn't feel a jolt but rather a slight rumble from the floor that just kept growing until the walls started rattling violently. Masako knew this was going to be bigger than the usual quake and started sobbing in the next room. We crouched under her desk together as she yelled out for her father (who died when she was 8). The shaking didn't stop. More precisely, it gradually changed to swaying, but the swaying was much broader than in the past. The movement wasn't as terrifying as the noise—a massive creaking sound. And it went on for more than a minute.

A commonly held truism in Japan says that most people who die in an earthquake are crushed by falling furniture. Actually, that's not true: most die from collapsed structures, but the vast majority of these structures are wooden one-family houses. Still, there is something to be said for the falling furniture theory. Because so many Japanese residences have little if any storage space, homes are filled with tall, heavy wardrobes and bookcases, and if they're not fixed to the walls in some way they will fall over. We don't have much in the way of possessions, but the bookcases we bought are the type that attach to the ceiling, so nothing fell over during the quake except a floor mirror in the bedroom, and that didn't break. The TV stand, however, which is on casters, would have moved all the way across the living room if it hadn't been tethered to the antenna outlet.

The only thing damaged in the quake was our peace of mind. Though I now have confidence in the integrity of our building, I don't want to live here any more if it means the possibility of having to go through that again, or worse. Which is a shame, because I like this apartment. It's well laid out, brighter than any place I've ever lived, and the view of Sumida River and the mountains of Nagano and Yamanashi is breathtaking. Of course, an earthquake can be just as scary when you're living on the first floor, but being on the ground is a slightly more reassuring situation, since after it's over you can get out of your building easily. When the shaking stopped, we were basically stuck on the 24th floor. The elevators automatically stop in an earthquake and can't be restarted until a technician arrives to turn them on again, and that could take hours. Having two cats (not allowed, thanks for asking) makes it even more difficult to get out. We have to put them in carriers and then schlep them down 24 floors in a stairwell that may likely be crammed with other people trying to escape. And if we stay, what if the water, gas and electricity are cut off? Or, even worse, a fire breaks out?

These were possibilities we'd considered ever since we moved in here but didn't contemplate seriously until the day after the quake. It may be a safe building, even in a monster quake, but the attendant disadvantages make the prospect of such a quake almost as terrifying as a structural failure.

And one more thing. The so-called building disaster team did nothing after the quake except apologize about the elevator. We live in a UR residence, meaning a semi-public apartment building, which is why the structure was state-of-the-art when it was built. But management is sorely lacking. We have never received literature outlining what we should do in a disaster. Apparently, we are supposed to get that from the public sphere. We're supposed to know that stuff ourselves.

But probably the saddest realization came when Masako went out into the hallway to see if any of our neighbors might need help. Ever since the couple who lived in 2409 moved out a year ago, we don't know anyone else on our floor on anything like a name basis. No matter what you hear about the cohesion of Japanese society, it means less when they reside in a vertical community: they don't even greet one another in the elevator. Even in fear, they keep to themselves.

Philip Brasor
Tokyo

タテ型コミュニティ

　アメリカ人右翼のトークショー司会者、グレン・ベッグや、東京都知事の石原慎太郎が言う「天罰」などという戯れ言を、僕はもちろん信じていない。だが、次のことは宇宙のブラックジョークとして楽しめる。
　3月11日に日本の東北地方を襲った大地震は、引っ越しシーズンのまっただ中にやって来た。日本の会計年度と学年度は4月1日、あるいはその時期に始まるため、多くの人たちが3月中に引っ越しをする。転勤や大学入学、あるいは他の人たちがそうしているから、という理由で。そのため、地震のあとの週末には、私たちが住む東京の下町にある38階建てのマンションの外にトラックが何台か止まって、引っ越してくる人たちの家具を運んでいた。幸運なことに、貨物用エレベーターは12日の朝までには運転を再開していたが、この新しい住人たちは彼らの新しい部屋の中に立ち、多くの余震で部屋が揺れているとき、何を思っていたのだろうか。
　もしかすると彼らは以前、高層ビルに住んでいたことがあるのかもしれないが、いずれにせよこの地震は、ある理論を部分的に試すことに役立った。この耐震構造は実際に大地震を耐え抜くことができるのだろうか？　もちろん僕らが経験した地震の震源地は、岩手県沿岸部から100キロほど離れている。しかし、報道によると、この震源地に一番近い大都市、高層ビルが立ち並ぶ仙台では、崩壊したビルはなかったという。技術は機能しており、たしかに命や財産を救ってくれはするものの、もっとやっかいな問題は解決していない。高層ビルにいて大きな地震を経験したら、もう一度それを経験したいとは思わないはずだ。
　午後2時46分に地震が襲ったとき、僕はメールを書いていた。この24階に10年以上住んでいて、十分に地震を経験してきた。普通なら、不安をかきたてるような突然の揺れから始まり、そしてマンション全体がうんざりするほどやんわりと揺れる。私の理解では、日本には高層ビルのための技術が2種類ある。ひとつはビルに柔軟性を持たせて設計する。建物全体がエネルギーを吸収し、骨組全体を通して均等に分散する。住む場所が高くなるほど、揺れはより幅広く、そして長くなる。もうひとつ、こちらはより高価だが、エネルギーの多くを吸収する緩衝材が土台に含まれている。僕らは前者の建物に住んでいる。今回、突然の揺れは感じなかったが、むしろ床からゴロゴロとした音を少し感じ、壁がガタガタと激しく音をたてるまで、ただただ揺れは大きくなり続けた。マサコは、これがいつもの地震よりも大きくなるとわかって、隣の部屋で泣き始めた。僕らは彼女の机の下に一緒にもぐり込み、マサコは（彼女が8歳のときに亡くなった）父親を求め、叫んだ。振動は止まらなかった。より正確には耐震のための揺れへと変化していったのだが、その揺れは今までよりも、もっと振幅が大きいものだった。しかし、この揺れより怖かったのは、ギシギシと激しくきしむ音だった。それは1分以上続いた。
　日本では一般的に、地震で死ぬ人の多くは倒れてくる家具につぶされると考えられている。実は、これは真実ではない。多くは倒壊した建造物によって死ぬのだが、この建造物の大半は木造の一軒家なのだ。とはいえ、この倒れる家具理論について、一定の信憑性はある。ほとんど収納スペースがない日本の住居の多くは、重量感のあるタンスや本棚で埋め尽くされ、これらを壁に固定していなければ、倒れてくるのだ。所有物といっても僕らはそれほど物を持っていないけれど、以前買った本棚は天井に固定するタイプだったので何も倒れなかった。寝室のフロアミラーは倒れたものの、割れなかった。でも、キャスター付きのテレビスタンドは、もしアンテナケーブルが差し込み口に差し込まれていなかったら、リビングの向こう側まで転がっていただろう。
　この地震でのダメージはただひとつ、私たちの心の平穏だ。私たちの住まいの安全性について今は自信を持っているが、もう一度このような、あるいはこれよりもひどい経験をしなくてはならない可能性があるというのなら、もうここには住みたくない。僕はこの部屋が好きだから、残念だけど。間取りもいいし、今まで住んだどんな場所よりも明るいし、隅田川や長野や山梨の山々の眺めは息をのむほどだ。もちろん、1階に住んでいようと地震が恐ろしいことに変わりはないが、地上であれば少しでも安心できるし、地震が終わったら簡単に建物から出ることができる。揺れが収まったとき、僕らは24階に閉じ込められていた。地震の際、

エレベーターは自動的に止まり、技術者が到着して操作するまで運転は再開されず、動くまで何時間もかかる可能性がある。僕らは猫2匹を飼っている（もちろん許可されていませんよ。ご質問どうもありがとう）。これは脱出をさらに難しくしている。猫をかごに入れて、逃げようとする人たちでおそらくごった返している階段で、24階からのろのろと下りていかなくてはならないのだから。かと言って留まるにしても、水、ガス、電気が止まってしまったらどうなるのだろう？　あるいは、もっとひどいことになって、火事が起こったらどうなる？

こういった可能性はここに引っ越してきてから考えたことはあるが、地震の翌日まで真剣に検討してはいなかった。このビルはモンスター級の地震が起こっても安全かもしれないが、それに伴う高層ビルならではの不利な条件は、構造上の欠陥と同じぐらい地震の可能性を恐ろしいものにしている。

それからもうひとつ。このビルのいわゆる災害対策チームは地震のあと、エレベーターについて謝罪する以外、何もしなかった。私たちはUR都市機構住宅、つまり半公共のマンションに住んでいる。このビルの構造が建築時に最先端だった理由はそれだ。でも、管理は痛ましいほど欠けている。災害時にどうすべきかを説明するマニュアルを、僕らは一切受け取らなかった。どうやら公の情報源から、自分で入手すべきらしい。

だが、おそらく最も悲しい発見は、マサコが近所に助けが必要な人はいないかと廊下へ出ていったときに起こった。2409号室に住んでいたカップルが1年前に引っ越して以来、僕らは同じ階で暮らす住人たちの名前さえ知らない。日本社会の団結力についていろいろと話を耳にするだろうが、タテ型コミュニティに属するとこの団結力は弱まるのだ。エレベーターの中ですら、お互いにあいさつすることがない。恐怖に襲われていても、彼らは自分自身の中に閉じこもっている。

Philip Brasor
東京都

Voices

Growing up with a sibling who was diagnosed with cerebral palsy since childhood is something I can't explain in one word to make you say, "Oh, I totally understand what that's like now." But what I can tell you is the feeling of having my little sister tell me she's jealous of me because I can run in the park, to see her cry in her room, pulling her hair out in frustration with her left hand—the stronger of her two hands. That feeling, that hollowness. Because you are allowed to have, by the powers that be, what someone else (who is no less deserving than you) is denied.

Since March 11th, I've reminded myself that in taking action, it is important to remember that there are many people whose voices in times of emergency are ignored, perhaps more so than they are on a daily basis.

Who will speak for the afflicted elderly, children and disabled, both Japanese and non-Japanese? Where can they go? Who will listen and tell them that their needs are just as important as anyone else's, and begin to address them? Those who have a voice, needing to be expressed—who will make sure that the mouths they come out of are fed, not chapped from cold, not muted by standards of validity or worth?

Jessica Tomoko Perez
The Bronx, New York

声

　幼少時から脳性麻痺を患う妹と一緒に育った経験をたった一言だけの説明で、「ああ、それがどんなものか、今わかったよ」とあなたに言わせることはできないでしょう。ただ私があなたに話せるのは、公園の中を走り回れる私がうらやましい、という妹の話を聞かされる気持ち。そして彼女が自分の部屋で泣き、いらだちから左手（両手のうち強いほうの利き手）で髪の毛をむしっている姿を見てしまったこと……。この気持ち、このむなしさ……。神の御心によってあなたに与えられているものを、（あなたほどそれを与えられる資格がないというわけではないのに）与えられない人がいるのだから。

　3月11日以来、自分に言い聞かせてきたことがある。非常時には無視される多くの人々の声があり、その数はいつもの日常以上に多い、という大切なことを、行動を起こす際には覚えておかなくてはならない。

　日本人であるかどうかを問わず、被災した高齢者、子どもたちや障害者の声はだれが代弁する？　彼らはどこへ行けばいい？　だれが彼らの声に耳を傾け、彼らのニーズもほかの人のそれと同じように大切だと答え、それに対処する？　だれにも声があり、伝えたいことがある。その声が発せられる彼らの口に食事を与え、寒さで凍えないように守り、妥当性や価値といった基準によってその声を消してしまわないようにするのは、いったいだれ？

Jessica Tomoko Perez
米国　ニューヨーク州　ブロンクス

Waiting

When my smartphone chimed at 3 a.m. Friday in Ontario, bringing news of a massive earthquake in Japan, I woke Hiromi. Her parents were in Miyagi. She muttered something about calling them in the morning and went back to sleep. We'd spoken to her dad via video Skype only a few hours ago. It could wait.

　Morning came, and the TV showed images of cars washing under a bridge like ice floes on a spring river, fishing boats perched atop buildings, entire villages reduced to mud-covered rubble. We called and called to no avail.

　We knew Oji-san would have been at home in Wakayanagi, far enough inland to be safe from the deadly waves, but Oba-san was supposed to be in Sendai for a lecture that afternoon.

　The barrage of calls from family and friends began almost at once with my parents offering to cut short their southern vacation. "No need," we told them, "there's nothing to be done but wait." I went to work long enough to fill in my boss and was sent home to wait. Hour after hour, we watched the news. We stared at the horror on TV like rabbits on the highway at night, unable to look away from the oncoming headlights. But for us, that doom would never arrive, only constantly approach. All we could do was wait, chained by distance, helpless to act.

　Dozens called and emailed to express concern, sympathy, horror and support. Was there anything they could do? Did we need anything? No, there was nothing. Only waiting.

    Hours of anxiety stretched into days. The kids were fed at intervals and otherwise left in the care of Nintendo and Walt Disney. I cooked, monitored the news and answered the phone while Hiromi sat glued to NHK's Internet feed and kept up the hourly ritual of dialing through to a recording in Japan telling us our call could not be put through. Appetite and sleep became a distant memory. I'd give in to nervous exhaustion and medicinal vodka and doze fitfully for a few hours, rising to find her maintaining her vigil while the 24-hour cable news drumbeat of despair rolled on.

    I stumbled through work, so preoccupied I could barely string a coherent sentence together. Wednesday came and went without contact, the constant worry and not-knowing gnawing at our souls like a trapped rat. We stayed composed, knowing that the least breach of the emotional dam would mean a flood of panic.

    Returning from the office early Thursday, I sat down to try to work and saw that my father-in-law's cold, grey Skype icon had turned to bright, friendly green. His computer was back online. They had electricity. I hollered to Hiromi and she dashed to the phone.

    We called, and at long last, they answered.

    The waiting was over.

Kevin Wood
Hamilton, Ontario, Canda

待ちわびて

金曜日午前3時、オンタリオ州に住む僕のスマートフォンが鳴った。見ると日本で大地震が発生したというニュースが入っている。僕はヒロミを起こした。彼女の両親は宮城県に住んでいる。しかし彼女は、朝になったら電話をするからというようなことをつぶやいて、再び寝てしまった。そのときは、ほんの2、3時間前にスカイプのビデオ電話で彼女の父親と話をしたばかりだったし、それほど急ぐこともないと思った。

朝になってテレビをつけると、画面には、まるで春先の河川に浮かぶ流氷のように橋の下を次々と流されていく車、ビルの屋上にまでうちあげられた漁船、そして村全体が泥だらけのがれきの山と化している光景が映し出されていた。電話をかけ続けても、まったく通じない。

妻の父親はこの多数の死者を出した津波からは十分遠くの内陸にある若柳の自宅にいるのはわかっていたが、母親はその日の午後、講義に参加するため仙台にいたはずだ。

僕たちのもとには、ほぼ一斉に家族や友人から電話がきて、僕の両親は南での休暇を切り上げて帰ると申し出た。しかし僕たちは、「その必要はないよ。今は待つ以外、何もできないから」と告げた。僕はその日、上司に状況を報告するために一応出社したが、すぐ家で待機するよう言われ帰宅した。そして何時間もニュースを見続けた。真夜中の高速道路で迫りくる車のヘッドライトの光に硬直して動けないウサギのように、そこに映し出される恐ろしい光景に釘付けになる。しかし、目の前の悲運は絶えず我々に訴えかけはしても、決してここまで届くことはないのだ。絶対的な距離を隔てて、自分たちはただ待つこと以外は何もできずにいる。

その後も心配やお見舞い、動揺や慰めの言葉が多数、電話やメールで寄せられた。彼らは、何かできることはないかと聞いてきた。何か必要なものはないか、と。いや、何もない、と僕らは答えた。待つことしかできない。

不安の時は数時間どころか、数日間に及ぶこととなった。食事のとき以外、子どもたちの遊び相手は任天堂とウォルト・ディズニーに任せている。僕が食事を作り、ニュースから目を離さず電話に応答する間、ヒロミはNHKのネット情報にかじりつく一方で、「現在電話は繋がりにくくなっております」という自動音声にもひるまずに、まるで儀式のように毎時間電話をかけ続けた。食欲も睡眠も、いつしか意識から遠のく。僕自身は精神的な疲れと薬代わりのウォッカに負けて数時間うたた寝をすることはあったが、目を覚ますと彼女は一睡もせずに、絶え間なく流れる絶望的なニュースを24時間ケーブルテレビで見続けていた。

僕はなんとか仕事をこなしてはいたものの、頭がいっぱいで会話もおぼつかなくなっている。水曜日になっても連絡は取れないまま、収まらない不安と、何もわからないやるせなさが、追い詰められたねずみが檻をかじるように、少しずつ僕らの心を蝕んでいった。それでも、わずかにでも感情のコントロールを緩めたらパニックに陥ってしまうとわかっていた僕たちは、とにかく落ち着こうと努力した。

木曜日、オフィスから早めに戻った僕は、仕事を片付けようとパソコンに向かった。そのとき、これまで冷酷なまでに灰色のままだった義父のスカイプのアイコンが、明るく親しみのある緑色になっているのに気づいた。彼のパソコンがオンライン状態に戻っている。電気が通じている証拠だ。大声でヒロミを呼ぶと、彼女は急いで電話に飛びついた。

電話をかけ、長い長い呼び出し音のあと、ついに電話が通じた。

もう待つのは終わりだ。

Kevin Wood
カナダ　オンタリオ州　ハミルトン

Want

I have been around Tokyo for 15 years and I feel I am needed here now more than ever.

The decision whether to stay is the most complex one I have ever had to make in my life. Japan is my adopted home. I would not leave a burning house alone if my family were still inside.

Our house is not as yet on fire but I need to be available in the event it does go up in flames. We as a community don't owe it to Japan. But when I think of the Fukushima 50 risking life and limb, when I think of the children now without parents in the Tohoku region, when I think about the untold damage to the region far beyond the scale of the New Orleans flooding, this is simply where I need to be.

It's where I want to be.

Dan Castellano
Tokyo

ここにいたい

首都圏に住むようになって15年経ちますが、いまほど、この地で必要とされていると思ったことはありません。

ここに残るかどうかという決断は、私がいままでの人生で下したなかで、もっとも複雑なものでした。日本は私にとって第二の故郷です。燃えさかる家に家族を残してひとり逃げることはできません。

もちろん、私たちの家にはまだ火の手は及んでいませんが、もしそうなったとき、私はその場にいて役に立てる人間でありたいと思っています。外国人としてそういう義務があるわけではありませんが、ただ、命がけで復旧作業をしている原発の作業員たち（当初Fukushima 50と呼ばれた）のことを考えるとき、親をなくした東北地方の子どもたちのことを考えるとき、あのニューオーリンズの洪水の災害規模をはるかにしのぐ、未だ明らかにされていない被害のことを考えるとき、私はただ、ここにいなければならないと実感するのです。

この国こそが、私がいたいと思う場所なのです。

Dan Castellano
東京都

Window

All my Tokyos feel imaginary.

Once, in a cab, whipping along that elevated Tarkovsky expressway, I saw, through an uncurtained window, a man seated naked on the edge of a dark wooden table. Helmut Newton but for real somehow. Of no particular age, with corporate hair. Awaiting something I could not, would never, see, beyond the frame of mullion and concrete. And since then I have tried to fill an infinite depth, of moment, of field, with details I am unwilling to trust. That he was Japanese. Or not. That the table was mahogany, one end of a long dining or perhaps conference table, highly polished. That the room was somehow atemporal, though the décor Occidental (as our grandparents used to say). That he looked at his death, awaiting its approach. Or at some astonishing fulfillment of the heart, unwilling as yet to fully accept its arrival as fact. Or, ditto, some ultimate carnal pleasure. Or, given the night, given this city, the speed of the cab, Japanese cinema and Borges, simultaneously at all three.

"What was the most memorable thing you ever saw in a city?"

"A man, sitting naked on the end of an expensive-looking table. Through a window. In Tokyo. Perhaps the fifth floor. From a cab."

"Where were you going?"

"I have no idea. It was evening, already dark. Near Ark Hills, or just beyond."

"What made it memorable?"

"His stillness." [Becoming evasive] "It's difficult to explain."

The Tokyos I've invented, the fragments of them, and the Tokyos I've seen, the fragments of them. Rattling together now, marbles in a box. Since the earthquake, I have been restless in some very specific way. When I rise from this chair, a part of me wants to go there, to Tokyo. I don't know exactly why. Somehow London and Tokyo are the capitals of my imagination, with Manhattan and Los Angeles like space stations between them. I have lived in none of these places. I doubt I will. Their function is other. Oneiric. Engines of dream.

"'I didn't know whether to scream or shit.'" [Quoting lyrics, the band Television, but this isn't understood, and no doubt makes a strange impression]

William Gibson
Vancouver, BC, Canada

窓

私の東京はどれもすべて架空に思える。

あるとき、タクシーに乗って、タルコフスキーばりの高架ハイウェイを疾走していると、カーテンのない窓ごしに、一人の男が裸で黒っぽい木のテーブルの縁に腰かけているのが見えた。ヘルムート・ニュートン、だがいちおう現実。年齢不詳、ビジネスマンふうの髪。私には見えない、絶対いつまでも見えない何かを、窓仕切りとコンクリートの枠の向こうで待っている。そして以来私は、無限の深さを—時の、場の無限の深さを—自分でも信用する気になれない細部で埋めようとしてきた。一、かれは日本人であった。あるいはなかった。一、テーブルはマホガニーで、見えたのはよく磨いた細長いダイニングテーブルもしくは会議用テーブルの端であった。一、部屋はなぜか無時間の場であった、ただし室内は（我々の祖父母たちがよく言ったように）洋風装飾であった。一、男はじぶんの死を見ていた、死の訪れを待っていた。あるいは、心が何かとてつもなく充たされるのを見ていて、その充足の到来を事実としてしっかり受け入れる気にまだなれずにいた。あるいはまた、何か究極の肉体的快楽を見ていた。あるいは、あの夜、あの都市、タクシーの速度を想えば、日本映画とボルヘスを想えば、その三つともを。

「どこの都市でもいい、都市で見たもので一番記憶に残っているのは？」
「高価そうなテーブルの端に裸で座っている男。窓ごしに見た。東京で。たぶん五階。タクシーから」
「どこへ行くところだった？」
「まったくわからない。晩のことで、もう暗かった。アークヒルズのそばか、すぐ先」
「なぜそれが記憶に残った？」
「彼が静止していたこと」〔逃げるような口調になってくる〕「うまく説明できない」

私が捏造した一連の東京、それらのかけら、私が見た一連の東京、それらのかけら。いまでは一緒にかたかた鳴っている。箱にしまったおはじき。地震以来、私はひどく具体的な落着かなさに囚われている。この椅子から立ち上がるとき、私の一部がそこへ、東京へ行きたがる。理由はよくわからない。ロンドンと東京はなぜか私の想像力の首都なのだ。マンハッタンとロサンゼルスがそのあいだに、スペースステーションのように位置している。私はそのどこにも住んだことはない。これからも住むとは思えない。それらの役割は、他であること。夢であること。夢の機関。

「わめけばいいのかクソすればいいのかわからなかった」〔バンド〈テレビジョン〉の歌詞の引用だが、相手にはわかってもらえず、明らかに妙な印象を与える〕

ウィリアム・ギブスン
カナダ　ブリティッシュコロンビア　ヴァンクーヴァー

Mari Kurisato

2011/03

Test

The Great Tohoku Earthquake has brought an unprecedented amount of damage in its wake. Something like a magnitude 9.0 earthquake, let alone a large-scale tsunami, was the worst disaster seen in 400 years. And then on top of that is the crisis that struck the Fukushima nuclear power plant, leading to radioactive materials being released.

Surely, isn't there something that this latest earthquake disaster, this so-called "triple setback" to our nation, is coercing us to do? For me, I can think of it as nothing less than The Invisible Hand leading us to The Test. In other words, this Test is of our spiritual resolve and strength in the face of adversity.

So, what exactly is being tested by this "suffering?" Who exactly? Why exactly?

Along with the victims themselves, countless people are ceaselessly asking, what meaning does this latest, almost unbelievable, suffering carry at its end? Some ask through religion, others through philosophy and still others take it as predetermined fate.

But, for myself, I don't see it as either asking philosophically, or arguing on religious grounds, to say nothing of taking it as mere destiny. The reasoning being that: It Has No Meaning. What is being tested for all of those left is the question: "Can I be a good person or not?" Thusly, what we must think is, what exactly makes a good person?

When they speculated that there might be a shortage, who so shamelessly spent money for unnecessary hoarding?

Who sold currency in the ensuing inflation after the quake?

Did you have fun consciously writing posts fanning the flames of doubt from the comfort of your warm room?

Do you just donate a pittance with a solemn face while leaving the rest for nature to run its course?

Do you only worry about the radiation while putting the land itself at a distance?

Are the survivors strangers to you, if they are not your family or friends?

In the end, is this all the responsibility of the government?

There are planned blackouts but you're not conserving power, are you?

You complain but you never raise your hand, do you?

You're just waiting until someone decides something, aren't you?

Can you show that type of behavior to children?

"But I'm different!" Are you able to say that?

And if you can say, "I'm different!" just exactly in what way are you different?

Even if it's just a little bit, I think it's fine. Not even completely different is OK, as long as you aren't lying.

For all the forced answers that have been readied, for all the grandiose assertions, all I can hear are mere excuses.

Isn't this test for us to see whether or not we can start to become Good People?

To be a Good Person, it requires neither showy performances, nor great self-assertiveness, nor fancy rhetorical arguments nor any great technique; but instead and rather intangibly, a soft but composed and sincere definition.

One by one, as we stand collectively in this, we can start to define ourselves as Good People.

In our desire to be Good People, a new power and order can take form.

As our unprecedented hardships are ever accelerating, it is a pressing trial on Japan and the Japanese people.

Is there nothing we can do but drop out of the running, one by one, and shut down?

Or can we use power and order to hold ourselves together, shift down a gear, and forge on?

To yourself, myself and all Japanese people, I pray for us all to be Good People.

Yushi Tabe
Tokyo

試練

東北関東大震災は、日本に未曾有の被害をもたらしました。

マグニチュード9.0の揺れと、それに伴う大規模な津波は、400年来最悪の災害と推察されています。加えて、福島原子力発電所の大規模な被災と、放射性物質の漏洩事故。

まさに、日本国に「三重苦」を強いることとなった今回の震災とはいったい何なのでしょうか？　私には、「見えざる手」による「試練」にほかならないように思えます。「試練」とは、すなわち、逆境に直面したときの心の強さや力の程度を試すためのものなのです。

では、今回の「苦難」で試されているのは何なのか？　だれなのか？　いったいなぜなのか？

被災者を含めた数多くの人々が、理不尽とも言える今回の苦難の果てにあるものの意味を激しく問うているに違いありません。ある人は哲学的に、ある人は宗教的に、またある人は運命的に。

でも、私にとっては、それらを哲学的に問うことも、宗教的に論じることも、ましてや運命として受け止めるということも本意とするところではありません。なぜならば、「意味がない」から。試されていることは、残されたすべての人々が「良き人たれるや否や」、考えなければならないことは、ならば「良き人とは何ぞや」ということ。

物資が不足するかもしれないという憶測から、金にあかせて必要のない買占めをしたのはだれですか？

震災直後の円高でまた金儲けですか？

安全で暖かい部屋から意識的に不安を煽るような書き込みをするのは楽しいですか？

ちょっぴりの義援金と自粛ムードに合わせるだけで、あとは成り行き任せですか？

放射線被曝の疑いが懸念されるだけで陸の孤島扱いですか？

身内でも含まれていない限り、被害者はただの他人ですか？

結局、責任は政府ですか？

計画停電だけど節電なんかやってませんよね？

文句は言っても、決して手は上げませんよね？

だれかが決めてくれるまでは待ちですよね？

そんな姿を子どもたちに見せられますか？

「私は違う！」と断言できますか？

「違う！」と言うのなら、何がどう違いますか？
あいまいでもかまわないと思うのです。不完全であっても、不誠実でさえなければ。
無理やり答えを用意して、ことさらに主張することは単なる言い訳にしか聞こえません。「良き人」であり
たい、と思えるようになれるかどうか、が試されているのではないでしょうか？　派手なパフォーマンスも、
自己主張も、理論武装も、高度なテクニックも必要のない、とってもあいまいで、柔らかいけれど、冷静で
誠実な定義。
一人ひとりが身の丈に合わせて定義していく「良き人」。「良き人」でありたいと願うことで生まれるパ
ワーと秩序。
未曾有の「苦難」は加速度を増して、日本を、日本人を試しにかかっています。
その速さについていけず、次々と振り落とされて休むしかないのか？
パワーと秩序によって自分たちを繋ぎ止めてシフトダウンし、進み続けることができるのか？

あなたも、私も、そしてすべての日本人が「良き人」たらんことを。

田部裕志
東京都

Acknowledgements

From thinking of the idea on March 18th to finishing the first completed draft on March 25th took far more effort than I'd imagined. Over 100 people worked on the project, none of whom I had met before. But thanks to Twitter, we were able to form a virtual newsroom that spanned the globe. I would personally like to give my warmest thanks to what quickly developed into the core team of editors—the Colonial Irregulars: Dan Ryan in Brisbane, California, M. Rosewood in New York and Sandra Barron in Los Angeles. This book also owes a massive debt to illustrator and stand-in designer Denver's Mari Kurisato, or Hail Mari as she became known, at least here in the Abiko bunker.

I'd also like to thank Jake Adelstein for staying awake long into the night to complete his article. And where would we be without Yoko Ono's support and William Gibson, who responded with such good humour to my sarcastic tweets cajoling him to join. He even abided by my absurd three-hour deadline. What a pro. What a gent.

But most of all, I want to thank everyone who donated a story or picture. Many didn't make it into this edition, purely from my inability to think and edit fast enough. Without them there could be no book. Finally, may I thank my long-suffering wife who worked tirelessly on this project, gave me love, cups of tea, and a kick when I needed it most.

Our Man in Abiko
25 March 2011

謝辞

3月18日にこのプロジェクトを思いついたときから25日のドラフト完成まで、想像をはるかに超える努力が必要でした。100人以上の方々がプロジェクトのために協力してくれましたが、一人残らず会ったことのない人ばかり。ツイッターのおかげでその方々を、全世界をまたぐ編集デスクにまとめることができました。個人的には編集チームの中心となったカリフォルニアのダン・ライアンさん、ニューヨークのM.ローズウッドさん、ロサンゼルスのサンドラ・バロンさんに特にお礼を申し上げます。そしてイラストレーター、またはときにデザイナーの代役も務めてくれたデンバーのマリ・クリサトさん（我孫子の制作本部では「聖マリ」というあだ名が付くまでになった）もこの本のために多大な貢献をしてくれました。

深夜までがんばって物語を仕上げてくれたジェーク・アデルスタインさんにもお礼を申し上げます。また、オノ・ヨーコさんの支援、私がツイッター上で皮肉めいたつぶやきで参加を迫ったウィリアム・ギブスンさんの快諾がなかったら、このプロジェクトはここまで及ばなかったでしょう。ギブスンさんは、3時間という私の無謀な締め切り時間まで守ってくれました。その紳士的な対応に頭が下がります。

しかし、だれよりもお礼を言いたいのはストーリーや絵、写真などを寄せてくれた方々です。私の思考回路や編集のスピードが追いつかず、結局この本に載らなかったものも多数あります。これらの投稿の数々がなければ、この本はもちろん存在しませんでした。最後に、疲れに負けず、愛情と茶を与え、必要なときに喝も入れてくれた私の辛抱強い妻にもお礼を言わせてください。

Our Man in Abiko
2011年3月25日

Acknowledgements for the bilingual edition

As with the English original, the Japanese text and bilingual edition of this book owe their existence to a large, scattered team of wonderful folk: 30 translators, numerous editors and checkers, and untold others who introduced friends or popped up to fill gaps or give advice.

As well as the translators, who made a huge contribution in record time, I particularly would like to thank Saiko Ena and Ai Kikuchi, the linchpins of the editing team, who worked long into the night to check and polish the text; Tetsuo Matsumuro, who offered invaluable editorial input; and Tomoko Ogawa and Sachiko Aoki, who checked translations and helped us get our style in order. Tamio Okumura, editor-in-chief at our publisher Goken, pulled team and book into shape and led the charge to meet the print deadline, while also contributing untold hours to the editing and checking process.

Professor Motoyuki Shibata of the University of Tokyo was a guiding presence who responded to many random emailed questions with spot-on advice; he contributes to the project a translation of William Gibson's "Window" that is a 300-word masterclass in the art. Ken Mogi responded to a Facebook message—the power of social media strikes again—with a foreword for this edition. And Barry Eisler showed one of the touches characteristic of #quakebook—the little bit more that everyone has given—in answering a query about the novel quote in his foreword by scanning in the relevant part of the Japanese edition and sending it back with his best wishes. The accumulation of those "little bits more" is the book in your hands now.

Gareth Edwards, editor of the bilingual edition
20 May 2011

2か国語版制作協力者への謝辞

先に出版された英語版をもとに2か国語版を出版することができました。英語版と同じように、さまざまな国や地域に分散したすばらしい方々がチームとして立ち上がったおかげです。実に30人もの翻訳者、10人近くの編集者、または友人を紹介したり、助言をくれたりした数えきれないほどの方々のご協力のもと、完成に至りました。

驚くべきスピードで和訳を完成させた翻訳者の方々にまず心からお礼を申し上げます。そして、編集チームの中心となり連日深夜まで編集作業に励んでくれた衣奈彩子さんと菊地愛さん、編集に際して重要なアドバイスをくださった松室哲生さん、翻訳チェックと表記の統一を行った小川知子さんと青木佐知子さんには特に感謝いたします。出版元である(株)語研の奥村民夫編集長は編集チームとこの本の両方をまとめ、印刷の締め切りに向けてみんなを引っぱり、自ら何時間も編集やチェック作業に協力してくれました。

東京大学の柴田元幸教授は何回も私の問い合わせに対して的確なアドバイスをくださいました。柴田先生によるウィリアム・ギブスン氏の日本語訳はまさに1,000字に詰まった翻訳のマスタークラスだと、私は読んだときに感動しました。茂木健一郎先生は、フェイスブックのメッセージに答え前書きを寄せてくださいました(ここでもソーシャルメディアの力が発揮されたわけです)。そして、バリー・アイスラーさんとのやり取りも思い出します。序文に出てくる引用は本人のどの著書のどの部分か見当がつかず、どうすればいいかと尋ねてみると、「よかったらこれを」と、日本語の文庫本から該当部分をスキャンして送ってくださいました。#quakebookに協力してくれた方々に共通しているボランティア精神を象徴しているように感じます。「もうちょっと、なにかしたい!」という皆さんの気持ちが、この本を完成に導いたのだと思います。ありがとうございました。

ガレス・エドワーズ、2か国語版編集責任者
2011年5月20日

English edition / 英語版スタッフ

Copy Editors

Lindsey Annison
Sandra Barron
Jesse Johnson
Joanne Greenway
M. Rosewood
Dan Ryan
Owen Schaefer
Jenny Silver
Vania Sofiandi
Aimee Weinstein

Translators

Hiromi Davis
Yoshiko Ikeda
Yuko Kato
Tomomi McElwee
M. Rosewood
Andy Sharp
Yoshie Sherriff
Fernando Ramos
@se7elndn
Shirabe Yamada

Designer

Edward Harrison

Illustrators/Designers/Photographers

James White
(English book cover design)
Gavin Strange
Mari Kurisato
Linda Yuki Nakanishi
Daniel Freytag
Fernando Ramos
Philipp Christoph Tautz
Brian Lynn
Yukiko Kurokawa

Advisors

Kevin Carroll
Roberto De Vido
Our Woman in Abiko
And many others

Bilingual edition / 2か国語版スタッフ

Editors / 編集者

Sachiko Aoki	青木佐知子
Gareth Edwards	ガレス・エドワーズ
Saiko Ena	衣奈彩子
Ai Kikuchi	菊地愛
Tetsuo Matsumuro	松室哲生
Tomoko Ogawa	小川知子
Tamio Okumura	奥村民夫

Translators / 翻訳者

Satsuki Ando	アンドウ・サツキ
Miaki Asada	浅田美晶
Kenji Chida	千田健二
Eriko Cousins	カズンズ・エリコ
Gareth Edwards	ガレス・エドワーズ
Akiko Fujimura	藤村明子
Satoka Fujita	藤田里香
Ayako Funakawa	舟川絢子
Naoko Hesse	ヘッセ杉山ナオコ
Chieko Irie	入江知恵子
Yuko Ishikawa	石川夕子
Yuko Kato	加藤祐子
Aya Kawai	川井綾
Harumi Kitagawa	北川晴美
Misato Matsuoka	松岡美里
Masafumi Matsumoto	松本匡史
Arisa Miyake	三宅亜理沙
Aki Miyatake	宮武亜季
Yuki Murata	村田有紀
Kaku Nagashima	長島確
Saeko Nagashima	長島佐恵子
Tomoharu Ogawa	小川知陽
Junko Rathmell	ラスメル純子
Asuka Scanlan	スカンラン明日香
Kana Shimizu	清水かな
Makika Sudo	須藤麻貴香
Akiko Suzuki	鈴木明子
Teppei Suzuki	鈴木哲平
Yuko Takeo	竹生悠子
Yuriko Yamaguchi	山口由利子
Motoyuki Shibata	柴田元幸

Book Design / ブックデザイン

Yuko Sawamoto	沢本佑子

Cover Illustration / 表紙イラストレーション

Mari Kurisato	マリ・クリサト

© Patrick Sherriff, 2011, Printed in U.S.A.

2:46 Aftershocks
午後2時46分 すべてが変わった
2011年10月20日　初版発行

編　者	quakebook.org
発行者	田中　稔
発行所	株式会社 語研
	〒101 - 0064
	東京都千代田区猿楽町 2 - 7 - 17
	電　話　03 - 3291 - 3986
	ファクス　03 - 3291 - 6749
	振替口座　00140 - 9 - 66728
表紙デザイン協力	山田英春
印刷・製本	Lightning Source, Inc.

ISBN978-4-87615-422-7 C0082
書名　246 アフターショックス　ゴゴニジヨンジュウロッブン　スベテガカワッタ
著者　クエイクブック　ドット　オルグ
著作者および発行者の許可なく転載・複製することを禁じます。

定価はカバーに表示してあります。
乱丁本、落丁本はお取り替えいたします。

語研ホームページ http://www.goken-net.co.jp/

CPSIA information can be obtained
at www.ICGtesting.com
Printed in the USA
LVIC042236180312
273643LV00006B